Hop King

Ezra Meeker's hop kilns, 1883.

Hop King

Ezra Meeker's Boom Years

Dennis M. Larsen

WSU
PRESS

Washington State University Press
Pullman, Washington

WSU PRESS
WASHINGTON STATE UNIVERSITY

Washington State University Press
PO Box 645910
Pullman, Washington 99164-5910
Phone: 800-354-7360
Fax: 509-335-8568
Email: wsupress@wsu.edu
Website: wsupress.wsu.edu

Library of Congress Cataloging-in-Publication Data

Names: Larsen, Dennis M., 1946- author.
Title: Hop king : Ezra Meeker's boom years / Dennis Larsen.
Description: Pullman, Washington : Washington State University Press, 2016. |
    Includes bibliographical references and index.
Identifiers: LCCN 2016023034 | ISBN 9780874223422 (alk. paper)
Subjects: LCSH: Meeker, Ezra, 1830-1928. | Pioneers--Washington
    (State)--Puyallup--Biography. | Businesspeople--Washington
    (State)--Puyallup--Biography. | Hops industry--Washington
    (State)--Puyallup--History. | Puyallup (Wash.)--Biography.
Classification: LCC F899.P94 L37 2016 | DDC 978/.02092 [B] --dc23
LC record available at https://lccn.loc.gov/2016023034

Cover image: Ezra Meeker's hop kilns in 1883, from his book *Hop Culture in
the United States*

Contents

Acknowledgments

I would like to offer special thanks to fellow Meeker scholars Ray Egan and Andy Anderson for their encouragement and critiques of early versions of the manuscript; to Karen Johnson, historical sleuth extraordinaire, for locating several of the illustrations used in the work and for proofreading the final version of the manuscript; and to my wife Pat for editing and reediting what I am certain at times seemed like a never-ending project. I offer final thanks to dozens of librarians and research assistants too numerous to mention, whose help was invaluable beyond description.

Preface

It has been eighty-eight years since Ezra Meeker passed from the American scene. His best-known legacy to our country is his twenty-five-year battle to save the Oregon Trail. But these efforts were just the final chapter of an already long and productive life. The story of his ninety-eight years has been only partially told, and primarily by Meeker himself. No comprehensive biography of Meeker's life has been written, a strange deficiency considering he left an impressive paper trail virtually everywhere he went. His name appeared in contemporary newspapers, court documents, and other public records almost from the time of his arrival on Puget Sound in 1853. When he burst onto the national stage in 1906 his name began to fill newspapers from coast to coast. No doubt some historians considered him a peripheral character in the story of Northwest development. If so they were most certainly wrong. Perhaps the flamboyant old-pioneer persona he created in his quest to save the Oregon Trail turned other historians away. Whatever the reason, his story remains mostly untold.

I discovered Ezra Meeker on a road trip to the Blue Mountains of eastern Oregon over a decade ago. An Oregon Trail kiosk at Emigrant Springs State Park told of his 1906 trek by ox team and covered wagon going east over the trail, setting stone monuments along the way. What began as a lark to locate all the remaining stone markers quickly escalated into a more serious search. The more I learned about Meeker the more intrigued I became with his life story. A decade later my workroom is filled with notebooks containing photocopies of his voluminous correspondence. Archival boxes are stacked in closets, chock-full of photocopies of contemporary newspaper articles about and by Meeker. On my bookshelves are everything written by him and most everything written about him. My computer's hard drive staggers under the weight of photographs, scans, and thousands of pages of transcriptions.

I set myself the daunting task of writing that long overdue biography. Since Meeker had already written pretty extensively of his pioneer years, that whittled my task down to the mere seventy years that remained. However, instead of picking up where Meeker left off, I chose to start a good way along in his life's journey. I first researched and wrote about his 1906 Old Oregon Trail Monument Expedition. Then I discovered a set of fascinating letters that Meeker wrote to his wife during his four years in the Klondike. That led to another book—a rather schizophrenic way of writing a biography, one might suggest. All the while I kept dabbling into his post-pioneer years—his hop-growing years. What I learned was that Meeker's story in these years was about much more than just growing hops. His most unexpected and meteoric rise to the top of the financial world followed by a fall of immense proportions is intimately entwined with the parallel story of the development of young Washington Territory as it grew into a state.

In December 1895 Ezra Meeker was facing the collapse of the empire he had built over the previous thirty years. He was on his way to London with a plan that he hoped might save the Meeker family from financial ruin. On Tuesday, December 10, he wrote his wife Eliza Jane from a steamship in the Atlantic Ocean telling her of his plan and noting her likely skepticism. "Building castles in the air I hear you say—well we will see; there is nothing like trying…I have been building castles in the air all along…"

Ezra Meeker's life can be easily compartmentalized into four periods of dreaming and castle building. The first is the story of his youth, his marriage and family, the 1852 journey west over the Oregon Trail, and pioneer days in Washington Territory. Meeker himself chronicled this time period in detail in his various books beginning with *Pioneer Reminiscences and the Tragedy of Leschi* written in 1905.

The second period covers the years 1860 to 1896, the rise and fall of his hop empire and his role in the growth of Washington Territory. No comprehensive history of this period of his life has been written; it is the focus of this work.

Next there was an interlude in the years 1897 to the end of 1901 as Meeker experimented with new careers for himself including a venture into mining that ultimately led him to the Yukon during the Klondike Gold rush of 1898, where he ran a grocery business in Dawson City until 1901. This part of his life has been covered in my book

Slick as a Mitten: Ezra Meeker's Klondike Enterprise, published in 2009 by Washington State University Press.

The final period of Meeker's life from age seventy to age ninety-eight, encapsulating his valiant effort to save the Oregon Trail and its story for future generations, is totally separate from the remainder of his life. It is almost as if a different man walked out on the stage after the loss of his financial fortune. This final segment, the Oregon Trail years, began to take shape in Meeker's mind after his return from the Klondike and commenced in earnest in 1906 with the grand adventure he called the Old Oregon Trail Monument Expedition. It ended with his death in 1928. This period of his life I hope to cover in a future volume.

Introduction

In 1852 when Ezra Meeker finished his arduous trek over the Oregon Trail there was little to distinguish him from any of the other thousands who had also made the journey. He arrived nearly penniless. His formal education amounted to less than six months in public schools. He was self-taught. Accompanied by his wife and infant son, he planned to become a farmer. There was no indication that he would become the author of over a dozen books and a columnist for two prominent Puget Sound newspapers, or run for political office multiple times, or found business enterprise after business enterprise. There was no indication that this young man in farm overalls would walk and talk at ease with the rich and famous, including financier Jay Cooke, activist Susan B. Anthony, five U.S. presidents, governors too numerous to mention, and noted businessmen from New York to London. There was no indication that he would become one of the wealthiest men, if not the wealthiest, in the territory.

Meeker was present at the birth of Washington Territory; indeed, his rise to the top of the financial world is intimately entwined with the development of the territory into a state. Almost single-handedly he showed the United States and the world that this sparsely populated corner of the country, some would say a backwater, was a place of considerable note and importance. And he did it by the most improbable of means. He grew hops in the Puyallup Valley, where today the crop is no longer grown. He turned a small, fledgling experiment into an economic giant. In the process he brought the region to the attention of the moneyed men of the East Coast and Europe, attention that resulted in tens of millions of needed dollars coming into the growing territory.

Meeker was present at many of the territory's milestones, large and small. He helped found libraries in Steilacoom and Puyallup. He facilitated the creation of the Puyallup Valley schools. His booklet *Washington Territory West of the Cascade Mountains* was the territory's first publication other than newspapers. He was a passenger and transported cargo on the inaugural run of the new railroad between Tacoma and Kalama. He was the primary opponent of those involved in the Chinese expulsion in the 1880s. He introduced the country to Washington Territory as the commissioner to the 1886 New Orleans Exhibition, the equivalent of a modern world's fair. He played an important but somewhat unnoticed role in the women's suffrage movement. And he became the largest exporter of hops in the United States, opening trade with England and Japan. The list goes on and on, but Meeker's role in these events has gone largely unnoticed. Meeker deserves long overdue recognition for the influential part he played in building the foundation of the modern state of Washington. That is the purpose of this work.

It is interesting to speculate on the source of Meeker's drive. He was a born risk taker with a pugnacious personality, and was characterized by some as ruthless in business dealings. People either appreciated him or hated and reviled him. There seemed to be no neutral ground, but he was not what one would call immoral in the manner of Gilded Age robber barons Jay Gould and James Fisk. Meeker was basically honest, although not averse to telling a lie or two on occasion, and he was self-righteous to a fault. He would battle hard and long, almost to the point of absurdity, with a rival, as witnessed in his dealings with Alexander Farquharson. The fact that he was a party to fifty-one civil court cases during territorial days offers further testimony to this characteristic. On the other hand he could be extremely generous and even sentimental. He had almost no interest in material things. The Meeker "mansion" was his wife's project, and he indulged her. He was content to live in his original log cabin long after he became one of the wealthiest men in the state and moved within the upper echelons of society with ease. Interestingly, he moved with the same ease in more modest society as well, and his most persistent sense of identity (until he became the "old pioneer" of his Oregon Trail years) was that of farmer. He was a constant promoter of the prospects of Puget Sound and plowed nearly every cent he made back into various projects that he felt would improve life in Washington, while also turning a profit.

Meeker faced much adversity and heartbreak. He lost his mother to cholera and his youngest brother to drowning in 1854. His son Thomas died as an infant in 1858. Another son became an alcoholic.

He lost a second brother in 1860 in a shipwreck off the California coast. He raised the surviving nephew as his own son, was overjoyed to witness his graduation from Cornell University, only to be crushed by the nephew's personal and business scandals. His long and loving marriage ended with his wife's death from dementia. He eventually found comfort in the Unitarian Church, but this was late in coming.

Meeker's life was a series of ups and downs. He prospered until calamity struck. But he always rose above it. The word "quit" was not in his vocabulary. Our story begins with one of the early calamities, the shipwreck of the *Northerner* on January 6, 1860.

EZRA MEEKER AT 23   BROTHER OLIVER AT 25

Ezra Meeker and Oliver Meeker. From *Seventy Years of Progress*

CHAPTER 1

Two Brothers

Ezra and Oliver

January 6, 1860. The wind was out of the south and was quite strong as Pacific Ocean winter winds often are. The *Northerner* had left San Francisco Bay just before dark the previous day bound for Puget Sound in Washington Territory. The steam engines of the three-masted side-wheeler with its sails billowing in the wind pushed the 1,102-ton vessel north at twelve knots. All day she had been running hard before the breeze and many passengers took this opportunity to come on deck and admire the magnificent scenery of the northern California coast.

For one of the passengers, thirty-two-year-old Oliver Meeker, this was familiar terrain. He had traveled this route in February 1854 on the SS *Peytona*. On that trip he traveled south from Puget Sound to the Isthmus of Panama and north to New York City. He and his brother Ezra, with Ezra's wife Eliza Jane and infant son Marion, had crossed the continent via the Oregon Trail two years earlier. They had arrived safely in Oregon Territory and were establishing a new home and a new life on Puget Sound in today's Washington State when a letter arrived from their father, Jacob Redding Meeker. "Boys, if Oliver will come back to cross with us, we will go to Oregon next year."[1]

Ezra helped Oliver raise funds to return east, and by April 1854 Oliver had reached his brother John's home in Eddyville, Iowa. While there, he married young Amanda Clement on April 23, after which he set out on his second trip over the Oregon Trail in three years. Along with Amanda, the party included Oliver's parents, Jacob and Phoebe Meeker, his brother Clark, and most likely his newly married sister Hannah and her husband Jesse Dunlap. These family members came from Indiana to rendezvous with Oliver in Eddyville.

This time Oliver, not Ezra, was the newlywed. It was, however, anything but a honeymoon. Oliver helped bury his mother who was struck down by cholera near today's Nebraska-Wyoming border. To compound the loss, his youngest brother Clark, age seventeen, drowned in the Sweetwater River near Devil's Gate, Wyoming. As the Meeker party struggled with illness and death, they fell behind the immigration of that year. James K. Hurd of Olympia, who had been out on the trail informing the emigrants of a newly built wagon road over the Cascade Mountains into Puget Sound via Naches Pass, heard from the Oregon Trail grapevine that the Meeker party was belated. Upon his return to Olympia, Hurd sent word to Ezra, who immediately started east over Naches Pass, met his family near the Columbia River, and guided them home.

Oliver and Ezra were about as close as brothers could be, an inseparable team. On arriving in Oregon in 1852 they opened a boarding house together. Shortly after, they floated a log raft down the Columbia River from today's Kalama, Washington, to an Astoria, Oregon, sawmill in an effort to raise needed cash. In the spring of 1853 they scouted the Cowlitz Trail north to Puget Sound. This adventure was followed by a whaleboat exploration around Puget Sound. The brothers moved north restlessly, building and abandoning log cabin homes at Kalama and McNeil Island, Washington Territory, before finally settling on side-by-side farms in the Fern Hill district of today's Tacoma, Washington, in early 1855.

The Puget Sound Indian War, or the 1855-56 Treaty War as it is called by modern historians, forced the families back to the safety of the village of Steilacoom on Puget Sound, where Jacob Meeker and his sons opened a store—J. R. Meeker & Sons—near the close of the conflict. All three men had farms nearby, but they weren't particularly prosperous, as is perhaps evidenced by Ezra's naming his farm "Swamp Place." The store however was making money, and the brothers supplemented their income with other schemes, for example loading cows on a barge they hauled north to Bellingham Bay to feed the Fraser River Gold Rush prospectors in 1858. Both brothers were involved in establishing the Steilacoom Library Association. About the only thing they hadn't done together was enter the political arena. Oliver had twice been elected to the House of Representatives in the territorial legislature. Ezra's energies, for the time being, went elsewhere.

In early 1859 the Meekers built what the local newspaper called a "commodious addition to their old store." Around mid-November the sailing ship *Ork* arrived in Steilacoom from San Francisco with a supply of merchandise for the newly expanded business—merchandise that was often sold before it could even be removed from its packing containers.[2]

With this success, the Meekers decided to take a risk. It was evident that there was a huge demand for goods from San Francisco. If the expense of the middleman were eliminated, potential profits would be even higher. The partners pooled their funds, borrowed more, and sent Oliver south to buy goods—enough to more than fill the shelves of their expanded store. Virtually everything the three men owned was resting in the hold of the *Northerner* that January day as Oliver headed home flushed with success. Their gamble was about to pay off. Then things went terribly wrong.

THE SINKING OF THE *NORTHERNER*

It was nearly four p.m. when the *Northerner* struck the small rock called Blunt's Reef about two miles off shore near Cape Mendocino, California. The shudder at first attracted little notice. Captain Dall, who was on deck, thought they had struck a whale, but he sent his First Officer, Mr. French, below decks to check for leaks. French found a fifteen to twenty-foot breach and water pouring into the hold. Captain Dall gathered the male passengers on deck, told them what had happened and asked for their help with the pumps. In short order they were pumping 12,000 gallons of water per minute out of the hold. Since the *Northerner* was only twenty miles from Humboldt Bay, the captain had hopes that they could reach the safety of that harbor before the ship sank. Three and a half miles north of Cape Fortunas the engineer sent word that the pumps were not keeping pace with the incoming water and that the boiler fires were about to be drowned. Captain Dall then decided that their only hope was to beach the ship and he accordingly ran her into the shore.

WRECK OF STEAMSHIP "NORTHERNER"
From a drawing made by a survivor.

"Wreck of the Steamship Northerner." Note the rescue line to shore. *Lewis & Dryden's Marine History of the Pacific Northwest*

The women and children were brought on deck and, along with the men, braced themselves for impact when the ship struck offshore rocks. After the initial collision the *Northerner* bounced along the rocks. The situation was frightful and desperate. It was clear to all that the ship could not long survive the pounding. Two lifeboats, loaded with women and children, were lowered into the crashing breakers. One capsized immediately and seven of the nine occupants drowned. The other, commanded by First Officer French, successfully reached the shore. After unloading the passengers, French and two assistants fought the breakers back to the ship where they were given a line to run to the shore. Almost immediately the lifeboat was hit by a huge wave, the line dropped, the boat capsized and was driven under the ship. When it popped out on the other side French was gone. The two assistants swam the boat to shore. The crewmen made several unsuccessful attempts to get the lifeboat back to the *Northerner* before giving up in exhaustion.

At this point Captain Dall dropped an anchor to keep the ship from drifting further down the reef and she became stuck fast in the sand and rocks about a quarter mile from shore, the pounding surf beginning to break her into pieces. Amid the chaos, a third lifeboat was somehow lowered and a rope got to shore, where it was made fast. Repeated efforts to row the lifeboats back through the surf to the *Northerner* failed. Captain Dall told the passengers to take the line and try to save themselves. One by one the men tried the line, only to be ripped off by the raging surf or dropping off from exhaustion. This effort went on from ten p.m. until two a.m., with rain coming down all the while. Captain Dall's cabin boy was given $500 in coins to guard shortly after the ship struck. When his turn came to grab the line Captain Dall told him to drop the money. The boy refused and was washed off the line and supposed lost. By some miracle he made it to shore with the $500 intact. Captain Dall was the last to take the line. About half way across he too was ripped off and plunged into the sea. Unlike others he was able to swim to the shore. Eventually the *Northerner* broke into pieces. Some half dozen passengers who refused the line drifted to shore and safety by hanging on to the floating fragments of the ship. One crewman cut a horse loose from the wreck and clung to the mane as it swam to shore.

Shore rescuers scooped up the exhausted survivors and took them to a nearby settlement where they were given shelter and dry clothes. The morning found the wreckage scattered for miles along the beach. Of the 107 people on board, thirty-eight passengers and crew died that night. Fourteen bodies were found washed up on the Centerville Beach. Only two were identified by name in the local press. A large pit was dug five feet deep behind a nearby hillock several hundred yards from the beach, and the dead were wrapped in sheeting and laid side by side with their heads to the east. The grave was enclosed with spars and marked with a cross. Perhaps among them was Oliver Meeker. A few bodies were recovered elsewhere along the coast, but half of the victims were lost to the Pacific Ocean, their bodies never recovered. The following day the survivors were taken to the town of Eureka in Humboldt Bay where they were put on the *Columbia* to continue the journey north.

Word that the ship had gone down reached Olympia and Steilacoom on Sunday, January 14, when the *Columbia* docked in Olympia with the *Northerner*'s surviving passengers aboard.[3]

It was left to Ezra to close up the details of his brother's life. On January 20 a probate notice appeared in the Steilacoom newspaper.[4] This was followed by an announcement of a memorial service.[5]

Of immediate concern following Oliver's death was the welfare of Oliver's widow Amanda and their young son Frank. Three family options were available to aid the widow and her son. Ezra's sister Hannah Dunlap and her husband Jesse and children lived on an adjoining land claim. They had most likely traveled west over the Oregon Trail in 1854 with Amanda and Oliver. However, Ezra was never close to Hannah's family. Religious issues divided them and it was unlikely he would ask for help from that quarter. Ezra's father, Jacob Meeker, now fifty-five years old, lived several miles away and had remarried, inheriting six young stepchildren in addition to starting a new family of his own. Providing for Oliver's widow and son was a burden he was not prepared to assume. The duty was clearly Ezra's, and it appears he accepted it willingly. According to the 1860 census, Amanda and Frank moved into Ezra's cabin on the Fern Hill farm. It was no doubt crowded with Ezra, Eliza Jane, their three children, Marion, Ella, and Caroline, and an otherwise unidentified boarder, Thomas Mallit, all squeezed in.[6] Interestingly the census taker listed Ezra's occupation as "butcher," perhaps reflecting one of the jobs he held at the family store in Steilacoom. Also living there was another family member whom the census taker chose not to count.

In the winter of 1854-55 a party of twenty Snohomish Indians consisting of two families appeared at Steilacoom with their canoes. Ezra noticed that the youngest child in the group was being constantly "picked at" by the older children. Upon inquiring if the child was a slave Meeker was told no, he was an orphan. He was then asked if he wanted to purchase the boy. Meeker declined the offer, but suggested that if the boy wanted to move into the Meeker household, he would be welcomed. There was much discussion among the parties involved and warnings from neighbors that Meeker was simply asking for trouble. But in the end the boy made the move and everything turned out well. There was a problem with his Indian name. The Meekers simply could not pronounce it and soon took to calling the boy "Jim." The name stuck and Jim became part of the Meeker household.[7]

SWAMP PLACE

For a time after Oliver's death Ezra retreated to his farm at "Swamp Place." The farm had few neighbors, with the closest being two miles distant. Two of the neighbors were bachelors. Of course, with such isolation, there were no schools nearby. Each morning Meeker would rise at four in the morning and from five until breakfast at six o'clock Marion, Ella, and Jim did their lessons at the kitchen table. Occasionally Eliza Jane would help out. When Amanda moved into the Swamp Place cabin she assumed the role of teacher and added Frank to the roster of pupils.

At least once a month Meeker trekked from Swamp Place to Steilacoom to attend meetings of the library board. He became a life member early on, and the library remained an important part of his life. The minutes of those meetings testify to his early appreciation and understanding of the need for public libraries.

As the year wore on new business ventures for Ezra and his father proved to be less than successful. J. R. Meeker & Sons hoped to secure the contract to supply beef for the garrison at Fort Steilacoom. It seemed a potentially lucrative contract. Accordingly the Meekers purchased a number of cattle at an average of one hundred dollars a head. Butchered beef was then retailing at twenty to twenty-five cents a pound. The *Puget Sound Herald* on June 29 reported a price plunge. Those cows purchased so dearly were now worth forty dollars, and prepared beef was retailing at twelve and fifteen cents.[8]

Meeker had better luck when he tried his hand at selling apples that fall. There was enough demand locally to sell hundreds of boxes, but it all had to be brought up from the Columbia River by ship. It seems the entire Puget Sound supply came from the orchards of Harry Darby Huntington at Monticello (today's Longview, Washington). Meeker became Huntington's local agent and on August 31 received his first shipment. The first box was delivered free to the editor of the Steilacoom newspaper, who gladly informed his readers that they were the finest apples he had ever tasted.[9]

Financial recovery for the Meeker family seemed a long way off and the future looked anything but promising. Ever the optimist, Meeker refused to see it that way.

CHAPTER 2

Politics and the Law

POLITICS

In 1860 Ezra Meeker stepped into the political arena for the first time when he attended the Republican convention in Olympia and gave the nominating speech for William Henson Wallace for territorial delegate to Congress.[1] Wallace went on to win the general election. He served until March 1863 when Lincoln appointed him as the first Governor of Idaho Territory. In 1864 Wallace went back to Congress, this time as the delegate from Idaho.[2]

In 1861 Meeker threw his own hat into the ring, vying for a position in the territorial legislature. The Pierce County Republican Convention met at the Methodist Episcopal Church in Steilacoom on June 1 and nominated Meeker for a seat in the Territorial Council (Senate). Initially, four candidates were in the field: Ezra Meeker, Frank Clark, George Parkinson, and William. H. Wood. (Wood later dropped out of the race.) The candidates traveled the county resting "neither night nor day," campaigning and defining their positions at public meetings. The local newspaper reported, "At these meetings the claims of the rival candidates were contested with much warmth, but with good feeling on all sides."[3] In fact, the campaigning was less than cordial. On July 2 Meeker penned a letter to the editor of the Steilacoom newspaper complaining that Frank Clark was circulating a story claiming Meeker was pledged to making Olympia the territorial capital rather than Steilacoom, and placing Olympia's newspaper in charge of public printing.[4] Meeker went on to accuse Clark of breaking promises about campaigning in Sawamish County (now Mason County) and general "rascality and underhandedness."[5]

Meeker lost. Frank Clark was elected to the Territorial Council in August. This was the first of many efforts Meeker would make to

9

obtain political office and the first of many defeats. In addition to lacking the political charm of his brother Oliver, he had a temperament
that attracted enemies, political and otherwise. In 1865 Meeker served
as the Door Keeper for the Territorial House of Representatives, an
appointed position.[6] In 1869 he ran for the office of Pierce County
Surveyor and lost.[7] Some sixty years later Meeker would make a second attempt to run for the legislature, again losing. In the interval he
would run for Congress and lose, and campaign three times for mayor
of Puyallup, winning twice.

MEEKER VS. CLARK

In the Washington State Digital Archives maintained by the Secretary
of State's Office is a web page called "Frontier Justice." It is a compi-
lation of civil and criminal court cases from the earliest days of the
territory through statehood. Ezra Meeker's name appears fifty-three
times in that database, either as a plaintiff or defendant. All but two
of these appearances are in civil cases involving disputes over money,
contracts, and the like. In 1860 Meeker appeared as the defendant in
criminal case PRC-944.

Frank Clark accused Meeker of "putting up and maintaining highly
obnoxious and nefarious posters in the rear of Messrs. Balch & Rogers
and Mr. George Gallagher's places of business in the town of Steilacoom." Clark demanded that "said nuisance be abated and the parties
maintaining this nuisance be dealt with according to law." Court documents do not describe the content of the posters but one can sur-
mise they were not flattering to Clark's reputation. Were they Meeker's
doing? It is certainly not difficult to believe he had at least a hand in
them, but he entered a not-guilty plea. The presiding judge, however,
decided the case without Meeker's testimony, so his side of the story
went unrecorded. To understand this courtroom dynamic one must
step back a little in time to examine a history of tangled animosities.

On November 17, 1856, Meeker served on the jury that was hearing
the trial of the Nisqually Indian Chief Leschi who had been accused
of murdering Abram Benton Moses at the start of the Puget Sound
Treaty War. Antonio B. Rabbeson was the chief witness for the pros-
ecution during the trial and Meeker firmly believed that Rabbeson
committed perjury on the witness stand. Accordingly, he refused to

vote to convict Leschi, resulting in a hung jury and a second trial. There is little doubt that afterwards Meeker made his views about Rabbeson known to the community, and he made the charge in print when he published *Pioneer Reminiscences and the Tragedy of Leschi* in 1905. The second trial found Leschi guilty, and he was sentenced to be hanged on June 10, 1857. The case was appealed to the state supreme court and the verdict was upheld.

Meeker wasn't alone in thinking Rabbeson committed perjury. Father Rossi, a Catholic missionary who served in Washington Territory from 1856 to 1860 wrote: "[Leschi] was hanged, and he underwent his punishment with heroic courage. In his last moment he cried out, "I pardon everyone!" and that is truly Christian. But, unfortunately he added one exception, which distressed me a lot. It was the only witness who had given evidence against him [Rabbeson] and who, as everyone knew, had never told the truth in his whole life."[8]

Two primary issues arose in Leschi's trail. First, did Moses' death occur as the result of an act of war? If so, it would not be considered murder. (Moses was a volunteer under the command of the U.S. Army and died in a skirmish with the Indians.) Second, was Leschi actually the person who killed Moses? However, the jury was not instructed to consider the act of war defense at the second trial. At the second trial Rabbeson testified that he personally saw Leschi at the "scene" of Moses' death. Meeker and Rossi believed this was a deliberate lie, as much evidence suggested it was physically impossible for Leschi to have been where Rabbeson claimed he saw him.

Meeker's argument that Leschi was judicially murdered, aided by Rabbeson's perjury, which he voiced in *Pioneer Reminiscences*, was met with a firestorm of criticism when it was published, primarily from University of Washington history professor Edmund Meany who attacked Meeker in the local press with counterarguments and insults. Historian Clinton Snowden writing in 1909 sided with Meany. Characterizations of Leschi as a "not good Indian" appeared in publications such as the *Oregon Historical Quarterly* as late as 1949. Pulitzer Prize winning author Richard Klugar in his book *The Bitter Waters of Medicine Creek* chronicles the multi-year effort to clear Leschi's name. On December 10, 2004, a special court headed by Washington State Supreme Court Chief Justice Gerry Alexander concluded that the murder of Abram Moses occurred during war, and that "Leschi should not, as a matter of law, have been tried for the crime of murder." The special court went on to exonerate Leschi.[9] Ezra Meeker undoubtedly would have approved.

With this background in mind, it surely vexed the Meekers that the perjurer, Antonio B. Rabbeson, on board the *Northerner* when she went down off Cape Mendocino, survived while Oliver Meeker did not. Then, through a stroke of ill fortune, Meeker found Rabbeson, who was serving a term as the Justice of the Peace, acting as the trial judge in his courtroom contest with Frank Clark.

Meeker entered a plea of "not guilty." Frank Clark began questioning those who had signed the poster, all apparently Meeker allies and citizens of Steilacoom. He made it through about a third of the witnesses and rested his case. Rabbeson immediately issued his verdict and exacted his revenge, declaring Meeker "guilty as charged of maintaining a public nuisance," and ordering him to "abate and discontinue the said nuisance," pay a bond of $150 and court costs of $40.50.[10]

Since there is no record of a conviction in the Washington State Archives, it is assumed that the Justice Court reversed Rabbeson, most likely on First Amendment grounds.

After surviving the sinking of the *Northerner*, Rabbeson found a way to further infuriate both Ezra and Eliza Jane. It is not known how Rabbeson came to be appointed the administrator of Oliver's estate rather than Ezra or his father Jacob Meeker, but it surely would have compounded their distress in the aftermath of Oliver's death.[11] Years later Meeker recounted an incident in which an individual (clearly Rabbeson) whose name "shall remain in oblivion where it belongs," came to their door with legal paperwork associated with Oliver's estate.[12] After Eliza Jane signed the papers, she coolly dismissed him: "now Mr, ----- you must never again darken the door of this house." The two men remained enemies for decades.[13]

Meeker was also in court in February 1861, this time trying to collect money owed by Benjamin Morris Spinning and his brother Charles H. Spinning to the store and Oliver's estate.[14] In a true stroke of irony, Ezra's attorney was Frank Clark. With an out-of-court settlement resolving the dispute, Meeker's time of living and working in Steilacoom was about to end.

CHAPTER 3

A New Start

At the end of October 1861 Meeker closed out the Steilacoom store. The local newspaper reported, "The sale of the remaining goods of the late firm of O & E Meeker, commenced last Saturday, will be continued next Saturday. Only about half the goods were sold last week."[1]

John Valentine Meeker. *Author's collection*

Meeker started the New Year embarking on yet another new business venture, this time the making of soap and candles. His goal, as always, was large. He hoped to supply the needs of all of Puget Sound. He studied the art of making these products with a person engaged in the business, then partnered with his older brother, John Valentine Meeker, to sell at a price lower than the San Francisco imports the citizens of Puget Sound were currently relying upon. The *Herald* said, "The soft soap now advertised…is pronounced an excellent article by those who have used it."[2] The business opened in March and was soon producing thousands of pounds of soap.[3] By April it was reported that orders were coming in faster than they could be filled.[4]

THE CUSTOMS COLLECTOR

Ezra Meeker's sometimes impulsive and pugnacious nature got his name into the local papers on another matter. He engaged in a nasty verbal spat at the start of the year with Victor Smith, the United States Customs Collector at Port Townsend, even though the issue concerned his father. Jacob Meeker had been serving as the Surveyor of Nisqually District, a position that despite its name had nothing to do with surveying. Jacob's title made him the assistant customs collector for south Puget Sound. Early in 1862 a letter from Salmon P. Chase, Secretary of the Treasury, dated October 30, 1861, reached Jacob informing him that the Customs Collector at Port Townsend had determined that the position of surveyor of the Nisqually district was no longer needed and that Jacob's commission was thereby revoked.

Jacob had argued prior to receiving this letter that Puget Sound needed six collection districts and that customs revenue could be collected at half the expense currently incurred if these districts were created. Apparently Ezra let Smith have a piece of his mind in a rather public fashion about the termination of his father's position,[5] prompting the following response that Smith sent to the *Puget Sound Herald* rather than directly to Jacob Meeker. Smith wrote that he had not recommended the abolition of Jacob's position but only for its removal to Port Townsend, and that it was President Lincoln who ordered the position closed. He went on to say:

> And I am the more anxious to offer you what would, under all the circumstances, be the most desirable place for you [Jacob Meeker] in the District, because it affords me the additional satisfaction of having a coal of fire on the head of your son Ezra, who in an ill-advised moment, has been led to assist and countenance the most shameless attacks upon the Collector of this District and the honored head of the Treasury Department. Even as late as Friday night last he was guilty of loudly endorsing and applauding the foul articles in the *Northwest.* These last will not injure me, nor yet the Secretary. *No mention has or ever will be made to the Department regarding Ezra's conduct.*[6]

Smith followed up by appointing Jacob as Surveyor of Port Townsend, in effect forcing him to move to north Puget Sound. As Smith probably expected, Jacob declined and the *Herald* said, "The next welcome intelligence we shall receive will probably be Victor's removal, and the appointment of some person more competent in his stead."[7]

A NEAR TRAGEDY

The Meekers were in the news again on August 14 when the *Herald* reported a near tragedy. Their daughter Ella, age eight, was found floating in the waters of Puget Sound behind her home partially supported by a piece of board. "Had it not been for the timely discovery of her situation by Mr. Sherwood, she would inevitably have been drowned, as her strength must soon have been exhausted."[8]

Ella's rescue was one of the few bright spots in an otherwise dreary existence. The Meekers were not prospering in Steilacoom. Ezra's brother was dead, the store closed, and the election lost. The soap business, for unknown reasons and despite a promising start, was not doing well. The farm at Swamp Place was not doing well either. In the fall of 1861 Meeker lost his entire potato crop to an early frost. Financially the family was at rock bottom. Meeker made the not too difficult decision to start over in a new location. The question was where?

THE MOVE TO PUYALLUP

Ezra and Oliver had briefly looked at the Puyallup Valley during their exploratory whaleboat trip around Puget Sound in June 1853. Meeker's memory of the valley from that trip was simply of huge trees everywhere, and that it would be a daunting undertaking to clear this land. His second visit to the valley came during the Indian war. In November 1855 just days after the outbreak of hostilities, Oliver, Ezra, and fifteen other pioneers formed a company of volunteers under the command of Captain John Carson whose purpose was to retrieve the possessions and livestock abandoned by settlers fleeing to Fort Steilacoom for safety. It was Meeker's only military experience and it lasted a week. However, the effort allowed him to take another look at the valley farms. His next opportunity came five years later. The Indian war had driven out most of the original valley settlers and few had returned. One who did return was John Carson, the commander of Ezra's military unit in 1855. Carson established a ferry on the river and in 1860 Meeker ventured north to the Carson place. This time his visit was a bit more leisurely and it allowed him to examine more closely the possibilities of the valley.

Among those living in the Puyallup Valley at this time was a man named Jeremiah Stilley[9] who had taken a squatter's claim on a quarter section of land on the south side of the river. Stilley constructed a cabin sixteen feet square and eight feet high set among the giant trees but had cleared little land. He had come west to Feather River, California, in 1857. Sometime later he moved north to Washington Territory. Meeker later wrote that he hadn't been there long enough to grow a crop.[10]

Stilley became part of the extended Meeker family in a rather roundabout way. Ezra's father, Jacob, arrived in Washington Territory a widower, his wife Phoebe having succumbed to cholera on the journey west. A woman named Nancy Burr also traveled west over the trail that year and was just ahead of the Meeker wagon train when her husband (David Solomon Burr) also contracted cholera and died. The twenty-seven-year-old widow continued on to Puget Sound via Naches Pass in company with her sisters, who were married to Thomas Headley and Henry Whitsell respectively, and who eventually settled in the Puyallup Valley where they took Donation Land Claims. Nancy Burr arrived in Steilacoom in the fall of 1854 with six young children ranging in age from ten years old to an infant who had been born on the plains. That winter in Steilacoom she and Jacob Meeker met, and on March 2, 1855, they married. Suddenly Ezra had a stepmother and six stepsiblings. One of those stepsiblings, Mariah Angelina Burr, married Jeremiah Stilley on September 6, 1862.

In the meantime, in the late summer of 1862, just before Jeremiah Stilley married into the family, Ezra and Eliza Jane, Marion, Ella, Carrie, Jim, Amanda, and Frank packed up their meager possessions and walked the seven miles to the Puyallup Valley "without a team, without a wagon, without money, and with but scant supply of household goods and clothing."[11] They brought with them seven cows, a steer (Harry), a few pigs, and a dozen or so chickens. Ezra traded a cow to another valley resident, Robert Moore, for a steer named Jack to make a team so he could once again start clearing land and planting crops. The three adults and five children moved into Jeremiah Stilley's tiny cabin and began to rebuild their lives.

Stilley either sold his cabin to Ezra, traded it for Meeker's Steilacoom dwelling, or simply abandoned it and let Meeker take possession. The latter possibilities are more likely since Ezra had little money at that time with which to make a purchase. No government survey was made in Puyallup until 1864. Until then, all claims on public land made outside of the original Donation Land Act were mere squatter's claims that had no legal standing under the law. There were few complications, however, since those who arrived in the valley after the Indian war respected the boundaries of the handful of donation land claimants still there and squatted elsewhere. Meeker said that after the completion of the first survey by James P. Stewart and George W. Sloan there was a rush to the land office in Olympia, the Donation Land Claim folk to document they had "proved up" their claims and the Homestead folk to make application for their rights.[12]

As the Meekers had already filed a donation claim on their Swamp Place property, Ezra needed to make this claim under the Homestead Act, which required a $16 fee. Fearing someone might preempt him, Meeker walked some thirty-three miles to Olympia where he could file by putting one dollar down and paying the remainder several months later. He wrote that it took him a good while to raise the other fifteen dollars.[13] And the new homestead claim was not contiguous as Meeker explained in a February 1912 letter to his daughter Carrie. "I bought Williamson out so as to get my claim a square quarter of section and not all long and no wide or else made up of fractions."[14]

Ironically, on January 1, 1863, Ezra and Eliza Jane received their "patent" from the United States of America for their 325.21 acres in Swamp Place.[15] Oliver and Amanda's patent arrived at the same time. They now owned the farms they had just abandoned. Amanda deeded Oliver's acres to Ezra to hold in trust for her son Frank.

Jacob Meeker also pulled up stakes, taking up a Homestead claim in 1863 across the Puyallup River from Ezra in what is today the city of Sumner, Washington, and not too distant from Nancy's sisters, Mrs. Headley and Mrs. Whitsell.[16] Accompanying Nancy to her new home were three of the children from her first marriage.[17] Nancy and Jacob had four offspring of their own, but only the two youngest, Malinda Meeker born in 1863, and Aaron Meeker born in 1865, survived to adulthood.

A third Meeker family also made the trek to the Puyallup Valley— the family of John Meeker. John (Ezra's older brother) had married

Mary Jane Pense in Indiana and moved to Eddyville, Iowa, on the Des Moines River in 1851. The couple's first child was born there and John taught school in Eddyville until 1859. That October John and Mary Jane decided to follow the rest of the family to Puget Sound. Attempting to avoid an arduous journey over the Oregon Trail, the John Meekers nonetheless found themselves entangled in an arduous journey of their own. The family took a train to New York where they boarded the steamer *North Star* bound for the Isthmus of Panama. They were shipwrecked shortly after their departure on one of the Bahamas, a sandy key about two miles wide and ten miles long, and remained on this uninhabited island for six days. Help was finally obtained from Fortune Island, fifty miles distant, and the Meekers, thinking they could now continue their journey, found themselves summarily deposited in Jamaica. They eventually made their way to Aspinwall (now Colon), Panama. A railroad took them across the Isthmus, and the steamer *Cortez* got them to San Francisco. After a rest of five days, they embarked on the final leg of their trip on the steamer *Northerner*, arriving at Steilacoom on December 10, 1859. A journey that usually took less than a month took John Meeker's family two, and Mary Jane and the baby were seasick most of the time. A month later John's brother Oliver would embark on a trip from San Francisco north to Puget Sound on what turned out to be the final voyage of the steamship *Northerner*.[18]

John Meeker found immediate employment in Steilacoom as a teacher conducting classes in the Willis Boatman house. The next year he taught at the Byrd schoolhouse near Fern Hill. By 1863 when he was able to file for his Homestead claim adjacent to Ezra's in Puyallup,[19] John's family had expanded to include four additional children.[20]

Throughout the years 1862 to 1864 Meeker worked long hours clearing his land and establishing his new farm. He transplanted his Swamp Place orchard, and planted raspberries and blackberries along with what he called ladyfinger and kidney potatoes. The valley soil was rich and the plantings prospered, and by the second year they were bearing fruit. In 1864 Meeker built another cabin adjacent to and of the same dimensions as the one built by Jerry Stilley, leaving a space of five feet between them for a double fireplace and chimney. The fireplace was constructed out of pumice or, as he called it, lava rock.

At first the cabin was papered with newspapers but later this reading material was replaced by real wallpaper. Eliza Jane planted an ivy vine next to the entry between the two cabins. It climbed to the top of the roof and invaded the sitting room and today, more than one hundred and fifty years later, it still grows on the site of the cabin.

Despite the move inland, the family's ties to Steilacoom were not severed. Eliza Jane returned there briefly to give birth to her third son, Fred, on December 13, 1862. Their second son, Thomas, had been born in Steilacoom on December 2, 1857, and died there November 3, 1858. And again on New Year's Day 1863 Meeker walked the rough road sixteen miles round trip from the valley to town to attend the year's first meeting of the Steilacoom Library Association.

Surveying

As a source of income to supplement the produce of the farm, Meeker relied on a skill he learned in Iowa during the winter of 1851—surveying. He was competent enough in the trade to be given a contract (Number 89) on September 22, 1866, by Selucius Garfield, the Territorial Surveyor General, to do a number of surveys in the final quarter of the year. Meeker went out often that fall with a crew consisting of C. C. Hanners, chainman, and Marion Meeker, Frank Meeker, Lynus Burr, and Edward Ross as assistants.[21] This crew did surveys in Thurston County, where they spent a considerable amount of time surveying the Thomas Chambers claim before moving north into Pierce County.

In 1867 Meeker was appointed Washington Territorial Deputy Surveyor and in that capacity surveyed a good portion of Pierce County and parts of King and Thurston Counties. One 1868 survey that he no doubt found interesting was the claim of his sister Hannah Dunlap and her husband Jesse. He subdivided their original 320 acres into several saleable parcels. Meeker also surveyed Swamp Place.

In addition to working outdoors in inclement weather and being away from home for long periods, the job at times presented other difficulties. Early in his surveying contract Meeker was assigned to subdivide the township bordering the Muckleshoot Indian Reservation. The survey nearly led to conflict. Meeker was stopped by some fifty or sixty Indians, who seized his surveying chain, and who "forbid him to proceed any farther."

The tribe was certain that the survey meant that their land was about to be taken away from them. The two groups camped a little ways apart that evening. In the morning Meeker began three days of negotiations, which included a trip to Olympia, to reassure the Muckleshoots that the purpose of the survey was not nefarious. The situation was satisfactorily resolved, and the tribe actually ended up helping with the survey.[22]

Over the years 1866-1868 the lands of Puget Sound settlers Delin, Judson, Thomas, Brannan, Byrd, Neasson, Bradley, Rigney, Daugherty, Dunlap, and many others were surveyed by Meeker and his various crews. In 1871 John Meeker took over the title of Deputy Surveyor and with a crew made up of John Boatman, Charles Boatman, and M. H. Elder continued the surveying of the Puyallup Valley and vicinity.

FAMILY MATTERS

On New Years Day 1867 the Meekers celebrated a wedding in the family cabin, that of Amanda Clement Meeker to Benjamin Franklin "Frank" Spinning. Ezra and John Meeker both signed the marriage papers as witnesses.[23] Amanda and her new husband moved to Steilacoom and later to California. Eleven-year-old Frank Oliver Meeker, however, stayed behind under the care of Ezra and Eliza Jane.

The birth of Ezra and Eliza Jane's last child, a daughter named Olive Grace, on October 24, 1869, also took place in Puyallup. Six days later Ezra's father Jacob Redding Meeker died in the neighboring town of Sumner.

CHAPTER 4

Birth of the Puyallup Valley
Hop Industry

As in war, the victor gets to tell the tale. And what proves true for war also proved true for hops. In the late 1800s Ezra Meeker was the dominant hop grower in the Northwest—and perhaps in the United States—and, as a result, a very wealthy man. Newspapers around the country conferred upon him the title "Hop King." And for a number of years he was indeed the "King." As such, Meeker's version of the origins of the Puyallup Valley hop industry has pretty much become accepted history. But other players in this tale deserve much more recognition than has thus far been accorded them, starting with Ezra's father, Jacob, and a family named Wood. And a thorough examination of that history tells us that the "Hop King" got some of his facts "mixed up" when telling the story.

The First Hops

The story is complex and somewhat controversial; so let us begin with what Meeker wrote in his 1883 book *Hop Culture in the United States*.

> Jacob Meeker, who did not live to see the importance of his work, was the pioneer in the business of hop-growing in Washington Territory. Charles Wood, familiarly known as "Uncle Charlie," a small brewer, residing in Olympia, furnished the cuttings or sets from his garden, and encouraged the enterprise by promising to buy the hops. The roots (about half a bushel) were packed fifteen miles, by J. V. Meeker, on his back to the spot where they were planted, and which to this day is about the centre of the great hop growing region of the Puyallup valley.
>
> These were duly planted in the spring of 1866, and yielded, the first year, one hundred and eighty-five pounds, and were sold to

"Uncle Charlie" for eighty-five cents per pound. This "first crop" was cured in the loft over the living room. The poles were carried to the barn and chairs provided for the "women and children" to sit while picking.[1]

This account was repeated by Meeker over and over in newspaper articles, in lectures, and in his various books for the rest of his life. However, over time, one subtle change appeared, apparently unnoticed by historians. In later versions, the year 1866 became 1865. A reexamination of the early history of the hop industry in Washington Territory offers an explanation as to why this occurred. But first let's look at the story of "Uncle Charlie" Wood and correct that error.

Isaac and Charlie Wood

The Wood family came west to Oregon in 1851 and made their way to Puget Sound. Isaac Wood filed a donation land claim in 1853 in what was then called Woodland, but that is known today as the city of Lacey.[2] Like many pioneers, he also established a business to supplement his farm income. Isaac started a small brewery in Olympia at Fourth and Columbia, in the heart of that infant city, and he put his family to work. His two oldest sons, James and John, were sent to the brewery to learn the business. His third son, Charles, was sent to Tyrus Himes' shoe shop to learn that trade. It seems the fourth son, also named Isaac, stayed on the Lacey farm, and Wood's daughter, Mary, was married to LaFayette McMullen, the second territorial governor of Washington.

Exactly when Isaac started his brewery is in dispute. George Himes, the secretary of the Oregon Historical Society, said it was in the latter part of 1857. Himes should know because Wood gave him his first ever taste of liquor, something a young man is not likely to forget. In a January 11, 1915, letter to Ezra Meeker, Himes wrote:

> Isaac Wood started a brewery in Olympia in the latter part of 1857. His daughter Mary was married to Governor Fayette McMullen July 12, 1858, and I know the brewery plant was in operation several months before that, and made what the family called "cream ale." In fact, Mr. Wood, being the nearest neighbor to my father's family—his D.L.C. [Donation Land Claim] adjoining ours on the west—thought it a

neighborly act to send us some of the "Ale." That was the first I ever tasted, but aside from a mere taste it was never used.[3]

However, two stories appeared in the Olympia *Pioneer and Democrat* casting some doubt on tee-totaling Mr. Himes' timeline. The first, written in 1859, stated that Isaac Wood was about to build a brewery and had gone to San Francisco to purchase equipment.[4] The second story, written in 1861, announced "Mr. Isaac Wood has just completed his large brewery at this place, and is now making cream ale in quantities large enough to fully supply all demands."[5] This, of course, was three and one half years later than Himes wrote. A local online history identifies Wood's establishment as the Union Brewery located at Fourth and Columbia, a site that was then right on the waterfront. It gives 1859 as the opening date.[6]

Beginning with his first book, *Hop Culture*, published in 1883, Meeker continually misidentifies the brewer who supplied his father with the hop roots as Charles Wood of Olympia. Years later, this misidentification caught the attention of George Himes, who wrote to Ezra Meeker in August 1919:

> Having occasion today to refer to some question about "Hops," in response to an inquiry, I was almost "stunned" to see you allude on page 8 of your excellent work on "Hop Growing" to Charles Wood, familiarly known as 'Uncle Charlie,' a small brewer, residing in Olympia, furnishing the cuttings or sets from his garden, and encouraged the enterprise by promising to buy the hops.
>
> Now where did you get your information? Charles Wood was a shoemaker, and succeeded my father in that business. He began as a journeyman in my father's shop in the fall of 1859 and succeeded him in 1863. He never had any thing to do with the brewery in Olympia, unless it was to take a glass of beer occasionally. Isaac Wood, my father's nearest neighbor on the west, was the brewer, aided by his sons, James Revellan Wood, commonly known as "Dick" and John Wood.[7]

Four years after the publication of *Hop Culture* Meeker wrote a rather long article for the Tacoma newspaper in which he retold the story of Wood and his father. In this article he correctly identified the brewer as Isaac Wood, but incorrectly put the starting date at 1865.[8] However, the errors of name and date were continually repeated in his various books all the way through 1916 with the publication of *The Busy Life of Eighty-Five Years of Ezra Meeker.*

"Who's on First?"

It seems that the explosion of wealth generated by the Puyallup Valley hop industry generated other claimants to the title of "first." And this title was considered to be of such prestige to the early participants in the hop trade that it led to a liberal bending of the truth. In 1877 a Snohomish, Washington, newspaper sent two reporters to the Puyallup Valley to do a series of interviews and investigative reporting to sort out the question of who was really first. One visited the Thompson and Meade farms and one visited the Meeker hop yards. At Thompson and Meade's they were told:

> In the spring of 1865 Mr. L. F. Thompson sent to San Francisco and purchased twenty-five hundred hop roots for one hundred dollars. Mr. Thompson claims, that from the two acres they were sufficient to set out, all the hops now in cultivation in the Territory and Oregon, were derived. His neighbor Mr. Meade joined with him in the enterprise. They have been in partnership ever since. They claim also to have established the first regular hop yard in the valley, calling it the Pioneer Hop Yard of the Puyallup.[9]

The story obtained from Meeker said:

> Mr. J. R. Meeker, the father of E. Meeker was the first one to try the experiment in 1864. He set out a kind of hops that would yield less, and not grow as large as the hops now in cultivation. They had no regular hop house or other arrangements for carrying on business. Their experiment was so successful however that others followed their example.[10]

1864? Like magic, two years vanished in Ezra's telling, allowing Jacob Meeker to retain the title of "first." What the reporters really got right in their article was the first sentence: "The accounts are somewhat contradictory, as to whom the honor should be given for establishing this [hop] industry in that valley." Since this is the only mention of the year 1864 in all the hop literature of the valley, one suspects a game of one-upmanship. If Thompson and Meade decided to shave some years off the start of their hop enterprise to give themselves the honor of first, Meeker, hearing that they were claiming 1865 as their start date, probably decided to trump them by a year.

A second source, a Seattle newspaper, also reported in 1877 that Levant Thompson and Elijah Meade, Jacob's neighbors, planted in the year 1865. The writer stated that he had visited their Puyallup hop farm and wrote the following, "Messrs. L. F. Thompson and E. C. Meade are the owners of this fine place, and have been from the first. They entered upon the cultivation of the hop in 1865, putting in a few hundred roots they had obtained with great cost and trouble, and increasing the number planted each succeeding year since."[11]

The True Story or "Bottom Facts"

Keeping in mind that a complete record of crop sales has not come to light for these early years, and all the various claims and counter claims originate with the two parties claiming the title of "first," how do we get to the true story or the "bottom facts" as Ezra often wrote? Let us assume the year 1866 is correct for Isaac Wood's hop experiment and follow Jacob Meeker to find where the trail leads.

Sometime in late 1865 or early 1866 Jacob Meeker had a conversation with Isaac Wood about possibly growing some hops on his Sumner farm.[12] Jacob no doubt thought of this as a small venture, involving little or no risk, by which he might make a few dollars. Around March 15, 1866, Charles Wood, third son and shoemaker, brought three pecks, or gallons, of hop roots to Steilacoom. They were intended for Jacob Meeker. John Valentine Meeker, who had come to Steilacoom on some errand, picked them up and packed them on his back to his father's place.

Jacob, thinking this was an experiment for just one growing season, did not clear a field and plant the roots properly. Instead he planted the hop roots in his apple orchard between the rows of trees. Ezra wrote, "My father planted the remainder in four rows of about six rods in length, and in the following September harvested the equivalent of one bale of hops, 180 pounds, and sold them to Mr. Wood for 85 cents per pound, receiving a little over $150.00."[13] This was more money than his farm made in total for the entire previous year. It was a huge sum for that period of Puyallup Valley history and it drew attention.

Encouraged by his success Jacob decided to expand his acreage. He contracted with Erastus A. Light of Steilacoom who had some hop roots in his garden at the price of $125 per thousand.[14] Combining Light's roots with the runners from his pioneer patch in the apple orchard, Jacob had enough roots on hand to plant two acres of hops in the spring of 1867.[15]

Prices remained good and that fall Jacob sold a part of his crop to Isaac Wood and part to Captain Samuel W. Percival, another Olympia brewer, for seventy-five cents a pound. This crop yielded four hundred pounds to the acre, a pittance compared to what the valley hops growers were able to coax out of their soil a few years later. But it put six hundred dollars into Jacob's pocket after the 1867 harvest.[16] It was fortunate that Jacob began selling to a second brewer as Isaac Wood got himself into trouble that fall. He had been selling liquor to the local Indians and found himself arrested and in court.[17]

The next year (1868) Jacob raised a still larger crop, which he intended to dry in a small smoke house that he had built on his farm. In *Hop Culture* Ezra described what happened at that fall's harvest.

> For curing the second crop a small twelve by fourteen feet log house was duly fixed up. Closely chinked, daubed and underpinned, the earth banked up around the foundation so that not a breath of air could get in below the hops. On the roof, though of clapboards, and open, a formidable ventilator was erected; below a large stove was set, with pipe running around the room, of a capacity for a house of three times the size of the one in use.
>
> The writer will never forget the look of despair depicted upon the countenance of his father, when arriving on the ground, where he had gone to see "the new hop-house work," and found the upper room filled with fog and the moisture dripping back upon the hops. The old gent was in a "peck of trouble," as he said, declaring that he believed if the "durned thing" (referring to the house) "was turned bottom side up it would draw." After considerable persuasion he consented to tightening the roof and opening some holes under the foundation, when the fog immediately disappeared, and the "first kiln of hops" in Washington territory was speedily dried.[18]

The *Willamette Farmer* wrote that in 1868 Jacob Meeker "raised another and still larger crop, which he dried in a little smoke house.

A hop kiln and pickers in the White River Valley. Note the hop vines and clusters adorning the pickers. The back reads: "Washington Territory Views, W. S. Walbridge, Portrait and Landscape Photographer, Slaughter, Wash. Ter." *From the collection of the Schmidt House, Olympia Tumwater Foundation*

And the cured hops were marketed in Portland by his son Ezra, who sold them for 25 cents a pound."[19]

In *The Busy Life of Eighty-Five Years* Ezra wrote, "After having produced his third crop my father died, but not until after he had shipped his hops to Portland, Oregon."[20]

Thus we have the story of Jacob Meeker. No matter how one counts, the experimental crop set between the trees in the orchard could not have been planted in 1865 or earlier. Hops were picked in September; consequently what Ezra called Jacob's "third crop," the one produced just before his death in October 1869, was harvested in September 1869. Working backward, we find that the second crop was the four acres harvested in 1868 and the first crop was the two-acre harvest of 1867. This would put the experimental crop, with roots supplied by Isaac Wood and planted in the orchard, indisputably in 1866. There is no magical way of counting back that could produce 1865 as the beginning of Jacob Meeker's hop growing.

So did Messrs. Thompson and Meade win the medal? Two sources have already reported they planted in 1865 beating Jacob Meeker by at least a year. A cut and dried case, one might think. But the *Pacific Rural Press* of August 26, 1882, states that Thompson and Meade started their hop farm in 1867, as does the *Willamette Farmer* of August 11, 1882. John Meeker, who participated in the family hop business, also puts their start after Jacob. "Some two years after the first planting by Jacob R. Meeker, Messrs. Mead and Thompson, of Sumner, and Mr. E. Meeker, of Puyallup, caught the hop fever, obtaining roots for planting from California."[21] John, too, is slightly off on his recollection of dates. While Ezra did delay his first planting until 1868 (two years after his father's start) Thompson and Meade seem to have started in 1867.

According to the *Pacific Rural Press* article cited above, Levant F. Thompson's farm adjoined Jacob's. The $157.25 Jacob received in the fall of 1866 caught Thompson's attention.

> But after the first year's experience among the apple trees, he was not alone among his neighbors in hop culture. Knowledge of his success stimulated others to try. Adjoining the farm of Jacob Meeker was that of Mr. L. F. Thompson...who had the enterprise to go vigorously into the business. Mr. Thompson...formed a partnership with his near neighbor, E. C. Meade, and with A. R. Williamson,[22] for the purpose of sharing the expense and profits of what was then regarded as a considerable venture in planting on Mr. Thompson's land. They sent to Flint, a hop grower in Sacramento,[23] and bought 4,000 roots, which filled two barrels and stocked four acres of ground.

Again according to the *Pacific Rural Press,* the partners were late on everything that season. The roots weren't planted until May. The poles for the vines weren't placed until July, and the vines weren't trained until August. Nevertheless the crop came in at five hundred pounds to the acre, which was equal to yields in Germany where hops had been grown for centuries. This crop was sold at fifty-five cents per pound, twenty cents less than Jacob received from Isaac Wood. Still the partners grossed the enormous sum of $1,100. In 1867 this and Jacob Meeker's were the only two hop yards in the valley.[24]

Ezra had also seen enough to start making grand plans. He incorporated in 1867, forming E. Meeker & Company, a business which would be a Washington fixture for the next twenty-eight years.[25] But the new business got off to a rocky start. A con artist named S. B. Fargo swindled the firm out of $208. Meeker hired a man named F. P.

Stringing hop vines with horses. *From the collection of the Schmidt House, Olympia Tumwater Foundation*

Dugan to chase him down and retrieve the money. The nature of the con is unknown as was the outcome of the chase.[26]

The following year, 1868, in partnership with Anthony R. Williamson, who seemed to have switched loyalties from Levant and Thompson, Meeker planted his first real crop of two acres and grew what he called "a few hundred pounds" of hops.[27] It appears Ezra was the last to enter the race.

So who was first and does it really matter? It mattered a great deal to the participants in this so-called race, so much so that a reporter could not get an accurate history from any of them. Meeker started using the 1865 date in 1887, four years after he published what was likely the correct date of 1866 in *Hop Culture*, and he never looked back. No amount of playing with the calendar could bring in Thompson and Meade's first hop harvest earlier than 1865, and most of the evidence supports a date two years later. Thus, by virtue of the size of his eventual hop empire and the power it conferred upon him to tell the tale, it was Meeker's privilege to award the title to his father. He firmly closed the door on his competitors when he changed the date (unnecessarily, as it turned out). But why didn't he correct the mix-up between Charles and Isaac Wood? It would be a simple correction, true, but it would also call attention to the date change. It was best to let sleeping dogs lie. Only pesky George Himes pointed out the first error, and even he missed the second one.

So who was first? As thorough an examination as possible of the "bottom facts" produces this most probable sequence: Jacob first planted in 1866, Thompson and Meade in 1867, and Ezra in 1868. Thompson and Meade probably put up the first valley hop house in 1867 with Jacob erecting his in 1868.

The water is more than a little muddy, as they say. Meeker did his best to make sure that his father received credit for starting the industry, but years later couldn't resist putting in a small accolade for himself. He added to the story the detail that his brother stopped by his cabin with the bag of hop plantings on that fateful 1866 trip to his father's farm. While there, "I fingered out of the sack roots sufficient to plant six hills of hops, and so far as I know those were the first hops planted in the Puyallup Valley."[28]

It took some years, but from these humble beginnings an economic giant would grow. The initial hop profit of $150 earned by Jacob Meeker would within two decades become millions of dollars and in the process would transform the valley and the territory. The transition from log cabin to mansion for many of western Washington's citizens was about to begin.

A QUICK PRIMER ON HOPS

HOP CULTURE

IN THE

UNITED STATES

BEING A

PRACTICAL TREATISE ON

Hop Growing in Washington Territory,

FROM THE CUTTING TO THE BALE,

BY

E. MEEKER.

WITH FIFTEEN YEARS' EXPERIENCE OF THE AUTHOR, GIVING
MINUTE INSTRUCTIONS HOW TO PLANT, CUL-
TIVATE AND CURE THE CROP:
TOGETHER WITH
ELABORATE AND GENERAL STATISTICS OF THE HOP TRADE OF
THE WORLD, COST OF PRODUCTION, HOW TO START A
HOP YARD, BEST MODE OF PRESERVING HOPS;
WITH A SYNOPSIS OF ENGLISH AND
GERMAN METHODS.

To which is added an exhaustive article from the pen of
W. A. LAWRENCE, Esq.,
Waterville, N. Y., on Hop Raising in New York State.

WITH ILLUSTRATIONS.

PUBLISHED BY

E. MEEKER & CO..

PUYALLUP, WASHINGTON TERRITORY.

PRICE, $1.50.

Ezra Meeker's 1883 book *Hop Culture in the United States. Author's collection*

Hop Culture in the United States: Being a Practical Treatise on Hop Growing in Washington Territory from the Cutting to the Bale by Ezra Meeker was published in 1883 by E. Meeker & Co. Its selling price was $1.50. In 170 pages Meeker told the tale of hops, but he neglected to mention what hops are and what they are used for. Simply put, hops are the female seed cones or flowers that are produced by a hop plant. Hops are a staple ingredient of beer, supplying its distinctive bitter taste and acting as a preservative and antibiotic in the beer making process. With this information in hand let us see what Mr. Meeker had to say.

He began with a brief explanation as to why the crop did so well in Washington Territory. Two rivers—the Puyallup and White, each headed on the glacial slopes of Mt. Rainier—flowed into lowland valleys that were major hop producing areas. Meeker described the soil as a rich alluvial deposit 144 feet deep with no subsoil or hardpan, through which the roots of his hop plants, unchecked by any obstacle, could grow to find moisture. His own experience found some of those roots to be nine feet deep. He credited the rivers for this richness but did not suspect the role lahars, huge liquid mudflows pouring off the mountain and into its valleys over eons, also played in creating the depth of rich soil. Some four hundred years before, the Electron Mudflow had swept through the Puyallup Valley taking down giant trees and burying all under a sea of mud. Meeker further credited the mild climate, cool summer nights and not-so-warm summer days, and a long growing season for allowing smooth, constant growth of the hop plant.

Meeker went on to give the details of growing hops. Hop cuttings were planted in March or April in mounds called hills, and one or two poles were set upon each hill providing a place to which the vine could attach itself to as it grew. (Some growers attached the hop vines to strung wire or twine.) The plant produced annual vines that grew from a permanent root. These vines grew up to a foot a day and could reach a height of twenty-five feet. The ingredients for healthy plants were sun and water, with room to grow, and soil rich in potassium, phosphates and nitrogen.

The fragrant green cones, resembling small pinecones, were harvested in early September. The poles or strung wires were lowered to the ground to provide access for the pickers and the cones were placed in a large box and taken to hop kilns. These were barn-sized ovens where the hop cones were carefully dried. Hops were spread an even fifteen inches thick across the floor and dried at a temperature of 150 degrees with plenty of draft, which would cure the hops at a rate of approximately one inch an hour. Sulfur was burned under the hops at the beginning of the drying process, primarily to bleach out diseases and blemishes. Various experiments with temperature over the years, and trial and error in all aspects of the drying process, refined the curing.

The next step was to put the dried hops into 180-pound bags called bales via a machine called a hop press. These bags were made of hop cloth, a light material sufficiently stout to hold the hops but not heavy enough to incur large freight costs. From here the hops went into a warehouse awaiting shipment to a market or a brewer.

The quality of the finished hops decided their value, and they were given one of five grades starting with "fancy" at the top, followed by "strictly choice," "choice," "medium," and "low grade." To get the top rank of fancy, a bale could not be too dry and the aromatic qualities had to remain intact. But it could not be too humid either, as that made it susceptible to early rotting. Hops also had to be disease-free, clean, and have good color. All that remained was to sell the crop, pay the bills, and prepare to do it again the next year. Meeker made it sound easy. It was anything but, always a delicate balancing act dependent on weather, timing, experience, availability of labor, and a hundred other factors, not the least being luck.

Henry Weinhard's Portland, Oregon, brewery in 1888. *The West Shore Magazine*

CHAPTER 5

Suddenly Wealthy

Henry Weinhard and the Early Years

In 1869, the year of his father's death, Ezra Meeker had four acres of hops under cultivation that produced a decent sized crop. While in Portland, clearing up matters related to his father's estate, Meeker met beer brewer Henry Weinhard and struck up a business relationship that lasted for the next fifteen years.

Meeker said about Weinhard:

> I am indebted [to him] for my early knowledge of the quality of our hops and which gave me confidence to plant with an inspiring hand. Asking him during the settlement for the first crop, how many of these he could use the answer was, "Oh, I can use all you can make." When the third crop, weighing nearly 20,000 pounds came, he took them gladly; the fourth [crop of 33,000 pounds] did not stagger him, but when we reached nearly one hundred thousand pounds he "begged off," and stood aghast when in 1884 I told him I had raised three hundred and thirty-six thousand pounds, giving Washington the banner crop of the world. This yield came from 170 acres, and was enough to fill his brewery and warehouses from basement to garret, and to supply his wants for ten years.[1]

The fluctuation in the price of hops at first kept all but the bravest Puget Sound farmers away from the crop. By 1869 the price had dropped to 25 cents per pound, down from the 85 cents per pound of three years previous. In 1870 it plunged to just 4 cents per pound. The contract Meeker signed with Weinhard shielded him from these wild fluctuations and enabled him to get started in the industry under an umbrella of security. Weinhard ordered at least two hundred bales (or a total of 36,000 pounds at 180 pounds per bale) of cured hops every fall from Meeker for his Portland brewery. Meeker had to plant twenty to twenty-five acres of hop roots just to supply Weinhard's needs, and grossed an average of $9,000 yearly on this account alone.

Timing the sale of the hop crop was crucial, often determining a farmer's success or failure for his year of effort. In the early fall of 1879 a majority of the Puyallup Valley hop growers sold their crops in San Francisco for 22 cents a pound. A short time later the price advanced to 35 cents per pound. It was estimated that the valley growers who sold their 300,000 pounds of hops early lost $36,000.[2]

Thompson and Meade gambled on foreign markets and shipped their 1869 and 1870 crops to Australia. Instead of the expected profits, they faced losses as prices collapsed there as well. Their hop acreage had increased beyond the capacity of the drying kiln they built in 1867, but expecting the low prices to continue for the 1871 crop, they could see no reason to incur the expense of expanding their drying capacity. They decided to plow under two-and-one-half acres of their now twelve-acre farm. At this point the Meekers stepped in, with Marion delivering a proposal from his father (who was on the East Coast) to lease the acreage intended for the plow. The proposal was accepted and the land was leased to Meeker for $25 per year. The California hops planted there yielded nearly 2,000 pounds to the acre that year. Meeker sold the crop in the fall to Weinhard for 50 cents per pound and grossed $2,000 on this land alone.[3] If he had shipped his hops to the San Francisco market he would have received a price of 70 cents per pound and grossed $2,800.

Interest in hops grew slowly. Two more Puyallup farmers, James Stewart and John V. Meeker (Ezra's brother), had stepped gingerly into the business by 1871.[4] In December 1872 the Steilacoom newspaper reported that there were just thirty-seven claimants living in the Puyallup Valley and that they had a combined 1,360 acres under cultivation.[5] Hops, however, accounted for just 383 of those acres, or slightly more than a quarter. In 1872 the *Pacific Tribune* listed others who were in the business that year: Meeker, 50 acres;[6] Thompson & Meade, 40 acres; Ryan & Avery, 33 acres; Fred Clarke, 16 acres; Kincaid Brothers, 14 acres; James W. Law, 10 acres; Joseph R. Dickenson, 12 acres; Isaac Lemon, 25 acres; J. P. Stewart, 8 acres; A. W. Woolery, 11 acres; and about 150 acres owned and controlled by other parties.[7]

Growing hops was a learn-as-you-go business in the Puyallup Valley in those days since none of the parties involved had any previous experience with the crop; but with serious money to be made, the farmers who jumped in by necessity became quick studies.

Promoting Puget Sound

Meeker was born a risk taker and promoter. At the urging of Elisha T. Gunn, editor of the *Olympia Transcript*, he wrote a short book in 1870 titled *Washington Territory West of the Cascade Mountains*. While Gunn pushed Meeker to take on the project, he did not fund it. Marshall Blinn stepped forward and offered to loan Meeker $1,000 to cover the cost of printing 5,000 copies and finance a trip to New York City, where he hoped to sell them.[8] Meeker wrote, "I pondered this for a long time. A thousand dollars looked mighty big to me. I then was struggling with the heavy timber on my homestead…with no income in previous years, though I thought I saw daylight ahead in the hop business."[9] He pondered, then leaped. He wrote, "I believe this pamphlet (book, my friends persisted in calling it) was the first publication of any kind put out from Washington Territory other than newspapers."[10] As collateral for the loan, Ezra and Eliza Jane mortgaged their Fern Hill (Swamp Place) donation land claim property.[11] On December 5, 1870 at 3 a.m. Meeker (about to turn forty) left for New York with 2,500 copies of his book (leaving the other 2,500 copies in Olympia)[12] and a display of fifty-two varieties of pressed, winter-blooming plants put together by Mr. Harvey R. Woodard of West Olympia just for this project.[13] He also carried a letter of introduction to Horace Greeley, editor of the *New York Weekly Tribune*, from Beriah Brown, a *Portland Herald* editor.[14]

Meeker took the stage, or mud wagon as most called it, to Cowlitz Landing, a boat from there to Portland, and a sailing vessel to San Francisco. He was seasick for the entire ocean voyage, as he would continue to be on almost every sea voyage he undertook for the rest of his life. He wrote of that voyage that he did not "care whether the ship went down if I could only be relieved of the agony within me." And he "made a mental resolution that I would never—no, never—…go to sea again; I would walk a year first."[15] The completion of the transcontinental railroad in 1869 gave Meeker a new option for cross-country travel. He boarded a train in San Francisco for New York, and sitting upright in a rigid seat for most of the journey, arrived at his destination eight days later.

Here Meeker sought and received an interview with Horace Greeley whose newspaper he had read religiously for eighteen years. Greeley examined the flower collection and suggested that Meeker exhibit it at the New York Farmers' Club and write up a story about these wondrous plants. The story was published in Greeley's newspaper, picked up by others and eventually reached two million readers.[16]

It was an act of some boldness on Meeker's part, however, that made the trip a financial success. He made his way to the offices of Jay Cooke, Northern Pacific Railroad tycoon and financier. With booklet in hand Meeker asked for an interview. Meeker was held in an outer office while the booklet was sent in to Cooke for his perusal. Cooke came out and was immediately surrounded by people who had been waiting to see him. After a moment he turned to Meeker and asked if he could accompany him (Cooke) on the evening train to Hartford, Connecticut. Meeker agreed, scrambled to get his flowers and a supply of books and made it to the train just before it departed. He found Cooke on the train and took a seat beside him, whereupon Cooke promptly fell asleep. Meeker wrote, "For a moment I felt a little uncomfortable, wondering to myself if I had crowded myself beside one who did not relish my company."[17] When Cooke awoke Meeker's fears were allayed. Cooke had never met anyone from the Puget Sound country and took much interest in what Ezra had to say. He and Meeker toured New England, Ezra lecturing about Puget Sound and Cooke pitching bonds for the railroad to the audiences. At the end of the tour Meeker worked for a while in Cooke's Philadelphia office. Cooke also purchased all of Meeker's books (including those left in Olympia) with the intention of placing them on his trains as advertisements. In March 1871, Meeker returned to Puyallup and his hop business. On October 17, 1871, he repaid Blinn and satisfied the mortgage.[18]

The contents of the booklet are enlightening. Meeker gave a concise account of almost everything there was to know about western Washington in 1870. He began with a geographical description of the area and continued to an in-depth examination of the three major

WASHINGTON TERRITORY

WEST OF THE

CASCADE MOUNTAINS,

CONTAINING A DESCRIPTION OF

PUGET SOUND,

AND RIVERS EMPTYING INTO IT,

THE LOWER COLUMBIA, SHOALWATER BAY, GRAY'S HARBOR,
TIMBER, LANDS, CLIMATE, FISHERIES, SHIP BUILDING,
COAL MINES, MARKET REPORTS, TRADE, LABOR,
POPULATON, WEALTH AND RESOURCES.

Entered according to Act of Congress, in the year 1870, by E. Meeker, in the
office of the Librarian of Congress, at Washington.

BY E. MEEKER.

OLYMPIA, W. T.:
PRINTED AT THE TRANSCRIPT OFFICE.
1870.

This rare, original copy of Meeker's 1870 booklet was likely a gift
from Meeker to Naches Pass road builder Edward Jay Allen.
Hervey Allen Papers, 1831–1965, Special Collections Department,
Hillman Library, University of Pittsburgh

industries west of the Cascade Mountains—lumber, fisheries, and coal.
The principal cities were described: Olympia population 1,502; Steilacoom 300; Port Townsend 500; Seattle, too small to mention, but it

housed the territorial university. In fifty-two pages he simply over-whelmed the reader with statistics. But in 1870 there was no mention of hops or hop growing. That economic engine was still in its infancy. Meeker and a handful of others were about to impact those statistics in a major way.

THE INFANT INDUSTRY

Not much is known about Meeker's hop growing activities in 1872, but it wasn't in his nature to let money he earned lie around. We can sur-mise that he expanded his hop acreage significantly. Whatever he did, it must have entailed enough risk to set Eliza Jane's alarm bells to ring-ing. On July 17, 1872, she filed this with her legal papers: "Notice; Eliza Jane Meeker declares that the East 1/2 of Midland Gardens [Swamp Place] is her separate property and in no way is liable for the debts of her husband, Ezra M. Meeker."[19]

The various Meeker farms had fifty acres of hops under cultiva-tion in 1872. Assuming a yield of around 2,000 pounds an acre, these farms could have easily grossed $50,000 in 1872, split in some fashion between Ezra, John V., and Nancy Meeker. This was serious money and it inspired Ezra to spend—much on his family, but more on other enterprises. This spending is what, no doubt, alarmed his wife. Eliza Jane wasn't alone in her worry. Meeker's farming practices alarmed fellow members of the Puget Sound Farmers' Club as well. They responded with this warning. "E. M. Meeker writes under date of April 28th. 'I am head over heals [sic] in spring work, with six hands and two klootchmen[20] to attend to;' cultivating hops of course. The success of our friend last season in hop culture has, we fear, turned him from the true course in farming, never to rely on one branch alone. An early and severe frost would kill his hops and hopes in one blow. Specialties are not safe in the long run."[21]

Nearly half of the valley's thirty-seven claimants were growing hops by the end of 1872, with all but a few doing so on a small scale.[22] The following year, however, John Meeker wrote, "a perfect furor came on, and every one desired to plant hops, resulting in high prices for roots. Although I had sold the product of my own hop yard of 1872 for thirty cents per pound, yet I sold roots from the same ground in the spring of 1873 for considerably more money than I had received for the crop of hops."[23]

By the end of 1873, Ezra Meeker, who just five years earlier was surveying in the winter rains of Puget Sound trying to supplement a meager farm income, had become a wealthy man. That season he shipped twelve thousand pounds of hops to New York where they commanded "an advanced price."[24] He did so well with his 1873 hop crop that he was able to invest $13,000 in a new enterprise.[25]

Meeker determined that a store in the budding city of Tacoma would be profitable and provide a diversification from hop growing. He obviously intended the store to be well stocked, as in addition to the $13,000 worth of merchandise he brought with him by ship from San Francisco he also received twelve tons of goods by rail from Portland.[26] In a practice Meeker often followed after starting a business project, he turned the management of it over to someone else. This time his eldest son, Marion, was placed in charge of the store.[27] Beginning in December 1873 Meeker advertised his store regularly in the Tacoma *Pacific Tribune*.

FINANCING AND MARKETING

The hop business was, from the beginning, a high-risk enterprise. It required much capital to plant, harvest, and sell a crop, and it was capital the farmers simply did not have. Hop growers had to borrow large sums of money to produce their crop and finding financing was difficult. Meeker borrowed funds from wealthy individuals, using his land as collateral, and paid off the mortgages when he sold his crop in the fall. For example, in February 1874 the Meekers borrowed $1500 from John Gale, presumably to cover the costs of planting. In June 1874 Ezra and Eliza Jane borrowed a further $11,725 from Charles W. Prindle, presumably to pay the costs of harvesting and selling the hops. The two mortgages were paid off the next year. The Meekers were taking out and paying off such mortgages at least through 1877.[28]

Just getting cash to pay the workers required risk. The Indian hop-pickers insisted on being paid in silver coins. To obtain these coins Meeker deposited drafts with government agencies in San Francisco. In turn the government shipped silver coins by steamer in an amount up to one thousand dollars to Edwin R. Rogers' store in Steilacoom. The coins were shipped without freight charges since the government wanted to get silver into circulation in Puget Sound. All that remained was to get the coins to Puyallup. In *Uncle Ezra's Short Stories for Children,* Meeker describes one occasion when this was done. In 1876 he sent his thirteen-year-old son, Fred Meeker, to Steilacoom to retrieve the silver shipment. Despite his mother's concern Fred rode alone, making the sixteen-mile trip to Steilacoom and back. He returned safely to Puyallup the same evening with fifty pounds of silver stored in saddlebags that were strapped behind the saddle and hidden under a blanket. Ezra later admitted it was "risky" to send such a young boy on such an errand but said Fred was equal to the occasion.[29]

Other hop farmers turned to the enterprising houses of Corbitt & MacCleay of Portland and San Francisco for financing. The *Tacoma Herald* credited them with having "to a great extent, nurtured and carried the (hop) business, furnishing the necessary capital and facilities for conducting it, and that too, at a time when no other firm would probably have made such advances as they have."[30]

It did not take the Puyallup hop farmers long to realize that San Francisco was their gateway to the hop market. Washington Territory had only a few small breweries. Meeker had the corner on the Portland market with his arrangement with Henry Weinhard.[31] San Francisco Bay was the terminus of the transcontinental railroad and the route to the east coast markets, and its sizable population supported a number of local breweries. According to the Tacoma newspaper, by 1877 the market had expanded. "California, Oregon and Washington Territory hops, owing to their superior quality, have been for the past few years an important feature in the New York market."[32]

Getting the hops to the City on the Bay and then to the East Coast was not without difficulty and risk. Prior to 1873, when the Northern Pacific Railroad reached Commencement Bay in Tacoma, the closest real port to Puyallup was Steilacoom, a rough two-day round-trip wagon ride away. Some growers opted for a shorter but more difficult route to tidewater. They hauled their crops down an even worse road on the north side of the Puyallup River to the sloughs at its mouth. From there they boated them across Commencement Bay to the single wharf at Old Tacoma where they hoped to put

them on the occasional sailing vessel that might stop in. Most chose
the Steilacoom route. Everything going to San Francisco from either
point required a sea journey and all sea voyages carried the risk of
shipwreck.[33]

The valley farmers soon developed the practice of pooling the hops
bound for San Francisco into shipments escorted to the bay by one of
the growers, who would then be in charge of marketing it. In the fall
of 1873 the task fell to Meeker. By mid-decade as the hop harvest grew
larger, multiple voyages were required to move an entire season's crop.
In 1875 George T. Vining was the unlucky escort on one voyage. George
was a Puyallup Valley hop farmer, merchant, and father of seven.
He was also the last postmaster at Franklin, Washington (renamed
Sumner in 1875). Vining boarded the cargo ship *Pacific* on November
3, 1875, in charge of 363 bales of hops, the product of seventy-five acres,
about 10 percent of that year's crop. Off Cape Flattery at 8:00 p.m.
Thursday, November 4, in the midst of a rainstorm, the *Pacific* collided
with the sailing ship *Orpheus*, was breached and sank.[34] Vining was last
seen alive below decks trying to save the precious hops. He went down
with the ship. Meeker described the loss as a crippling blow to the valley farmers.[35] This was not an isolated instance. In October 1877 hops
shipped on the steamer *Constitution* were a total loss when she sank.[36]

Did Meeker ever have doubts? In 1877 when a report surfaced that
he intended plowing up his hop yards and getting out of the business,
he responded by planting more land with hops.[37] Despite the wild fluctuations in hop prices from year to year and difficulties getting the
crop to market, profits were still considerable and Meeker wasn't about
to give up this wealth.

Picking Hops

Throughout the 1870s and the 1880s the success or failure of a year's
work depended on getting enough pickers at the right time to harvest
the crop. Hop field hands, and especially pickers, were hard to come by.
By 1873 the non-Indian population of Pierce County was still a paltry
1700. Without the aid of Native American and Chinese workers most
of the valley hop crop would have died on the vine. But they came,

Puyallup Valley hop scenes. From *Harpers Weekly*, 1888.

initially by the hundreds, and eventually the thousands. How did this happen? Let us deal with the Native Americans first.

By July of each year the hop growers of Washington Territory had a pretty clear idea as to the expected size of that year's crop and of the number of pickers needed for the harvest. Accordingly they sent agents around to the various reservations soliciting pickers. The reach was far and wide. All of the Puget Sound tribes were contacted, as were those east of the Cascade Mountains.[38] The reach went north as well, up into British Columbia and even to Alaska, 1,800 miles away. In 1889 Ezra Meeker went as far north as Prince Rupert, British Columbia, to secure 150 Native American workers.

The watch began around mid-August. The burning question: would the Indians come? Meeker said they failed to appear in the needed numbers just once (1888), and as the size of the harvest grew so did the number of Indians who came almost by magic, knowing they were needed. Nervous agents were sent to Seattle to watch for the parade of canoes that would be coming down from the north. By the end of August the hop-pickers began to arrive. They came in families of men, women and children. Some of the canoes were large enough to carry a dozen or more people. "They presented quite a picturesque appearance, sailing along in line with their white sails bellying in the wind, and the bright colors of the Indians' garments contrasting strongly with the dark outline of their canoes."[39]

The Pierce County agents directed a portion of the migration to the mouth of the Puyallup River in Commencement Bay, where the canoes were paddled upstream as far as the Reservation Agency. There the Indians met the growers who brought wagons and teams to carry them and their baggage to the hop yards.[40] Others were directed to the Snoqualmie Valley and hop yards such as Wold's near Issaquah.

The numbers were huge. Historian Paige Raibmon documented that six thousand British Columbia Indians were away in Washington Territory's hop fields in 1885. This represented one quarter of the Native population of the province.[41] In 1886 four thousand hop-pickers were engaged in harvesting the hops in the Puyallup and White River Valleys. Meeker said, "[S]even hundred of these were white people, the remainder being principally Indians and a few Chinamen."[42]

Each grower's style in dealing with the influx was unique. At first Meeker tried to board his Indian workers. The Meeker women prepared food, set it out on tables, and called the workers to help themselves. A few did, and hoarded all the "grub." To solve this problem, individual portions were put on tin plates, but the plates were thought to be included with the dinner and were not returned. By the third year Ezra had the Indians setting up camp and boarding themselves for the hop-picking season. One financial perk unique to Meeker's hop farms was the payment of one dollar to each woman whose child was born on the farm during picking season. Meeker said one year he paid out seven dollars in such bonuses.[43]

In 1877 Native American Peter Stanup offered his view of a late-August hop harvest:

The Indians from down Sound[44] came to the Puyallup Valley... and found arrangements made for picking hops...the picking commenced, with 1,600 pickers on 400 acres of hops. The Indians were superintended on each field by Indian bucks, and the work continued till the first Saturday, when almost all of the males and females went to the Sumner race-track, to witness the races and other gambling business—all day till night, then the dance took place at Uncle Davies' stand and in the morning, on Sunday, at 11 o'clock, the Puyallup and Christian Klickitat and some of the Skokomish Indians made their church back of Grainger & Boatmans. Coke H. Stevise preached the sermon, while the rain was pouring on the multitudes; but still they would not stop till they got through; and the Tulalip Indians, Catholics, were holding church at Boatman's, while the Devil's followers were having their way at the race ground.[45]

It may seem counterintuitive that such a large migration of Native Americans into Puget Sound was tolerated and even welcomed when just years earlier the white settlers of Puget Sound were at war with the local tribes. The 1860s and 1870s were a time of escalating conflicts between the U.S. government and the western tribes. George Armstrong Custer met his demise at the Little Big Horn River in Montana in June 1876. The next year, in 1877, the U.S. Army was pursuing Chief Joseph and the Nez Perce. That same year hop growers in Washington and Oregon needed 2,700 pickers—the majority of whom were Native Americans. Were relations between Indians and whites in Puget Sound somehow exempted from the discord throughout the West?

Coll Thrush in his book *Native Seattle* offers an economic reason for the accommodation. He referenced an 1878 Seattle newspaper, "that predicted that after three or four weeks earning 'considerable money' from labor in the fields, the Indians 'will then return, on their way stopping at Seattle to spend the larger part of their earnings.' The movement of working Indian people—and not insignificantly, their money—in and out of Seattle was becoming part of the city's urban calendar."[46]

The *Tacoma Daily Ledger* reported on the 150 Prince Rupert Indians hired by Meeker in 1889: "These Indians will pick the whole of Campbell & Meeker's crop, consisting of fifty acres. In about three weeks, if there is no interruption—as they are paid $1 per box—they will have at the end of that time $4,000. The average crop being eighty boxes per acre this does not include bosses and pole puller, who are paid $2 and $2.50 per day, and in some cases even higher."[47]

Money provided incentive for all parties to behave themselves and get along for the month they were required to be in close contact. The

This photograph first appeared in William Bonney's *History of Pierce County*. Bonney labeled it, "Old Ezra Meeker Hop Yard, Puyallup, 1883, Indian camp in foreground." *Washington State Historical Society 2010.0.289*

local merchants anticipated a spending spree and it behooved them to play nice with their temporary visitors. The growers simply could not harvest without pickers, and the Indians, of course, wanted and needed the money. At the end of September the armada of canoes wound its way home to Canada and Alaska. The Puget Sound tribes returned to their reservations. In the main, the Native Americans did not outstay their welcome.

After all available Indians were set to work, growers began importing Chinese workers whom they paid ninety cents a day without board.[48] The Chinese hop workers also came from near and far. Those who had been working on the construction of the transcontinental railroad found themselves cut loose from employment with its completion in 1869. Many came to western Washington in the early 1870s to seek work on the railroad line being built here and migrated instead to the region's hop yards. Others went to Tacoma and Seattle where they found growers eager to hire them. Some were hired from out of state by Chinese labor brokers and sent to Washington by ship and rail. As mentioned above, in the early years of the industry the ratio of non-white to white workers was large, giving an appreciation of how much these workers were needed. The *Tacoma Herald* supplied the numbers for the hop-picking season on one farm. "Mr. Stone dries the first kiln of hops of any farmer in the Valley, this season, and his twenty-two Chinese and eight or ten white persons begin picking this morning and he dries his first kiln tonight."[49]

The workforce that picked the hop crop each fall was large, transient, and of diverse cultures and languages. Problems and misunderstandings were inevitable. The growers demanded that the boxes be free of leaves and branches and that the hops not be picked in clusters. Disputes about the quality of the picking often led to pay being docked, which in turn led to work stoppages by the pickers. An 1877 dispute with Chinese workers resulted in an appeal to "Quong Ti & Co., of Portland, who are responsible for the picking of hops have been telegraphed, and they are expected to see that the work is continued according to agreement."[50] According to Raibmon, the Native Americans were adept at using work stoppages to get higher pay and improve working conditions. As the white population of the territory grew, the friction increased, especially with the Chinese, who committed the sin of not leaving after the picking season. By the middle of the 1880s anti-Chinese sentiment reached a boiling point.

Years of Prosperity 1874-1879

Eliza Jane's worries about her husband's spending, prompting her disclaimer regarding his debts, proved unnecessary, as 1874 was a banner year for Puyallup Valley hops. The *Pacific Tribune* reported the crop was double that of the previous year, but demand still exceeded supply, resulting in prices between thirty and forty cents per pound, and farmers were grossing from $500 to $650 per acre.[51]

By the middle of the decade, hop growing in the Puyallup Valley had become a big business. In 1875 a meeting of the valley growers was held in Meeker's newly opened Puyallup store. There "it was ascertained that about nine hundred thousand pounds will be produced and that to gather this crop twenty-seven hundred pickers will be required."[53]

Throughout the rest of the decade the Puyallup Valley hop industry continued to expand and prosper. In 1876 over 1,700 pickers were needed to bring in that season's crop of four hundred tons.[53] Another thousand were needed in the remainder of the territory. Prices for the year, however, were as low as twelve cents a pound. Meeker faced other hazards besides low prices. While on a business trip to Portland that July he suffered a mishap. While preparing to mount a horse "it kicked him a terrific blow on the head, breaking the jawbone and knocking out a number of teeth."[54]

While a portion of the year's hops were sold to local breweries around Puget Sound and Portland, the majority were sent by ship to San Francisco and then by railroad across the continent. Puyallup Valley hops were now being sold in Midwest markets such as Milwaukee and St. Louis and on the East Coast in New York. As the large valley growers like Ezra Meeker were becoming wealthy men, more farmers began to enter the business. The names McCarty, Kincaid,

TOBACCO

At the end of the 1870s Ezra gave his wife yet another cause for worry as he planted eight acres of tobacco and began manufacturing cigars. This crop went nowhere. Meeker realized no "remuneration" and the experiment ended quickly, no doubt to Eliza Jane's great relief.

Then on April 20, 1882, Ezra wrote a letter that no doubt surprised and delighted his wife, and it had nothing to do with hops or business of any sort. Ezra announced that he had quit smoking cold turkey at age 51.

Meeker started smoking as a child when he would help his mother, a lifelong smoker, light her pipe. "That was before the time of matches…and mother…would send me to put a coal in her pipe, and so I would take a whiff or two, just to get it started, you know, which, however, soon developed into the habit of lingering to keep it going. But let me be just to myself…more than twenty years ago I threw away my pipe and have never smoked since, and never will.[55]

Meade, Woolery, Bonney, Bowman, Matthews, Van Ogle, Campbell, Thompson & Sons, Carson, Dickenson, Boatman, and Gardella began to appear in newspaper accounts as important valley hop growers, all competing with Meeker.

Not all the competition was friendly. In 1878 an attempt was made to burn Meeker's hop buildings. Fortunately a watchman discovered the fire shortly after it was set and little damage was done. Meeker told the local newspaper he thought the fire was set in an effort to get his pickers. He had just hired 120 Indian hop-pickers and if his buildings were burned these pickers would be thrown onto the labor market and "some irresponsible half-breed, Indian or white man might have obtained fifty or a hundred dollars for furnishing a given number of pickers on short notice."[56] Meeker wasn't the only grower to face arson. Later that month some of Levant Thompson's buildings were burned. Nathan and Benjamin Kelly of Elhi shared the same fate.[57]

In 1879, according to the U.S. Census, fifty-five growers in Washington Territory had planted 534 acres in hops with a yield of 703,277 pounds.[58] Over four hundred acres of those hops were in the Puyallup Valley. Farmers who ten years earlier were clearing trees, living in log cabins (the Meekers were still living in their cabin, and would be for another ten years), and scrambling to make a living were now looking at a very different future. It would be a future that tested their mettle.

First Ride on the Northern Pacific

Jay Cooke's Northern Pacific Railroad line from the port of Kalama on the Columbia River to its terminus at Commencement Bay on Puget Sound and the fledgling city of Tacoma was completed December 16, 1873. For years this railroad line was an orphan. It connected Tacoma to Portland, via a ferry at Kalama. But there was no connection between Portland and the eastern U.S. cities. Even so, it was a major event for the citizens of Puget Sound, as it was the beginning of the end of their isolation from the rest of the nation. And it was an event that Meeker was not about to miss.

John Sprague, the railroad superintendent, invited Meeker to accompany him on the first train (consisting of an engine, one passenger car, and one freight car) from Tacoma to Kalama.

> I think there were but eight passengers in all—Gen. John W. Sprague, Theodore Hosmer and wife, Harry and Pitt Cook, myself and wife, and our little 5-year-old daughter, Olive.[59]
>
> On the first train two small shipments of freight were carried, a shipment of fish from the salt seawater of Puget Sound to the fresh water inlet of the Willamette. The other a shipment of furs by myself...
>
> After that day, and for many months after, one train a day over to the Columbia river and return was sufficient to accommodate the traffic—a mixed train of one passenger and perhaps two or three freight cars.[60]

CHAPTER 6

Building a Town

Puyallup is Born

The settlement that grew around the Carson Ferry on the Puyallup River was for a time called Franklin. James Stewart, who arrived in the valley in 1859, is credited with using the name when he established a post office near the ferry in 1862.[1] (Franklin, New York, was his hometown.) Through 1874, mail for residents living on both sides of the river was addressed to Franklin, Washington Territory. Meeker recalled the renaming of the town: "We were all tired of the name Franklin, for there were so many Franklins that our mail was continually being sent astray. We agreed there never would be but one Puyallup; and in that we were unquestionably right, for surely there will never be another."[2]

The first post office named Puyallup was established on the south side of the river on September 3, 1874, in the home of Darius M. Ross, just west of Clark's Creek.[3] From this date on the Puyallup Valley would be home to two post offices, one on each side of the river. The Franklin post office on the north side of the river retained that name for another year, until September 20, 1875, when the U.S. Postal Service changed its name to Sumner. Unlucky George Vining, who died in the sinking of the steamship *Pacific*, served as Franklin's last postmaster, operating the post office out of his store.

On May 22, 1877, Ezra Meeker was named the Puyallup postmaster and he moved that post office into his store on the west side of Meridian Street.[4] Eventually the title of Puyallup postmaster passed on to Marion Meeker. Puyallup on the south side of the river and Sumner on the north side became established names in the mid-1870s and remain so to date.

Near the end of the decade Meeker immersed himself in civic affairs. On February 18, 1877, he recorded the plat for the future city of

Puyallup.[5] That same year he became a principle in the incorporation of the Puyallup Valley Cemetery Association and was elected to the committee that selected a site for the county fairgrounds, the forerunner of today's Washington State Fair.[6] In February 1878 Meeker was asked by the Pierce county commissioners to help run the election that chose delegates to write a state constitution.[7]

SCHOOL DAYS

Ezra Meeker placed a very high value on education. As a child in Indiana, his formal schooling lasted only a few months. However, he watched his older brothers pass through the grades and do their lessons at home. John and Oliver both attended school much more regularly than did Ezra, and no doubt some of their learning was passed along to their younger brother. Meeker later claimed that his real education came from reading Horace Greeley's *New York Tribune* for some eighteen years. Meeker was determined to secure opportunities that he lacked for his children and the children of the Puyallup Valley.

A Mrs. Carson had run a valley school in 1861, but there was none in 1862 or 1863. In those years the Meeker children received their education at home. In 1864 the valley residents erected a twenty- by twenty-four-foot log cabin school about a half-mile from Meeker's home, near the site of the present high school, on land donated by James Stewart. The pupils sat on a bench with a slanting shelf along the wall for a desk. Thus their backs were to the teacher who stood in the middle of the room. The windows were open slits covered with canvas. Twenty-four-year-old Amanda Meeker, Oliver's widow, was the teacher.[8] This was a subscription school. Amanda was hired for a three-month term at a certain sum to teach the children of those parents who paid the fees. Frank, Marion, Ella, and Carrie Meeker all attended this school. The next year John Meeker was hired to teach. Thirty-one children of school age lived in the valley in 1866, and the school term was extended to six months. The parents were charged four dollars per pupil and John Meeker was paid $280 to teach. Uncle John taught at the log cabin school until 1871 when he turned the reins over to Thomas Coon.[9] That year a new, slightly larger, school building replaced the log cabin school.

Thomas Coon was near the end of his junior year at Willamette University when he received an offer from Ezra Meeker to become the teacher at Puyallup.[10] Coon was born in Silverton, Oregon, Mary Weller Meeker's hometown. How he and Meeker crossed paths is not known—perhaps through Allen Porter, Mary's uncle, who was a long-time resident of the White River Valley near Puyallup.[11] Coon was seventeen years old when he accepted Meeker's offer. He obtained his teaching certificate at Tacoma in June 1871 through an examination that required him to provide a specimen of his handwriting and to state the name of the school he attended. He would find that seven of his pupils were older than he was. Coon recalled in 1921 that before the completion of a school building, class was held in a vacant house on Meeker land that had been used to store hops.[12]

This school session lasted six months. There is no record of who taught the Franklin school in 1872 and 1873, as Thomas Coon returned to Willamette University in Salem, Oregon, for two years. In October 1873 another valley school opened for four months a few miles up the river from Puyallup at Elhi (Alderton). Its teacher was Miss Delia McNeal of Salem, Oregon, who received one hundred dollars and board for her work.

On Thanksgiving Day, 1873, Eliza Jane Meeker organized a special event for the local school children of Elhi. Miss McNeal described the festivities.

> On Thanksgiving day we went to school as usual but just before noon, two wagons filled with people from the Franklin [Puyallup] neighborhood, drove up to the schoolhouse…Mrs. Ezra Meeker seemed to be chaperone for the crowd. They came in until the room was filled to overflowing when they brought out their baskets and produced a "Thanksgiving Feast" in which both pupils and teacher joined, thankful not only for the feast but for the kind hearts which prompted the visit.[13]

On April 12, 1874, the two valley teachers, Mr. Coon and Miss McNeal, married and "theirs was the distinction of being the first couple married in Tacoma."[14] That spring and summer the two teachers changed schools. Thomas Coon taught at a school on the north side of the river in today's Sumner and the new Mrs. Coon left Elhi and began a six-month term teaching at Franklin.[15]

According to Mrs. Coon, the school also served as a community center. "Debating societies met there and discussed the problems of the times. The Good Templars had their meetings on Saturday night and Sunday school and church came the following day. It was a common meeting ground for all regardless of creeds or politics."[16]

Interestingly, Ezra did not have his daughter Carrie attend the Franklin high school. She was sent to a boarding school in Portland where she completed her secondary education. Several years later Olive Meeker, Ezra's youngest daughter, completed her high school years at a boarding school in the San Francisco area. By 1877 there were 106 children attending school in Puyallup.[17]

A Library for Puyallup

Eliza Jane Meeker created Puyallup's first library in the Meeker cabin. For a number of years she kept her reading room open three evenings a week, and its sixty-seven periodicals could be checked out and taken home for up to a week at a time. Ezra gave Eliza Jane full credit for making this library a success.[18]

On December 12, 1880, Meeker and seven other Puyallup businessmen formed the Puyallup Library Association. Stock in the association sold for five dollars a share, and five thousand dollars capital was raised.[19] This was the second library association that Meeker helped start in Washington Territory, the first being in Steilacoom in the 1850s. A small room was rented on the corner of Pioneer and Meridian, and Frances McCoy was hired as the librarian at twenty-five dollars a month with the requirement that if she wished to take a vacation she had to find her own replacement.

In 1888 the city of Puyallup accepted a gift from Ezra and Eliza Jane of the land upon which their original cabin stood with the stipulation that the land could only be used as a park. Years later, when the city applied for a Carnegie grant to build a new library on part of what was then known as Pioneer Park, they needed Meeker's permission to do so. It was January 1912, and at the time Meeker was wintering in Texas as part of his second Oregon Trail Monument Expedition. The city officials located him and secured his permission. Meeker only asked that his old cabin be left untouched as he hoped to preserve it as a kind of a museum.[20] The new library opened in 1913.

SMALLPOX AND THE SHOTGUN QUARANTINE

In the first week of November 1881 the Northwest was hit with a smallpox outbreak. Cases were scattered as far afield as Dayton, Washington, and Portland, Oregon. The center of the contagion, however, seemed to be Pierce County, and in particular the city of New Tacoma. There were two deaths out of sixteen cases in that city within the week, three deaths on the nearby Puyallup Indian Reservation, and one in Steilacoom. Government authorities immediately quarantined the city. All rail traffic to and from New Tacoma was halted. The U.S. Post Office refused to deliver to or accept any mail from New Tacoma. Docking steamships refused to allow anyone from the city to come near, even to unload cargo. The New Tacoma City Council ordered its health officer to halt all traffic between New Tacoma and its immediate neighbor, Old Tacoma. The schools, both public and private, were closed and all public meetings cancelled. The *Pierce County News* stated that a "Report says that the telephone wires connecting the Tacomas [are] to be cut to prevent extending the disease."[21] Those stricken were confined to their homes and a flag placed in the front yard designating that the residence was quarantined.

Some residents of New Tacoma felt their city was unduly stigmatized. "The last issue of the *Olympia Transcript* has an article from a correspondent who states what Mr. So and so told Mr. So and so, how small pox originated in New Tacoma and he gets about as near the truth as such reports usually are."[22] It also complained about the interdiction of the mails.[23]

By mid-November the city health officer reported that he had visited fifteen cases and had learned of six more. A petition was handed over to the city council requesting that the Chinese not carry washing through the streets during the epidemic. The Council tabled it for future consideration but did order that the Chinese quarter be thoroughly searched daily and fumigated weekly.[24]

As panicky citizens began to flee to outlying communities, Puyallup, led by Ezra Meeker,[25] enforced the quarantine with shotguns. "Armed guards were posted at all entrances to Puyallup with orders to shoot."[26] "It was given out that no persons from the infected districts would be permitted to enter Puyallup. Some people were actually turned back."[27] This effort by Meeker to protect the city of Puyallup would be used against him by the editor of the *Ledger* four years later when he (Meeker) argued that the Tacoma City officials had no legal authority for the forcible removal of the Chinese. The editor threw the argument back in Meeker's face saying he had no legal authority to prevent the entry into Puyallup of Tacoma citizens during the smallpox scare, but he did it anyway.

By the end of the month the *Pierce County News* reported that the "small pox scare" was nearly over. "There has been but one new case in ten days. In all there are 16 cases and they are convalescent. But four flags are up and all danger is now past. Gen. Sprague, of N.P.R.R. Co., has sent a telegraphic request that the embargo on through travel be taken off."[28] Puyallup officials stated, "The quarantine against New Tacoma will be removed in a few days if no more cases occur there."[29]

William P. Bonney, at this time operating a drugstore on Pacific Avenue opposite Eighth Street, saw the epidemic as an opportunity. In a tiny room in the rear of his store, he offered a fumigation service that promised protection from the pox. The patient, or victim, sat in the tiny room, which was filled with fumes of burning sulfur, sucking in oxygen from a small hole cut in the door. At twenty-five cents per treatment, Bonney found himself quite busy. He also sold a tin box filled with carbolic crystals, to be carried about in one's pocket to protect from the contagion.[30]

The *Pierce County News* summed up the financial toll. "The pestilence has entailed a heavy indebtedness upon New Tacoma. The Common Council have estimated it in gross, at $5000 and has levied a special tax of one per cent on all taxable property to discharge the liabilities incurred. No doubt the Council will, in time publish an exhibit, showing the expenditures of the money raised for the small pox fund."[31]

CHAPTER 7

The Feud

Meeker's propensity to battle a rival to the point of absurdity is best illustrated by his dealings with Alexander S. Farquharson. The two men, who began their relationship as business partners, clashed repeatedly for nearly a decade, keeping the territorial courts quite busy. In actuality their disputes were incidental to the important growth and development that the two men fostered in the burgeoning territory.

FARQUHARSON VS. MEEKER

In the long feud between Alexander Farquharson and Ezra Meeker only Farquharson's side has been told, and Meeker was always the villain. Other than a contemporary letter or two, Meeker barely mentioned the incidents that Farquharson wrote so passionately about in his memoir. Careful research, however, has debunked Farquharson's version of many of these events.

Years after the feud took place Farquharson typed a memoir in which he told his version of the history that entangled the two men. That manuscript found its way into the collections of the Washington State Historical Society.[1] There it sat until Herbert Hunt wrote his *History of Tacoma* in 1916 in which he briefly summarized Farquharson's conflict with Meeker, using Farquharson's manuscript as his sole source. Edgar T. Short of the *Tacoma Times*, in a series of articles published in 1935 and again in 1941, told the story of this feud in great detail, again using Farquharson's manuscript as his primary source. Thus the version that became "accepted history" was Farquharson's. With that in mind, the tale begins.

The Stave Factory

Early descriptions of the Puyallup Valley mention the large cottonwood trees that lined the river. These trees, while presenting an obstacle to farming, would be a valuable commercial resource once cut—if a market for them could be found. In December 1875 Alexander Farquharson of San Francisco arrived in the Northwest with a plan to purchase cottonwood in large quantities. Cottonwood was used to make the binding hoops for the wooden barrels used as containers for California sugar being shipped to the East Coast. Farquharson had come north with an order for eleven million barrel hoops from the Peabody firm of San Francisco.

Farquharson arrived in Tenino on December 1 to meet with General Sprague, the superintendent of the Northern Pacific Railroad. The men discussed plans for shipping barrel hoops to San Francisco and building a stave factory somewhere on Puget Sound.[2] At the conclusion of their talk Sprague agreed to put storage sheds for cottonwood bolts (short logs) at shipping points along a railroad line that would be extended to Puyallup and the Wilkeson coalfields in the near future. Sprague also agreed to ship the bolts to the Tacoma factory by rail, where they would be fashioned into barrel hoops and sent twice a month to San Francisco. Farquharson then returned to California fully expecting to build his mill in Tacoma on land supplied by the Northern Pacific, and to contract with families throughout the valley to supply it with wood.

The following year in late November the local newspaper reported an event that would influence Farquharson's future actions. "Two contracts on the Puyallup railroad have been let. They comprise those nearest Tacoma, and have been taken by Messrs. Meeker and Mann."[3] Construction of the long awaited branch line from Tacoma through the Puyallup Valley was about to begin.

About this time Meeker wrote a letter to Farquharson asking him to come to Puyallup to look over the prospects for perhaps building his hoop shipping station and barrel stave factory in the valley. Farquharson promptly agreed.

Farquharson was irritated that the Northern Pacific would not give him the site he wanted for his mill in Tacoma. When Meeker offered him six cleared acres as a factory site for six hundred dollars

Farquharson accepted. In the following days Farquharson negotiated contracts with valley settlers for cottonwood timber at ten cents a cord on the ground or $2.50 delivered to the factory, contingent on the railroad being built. Attorney Frank Clark drew up the contracts that would clear the valley of cottonwoods over ten years, which was the life expectancy of the mill.

Two competitors, Kelly and Blackwell, who owned 320 acres of timber north of the river, tried to scuttle the deal. They offered Farquharson free land, free timber, and one thousand dollars cash to quit Meeker. They also tried to talk General Sprague into building the branch line on the north bank of the river instead of the south. It was a losing proposition as the land Meeker sold Farquharson was already cleared, while theirs was not, and James Stewart donated a thousand feet of his south-side property for a railroad right-of-way. Factory construction began in June 1877, although Farquharson threatened to build it on the Skagit River if there were any more problems. It was reported that the factory would employ forty men, that a train depot would be located nearby, and that Meeker was building a store there also.[4]

On June 6, 1877, the Northern Pacific railroad branch line being built from Tacoma to the Wilkeson coalfields reached the village of Puyallup. Transportation to tidewater and thus to the hop markets of the world became much faster and more efficient.

A CALM BEFORE THE STORM

July saw the completion of a water system producing thirty thousand gallons daily, supplying both the factory and the town's needs. The *Tacoma Herald* reported the details of the construction and noted the cost was one thousand dollars. It stated, "E. Meeker and A. S. Farquharson as superintendents, Prof. Bean, of the Academy, as civil engineer, and Marion Meeker [age 25] as constructor, have the credit for furnishing Puyallup with its first supply of water from the mountainside."[5] It was implied that Meeker and Farquharson were co-owners of the works. In fact the water works were owned solely by Meeker.[6]

The coming of the railroad to Puyallup in 1877 proved the catalyst for Meeker to open a general merchandise store and a livery stable there.[7] The first train to Puyallup carried equipment for the stave mill. The factory's initial two stave machines turned out twenty-five

Meeker's Puyallup store ca. 1879. *Courtesy of the Puyallup Historical Society at the Meeker Mansion*

thousand staves per day. Ten more machines were expected shortly. The *Tacoma Herald* stated, "One can imagine what the production of staves will amount to under such circumstances. All the available space in the yards will be occupied by piles of staves and it will require a small regiment of Chinamen to take the staves away from the machines."[8] The entrepreneurs were at work.

For a time all was harmony in Puyallup. The factory was running at half capacity but was expected to soon employ a full work force.[9] According to Farquharson, his first conflict with Meeker developed shortly after the factory opened. The dispute was over hauling cottonwood to the stave mill. Farquharson wrote that he was paying teamsters (his own men, some of Meeker's employees, and a few independent haulers) a dollar a cord to transport wood to the mill. The haulers demanded $1.50 a cord and went on strike. Farquharson accused Meeker of instigating the teamsters and claimed he broke the strike by threatening to use his own teams exclusively. According to Farquharson, the independent haulers caved in and went back to work, and when Meeker's teamsters refused to return to work he fired them.[10]

Fight Over Water

The stave mill needed a healthy supply of water to survive, and it was over water that serious trouble began. The spring that was the source of Meeker's Puyallup water works (known today as Maplewood Spring) also spawned a small stream that flowed across the southern half of Meeker's land. Ezra used the water for irrigation and watering stock, but the flow was so weak that the stream nearly dried up in summer.

According to Farquharson, Meeker originally charged his company $50 a month for the water used by the factory, but in late 1878 tripled the price to $150 a month. Farquharson wrote he wasn't about to pay the new rate, and that he informed Meeker he would file a homestead claim on the spring and re-route Meeker's intermittent stream off his property and use it for the factory's water supply before agreeing to the new charge. Meeker supposedly beat him to the punch by having a friend file for a homestead claim on the spring before Farquharson got his paperwork in order. Farquharson said he countered by digging a ditch that intersected the stream about a quarter mile east of Meeker's lands, diverting the water to the stave factory. The truth in all this is difficult to sort out. At this point two facts are certain: the water works were owned and controlled by Ezra Meeker, and Farquharson started to dig a ditch to divert water.

The two antagonists took their dispute to the territorial court on May 19, 1879.[11] There is no mention in the court record of anyone filing a homestead claim on the spring. Meeker simply testified that he had always used the water from the small stream that headed in the bluffs and that Farquharson was doing him harm by digging a ditch to divert that stream. He asked the court to enjoin any diversion of that water. Farquharson argued the ditch was not diverting any water, but was simply taking water that flowed into a bottomland swamp and that Meeker was suffering no harm. Meeker won the case and was awarded damages of $81.62 and court costs of $28.65 by Justice of the Peace George W. Boatman.

Farquharson wrote that he also clashed with Meeker in 1879 over a contract to log timber on the Davidson property that adjoined Meeker's on the east. Farquharson said he paid Meeker cash and requested that Meeker also pay the log haulers in cash, less what they owed at his Puyallup store. He went on to say that Meeker, instead, paid the teamsters in goods from his store, less what they owed. Enraged at what he considered a breach of contract, Farquharson determined to damage Meeker. He opened a competing store in Puyallup and sent his foreman to San Francisco to buy quality merchandise to stock it.

It took just six years to clear the Puyallup Valley of its cotton-wood forests and turn them into sugar barrels. The village of a few dozen families grew into a small city of 750 residents according to the 1878 County Auditor's Census.[12] And the Meeker-Farquharson conflict continued into the next decade, accomplishing little more than enriching the valley attorneys.

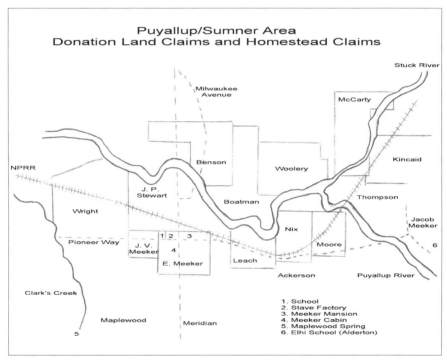

Over the years Meeker acquired much land beyond the illustrated homestead property. The new properties were primarily on the south side of the Puyallup River with the exception of a large holding in the White River Valley to the north. *Courtesy of Karen Johnson*

Ezra Meeker Charged with Larceny

There seemed to be no end to the bickering and the lawsuits, and the turmoil expanded to include friends, acquaintances, and business associates of both Meeker and Farquharson. The next major round of the Meeker-Farquharson feud flared up in 1883. This episode was conducted primarily through Farquharson's surrogates and business partners. Farquharson at first chose to stay in the background, appearing only peripherally in the court documents.[13] Ezra Meeker demonstrated once again his willingness to fight an opponent to the bitter end, highlighting the stubborn streak in his personality that created enemies and alienated so many. This time Meeker found himself facing a charge of felonious larceny.

The point of conflict was a piece of land called the Walker farm, located on the north bank of the Puyallup River where the ferry operated. John Walker died in 1871 and a few months later his widow, Margaret, moved to New York. Before she departed Margaret leased the farm to Augustus Gardella, a Sumner hop farmer. Gardella, in due course, moved into residence, and in November 1873 he reestablished the Puyallup River ferry under a license granted him by the Pierce County commissioners.

Mrs. Walker soon joined her husband in death and Ezra Meeker was named the executor of the estate. An heir, Miss Mary Walker, who was living in New York, put Meeker in charge of her Puyallup affairs. For several years Meeker collected the rent from Gardella and sent it on to New York. For reasons unknown, beginning in 1877, Gardella ceased making his rent payments. By March 1879 he had been in arrears for two years and owed the sum of five hundred dollars. Furthermore, his lease had expired. Meeker, acting on behalf of Mary Walker and with a legal court order, evicted Gardella. Following the eviction, Meeker leased the property from Miss Walker, who remained in New York. In 1880-1881 Meeker invested some fourteen hundred dollars in improving the property.

At this point Farquharson's father-in-law, William Wagner,[14] joined Gardella in an offer to purchase the farm for $5,000. Their offer was accepted and the deed sent to Puyallup, but an error resulted in the deed being returned to New York for correction. In the interval

Miss Walker received other offers of $8,000 and $10,000 for the farm, from persons unknown, which prompted her to renege on the deal and withhold the deed. Accordingly, Gardella brought suit against Walker.[15]

No doubt Gardella and Wagner were livid. It took little imagination on their parts to suspect Meeker's interference behind the scenes, and it's quite likely that one or both of the competing offers was his. On the other hand, Meeker was convinced that Farquharson was funding the effort to purchase the property out from under him. In fact, this assumption shortly proved to be correct.

Gardella, Wagner, and Farquharson, claiming their purchase was valid, leased a portion of the disputed land to a Mr. Morgan who built a storage shed on the property. Meeker responded by ordering his employees to empty the shed. This action resulted in an accusation of theft against Meeker, and a grand jury actually indicted him. Meeker was found not guilty at trial, but the battle over ownership continued. Mr. Gardella eventually prevailed, and on March 1, 1886, Meeker turned over the Walker place to his adversaries who immediately sold a ten-acre plat and advertised others.[16]

With the valley forests all logged by the summer of 1886, the stave factory, as expected, closed its doors. On June 22, 1886, the *Tacoma Daily Ledger* announced the removal of A. S. Farquharson and his family to Seattle.[17]

But the war was not quite over. On March 17, 1888, in the case of *A. Gardella vs. Ezra Meeker*, Gardella received a judgment of $3,050 in damages plus interest. Meeker appealed. On February 24, 1890, the Washington State Supreme Court reversed the judgment against Meeker and, once again, the true winners were the valley attorneys.

Farquharson's Tall Tales

It is obvious that Farquharson invented stories, some of them many years after the fact, to serve his own interests.

Tall Tale #1—A. S. Farquharson version: Sometime in 1877 he and Meeker stood together in the stave mill discussing a name for the town that was growing up on the south bank of the Puyallup River around the mill and train depot. Supposedly he suggested Meekerville and Meeker countered by suggesting that the town be named after Farquharson. Farquharson replied, "Then why not give it the Indian name, Puyallup? Nobody could object to that." Meeker said, "That's the very thing—we'll call the town Puyallup."[18]

Fact check: The area was originally called Franklin until 1874, when the U.S. Post Office officially adopted the name Puyallup. When Meeker formally platted the city on February 18, 1877, he recognized the name that had already been in official use by the U.S. government for over two years. Meeker wrote, "I consider it no honor to be the man who named the town (now city) of Puyallup. I accept the odium attached to inflicting that name on suffering succeeding generations by first platting a few blocks of land into village lots and recording them under the name Puyallup."[19] Only Farquharson (repeated by the *Tacoma Times* in 1941) mentions a role for himself in naming the city Puyallup.

Tall Tale #2—A. S. Farquharson version: William Kelly's hop house on the Buckley Road was burned down by an arsonist and Robert Sproul (Farquharson's factory foreman) was arrested and charged with the crime. According to Farquharson, Sproul was captured near his Carbonado property in the vicinity of the arson. He was then brought to the porch of Meeker's Puyallup store where a "mob" had gathered, listening to Meeker urging Sproul's lynching. In his story, Farquharson arrived at the hotel with armed men from his mill, confronted Meeker's lawless behavior, and threatened to hang Meeker if he didn't desist. In response, according to Farquharson, Meeker ran into his store, slammed the door behind him and locked himself in safety. This supposedly struck the would-be lynch mob with so much mirth that tensions collapsed and the crowd dispersed.[20] Farquharson claimed that he incarcerated Sproul in Mrs. Taylor's Puyallup Hotel and then brought him to his residence for breakfast in the morning before turning him over to the jailer. Farquharson went on to say that Sproul walked out of jail before his trial and made his escape to Canada.[21]

Fact check: Contemporary newspaper accounts and court records make no mention of such an event.[22] In fact, two barns burned on September 9, 1878, within twenty minutes of each other. However, the closest a contemporary newspaper came to mentioning a "mob" was to say, "People of the valley were greatly excited at the occurrence and went to follow tracks."[23] Indeed, a trial record exists.[24] Pages of court testimony held at the Washington State Archives make no mention of a lynch mob and cast cold water on Farquharson's claim that Sproul walked out of jail before his trial and made his way to Canada. The judge, Dr. Joseph Edward Gandy,[25] eight years later wrote an extensive article about the case and made no mention of a mob either. Instead Gandy pointed out that the circumstantial evidence against Sproul was so weak that despite being indicted by a grand jury, the prosecutor refused to continue the case and Sproul was freed.[26] Farquharson's memoir is the only mention of Meeker having any role in this affair, and it seems to be made up. At the very least, it would have been absurdly out of character for Meeker.[27]

Tall Tale #3—A. S. Farquharson version: Farquharson wrote that he chased Meeker out of his 1886 run for Congress by threatening to follow Meeker all over the district denouncing him.[28]

Fact check: This account is totally false and will be thoroughly discussed in Chapter 14. Meeker stayed in the race until the bitter end, losing in the voting at the state Republican Convention. As for Farquharson harassing Meeker, no evidence of this appears in any contemporary sources.

Truth-Telling

When Farquharson claimed he would not believe Meeker even under oath if Meeker had a financial interest in the outcome of a case, one is tempted to believe Farquharson might well have been describing himself. But could Meeker always be relied on to tell the truth?

Indeed, after years of researching the man, I have caught Meeker in a fabrication or two. When writing of his Klondike experiences in *Ventures and Adventures* he wrote, "I received a good ducking in my first passage through the White Horse Rapids, and vowed I would not go through them again, but I did, the very next trip that same year, and came out of it dry." The reader, of course, envisioned whitewater spraying over the boat, showering down on Meeker, and that is clearly what he intended the reader to think. However, in a letter to his wife he explained the ride was smooth and what little water came into the boat did not wet him but that he took a ducking from a rain shower as he had forgotten his raincoat.[29] A little literary license perhaps to spice up a story, or a harmless lie to his wife to quiet her worries? Who can say?

In another case, writing about his Oregon Trail trek of 1852 in *Pioneer Reminiscences*, Meeker included a passage that he knew to be untrue. That didn't stop him from printing it. In southeastern Idaho Thomas McAuley, who headed the wagon train in which Meeker was traveling, called a halt in their westward journey to build a toll road around an obstacle called Big Hill. Meeker wrote, "At that last camp we tarried together for many days...[before separating]"[30] McAuley's sister Eliza kept a diary that Meeker borrowed when he was proofing his manuscript. When he came to this section he discovered that he tarried one day, not many. In his response to Eliza he wrote, "I thought we had camped together longer...and maybe the cold facts will spoil a nice little story I have written. I am not sure but will let it remain."[31] Remain it did, though the "untruth" here was of little consequence.

Like any good politician or entertainer Meeker would occasionally "spin" stories to fit his agenda, as did his rivals. He certainly shuffled a few dates in order to ensure his father's legacy as the originator of the valley hop industry, but he had lots of company in doing this. Of course, the truth seems to be that his father really did deserve the title. Perhaps when Meeker's veracity is questioned the rule of thumb should be "trust, but verify."

Note the hop vines have been let down from the poles to enable picking. *From the collection of the Schmidt House, Olympia Tumwater Foundation*

CHAPTER 8

The Hop King

"Mr. Meeker, who has been felicitously styled the 'hop king,' is increasing his claim to that title…" *Tacoma News*, November 23, 1882

THE HOP EXPLOSION

Without a doubt 1882 was the watershed year for the Meekers and the Puyallup Valley hop business. There was an unprecedented worldwide hop crop failure that year. The only part of the world unaffected was the Pacific coast. Desperate brewers offered astronomical prices for West Coast hops. Offers of twenty-five cents a pound that seemed generous in 1881 were scoffed at in 1882. Fully one-third of the Puyallup valley crop sold that fall for a dollar a pound. Overnight the growers in the Puyallup Valley became rich. Meeker marketed one hundred thousand pounds of hops at an average price of seventy cents per pound, earning E. Meeker & Co. $70,000 gross and $62,000 net, or nearly two million in current dollars. His nearest rival Van Ogle sold his crop for $50,000, earning a net profit of $44,000.

Others realized smaller but still very significant incomes. Johnny Boatman's adventure with the incredible rising prices that fall entertained readers of the *Tacoma News*.[1]

> John, it appears, is the owner of some five tons of hops, which he has been holding for higher prices. A while ago, when hops were ranging in the neighborhood of sixty cents John, in a moment of weakness produced by the bewitching and intoxicating glances of his young bride's bright eyes, consented to give her everything above sixty-one cents for "her very own" for pin money. Now that "everything above sixty-one" cents amounts to four thousand dollars, the neighborhood, including Mrs. Boatman, is amused. John, they say, sticks up to his bargain like a man.[2]

But Mrs. Boatman may have had cause to complain after all. Apparently her husband held out too long for higher prices, a mistake that cost a good deal of her anticipated pin money.³

Meeker was on the road during the fall and winter of 1882–83. A Tacoma newspaper wrote, "Mr. Meeker of Puyallup is on a trip east, which may be extended to Europe."⁴ Meeker departed from Puyallup in mid-October for a journey to Waterville, New York, the center of the New York hop industry. He would not return until early June 1883. The European trip would wait one more year. While in Waterville, Meeker stayed with W. A. Lawrence, a major East Coast hop merchant. On this visit Meeker made a major study of the New York hop industry and in conjunction with Lawrence, he wrote *Hop Culture in the United States*, his second major literary work.⁵

Meeker's in-person dealings with the East Coast end of the hop trade would completely transform how he conducted future business. In the process, the Pacific Northwest hop trade was transformed as well. Prior to 1882 Meeker and other Washington growers had shipped their hops primarily to San Francisco. Here the local hops brokers mixed the Northwest hops in with California hops and sent them off to New York to be sold. That fall Meeker quietly shipped a large quantity of Washington hops directly to New York, bypassing California, and tried to personally sell them in that market. He was convinced that the Northwest hops were superior in quality to the California hops and should command a better price. But he got nowhere with the New York brokers. They would offer him no more than eighty-five cents a pound, which was less than hops were selling for on the West Coast at the time. An Oregon newspaper explained that Washington Territory was simply too remote for most eastern businessmen to take note of and "its products are gauged entirely by San Francisco and California."⁶

Accordingly, Meeker decided to bypass the New York hop brokers. He obtained a list of leading brewers and contacted some sixty-five of them. The brewers were unconvinced at first by Meeker's claims of the superiority of Northwest hops. To prove his point Meeker hired a noted chemist who did an analysis of the extract from the hops of New York, Bavaria, and Puyallup (but for unknown reasons, not California). The results came in strongly in favor of Puyallup hops, with New York samples producing 14.33 pounds of extract from a hundred pounds of hops; Bavaria, 15.50; and Puyallup, 17.16. With his proof in hand, Meeker sold some forty thousand pounds of his now proven high-extract hops directly to the brewers at prices as high as $1.05 per pound. He was now determined to cut loose from the San Francisco market. Henceforth Meeker sent his entire crop to New York direct, for a time employing Lawrence as his agent. In the process he forced the East Coast brokers to acknowledge Northwest hops as a distinct and superior commodity.[7] The completion of the Northern Pacific Railroad to Portland, Oregon, in the summer of 1883 made it eminently possible to enact his plan. By connecting to the existing Washington Territory line there was now direct rail service from Puyallup to the East Coast.

But Meeker did not completely abandon California. In 1881 he formed a partnership with his son-in-law, Eben Osborne,[8] titled Meeker, Osborne & Co. The two men began buying hops from local farmers and shipping them on commission around the country, wherever they could command the best price. This became a lucrative business in a short time. Meeker, Osborne & Co. opened offices in 1882 in Seattle, Puyallup, and at 311 Stockton Street in San Francisco.

Eliza Jane stayed in Puyallup through the winter months and joined her husband in the spring of 1883 to do some touring of eastern cities such as New York and Philadelphia. The letter below, from Waterville, describes the anticipated reunion from Ezra's perspective. We are left to speculate as to how the sentiments expressed were received by Eliza Jane.

> Dear E. J., When I got up this morning. I thought of you the very first thing. First, I found a button hole torn out of my shirt collar & could not use it. Next a hole in the toe of my socks, then next I found my pants pocket out of order—what on earth am I to do without you? How am I to manage all these things? I think you will have to bundle right up and come and take care of me, don't you...I don't know how long I will stay here, probably a week more. The flurry in the hop market made me fear going west at present and so I may now defer it until I hear you are coming and go to meet you at Omaha, and which is nearly half way; four days on the cars and one change would land you at Omaha. I don't now think I could get away from the east for two months and if so then think it would be best to stay

this summer and for you to come and make that long expected visit. What do you think?[9]

On May 1, 1883, Meeker wrote a letter from Philadelphia with advice to give to those who thought the fortunes made growing and selling hops the past year would be a permanent fixture. "These high expectations, even if well founded, beget extravagance in some, rashness in others, and can only result in ultimate loss to the individual and community. Hops are boomed to their certain death and extinguishment of value unless carefully handled, and not "rushed into" as one would rush into a mining camp, or for Tacoma corner lots, if you please, but rather must be handled more like one would handle dynamite—'with care.'"[10]

During Meeker's absence in the winter and spring of 1882–83 his son Marion and nephew Frank Meeker managed the family business, cleaned up after the fall harvest, and made preparations for the spring planting.[11] Ezra and Eliza Jane returned home around June 6 and were greeted with a surprise party in honor of their arrival.[12] Ezra had been away over eight months and Eliza Jane nearly four.

Hop Headlines

The main business of 1883 was hops. Meeker's warning that the crop should be handled like dynamite was totally ignored. Hop fever infected everyone. E. Meeker & Co. increased their hop acreage to two hundred acres, including fifty new acres along the White River near today's Kent, Washington. Most other growers followed suit. The *Tacoma News* provided the following list:

Van Ogle had 65 acres; Gardella 50 acres; L. F. Thompson 40; John Carson and A. Campbell, 40 each; J. P. Dickenson, Chris Helmbold and Boatman & sons, 30 each; John Kincaid, G. Ryan, E. Meade, and S. Woolery, each from 23 to 26; O. M. Annis, John Meeker, Chris Kincaid, D. M. Ross, B. Spinning, J. P. Stewart, A. J. Miller, R. Nix, Frank Young, and J. D. Gillham, from 13 to 20 each, and many others are credited with from 3 to 12 acres each.[13]

The *Tacoma Ledger* reported that over eight hundred acres of valley land were growing hops that summer, up 40 percent from the year before, and that around sixty farmers were now growing hops in the valley. Workers were needed to plant these new fields and to hoe the hop plants in the spring. Growers were offering fifty dollars per month for such services. Meeker estimated that he would need five hundred pickers to harvest his crop in September and that five thousand pickers would be needed for the entire valley. One dollar per box was to be offered to pickers, this being the same price as was paid in 1882. The average picker could make about $1.50 per day.[14]

The newspapers were full of hop news. Advice and predictions filled the pages of the *Tacoma Ledger*. It was claimed over a ten-year period growers could not fail in making money.[15]

In the spring the *Ledger* reported the vines in excellent condition, the soil all that could be wished, the weather fine, and buyers prowling the hop yards offering good prices. But it also noted that most of the growers intended to hold out until the harvest before signing contracts.[16]

The July newspapers fretted about the lack of rain and the damage the dry conditions were doing to the hop crop, and when rain finally came it got a front-page story. Reports from England were a regular feature, and it was worrisome to learn that "The weather in England was favorable and the hop vines are in good condition and promising." Another source of worry was that English brewers had resorted to a chemical substitute, probably a preservative, to offset the incredibly high prices they had to pay for hops. In the long run it was a failure as hops continued to be the number one choice for brewers as a preservative and for its taste.[17]

In July the *Ledger* canvassed five of the principal hop growers in the county and found that all but one thought yield would decline by one third due to the dry conditions. But the editors were pleased to note that the yield per acre in New York was a paltry seven hundred pounds and that prices were holding at 25 percent above the average. By August there was a whiff of panic in the air. "The market is going from bad to worse, with no signs of future improvement…There are no orders on hand from Eastern buyers."[18]

The *Ledger* then began to print very long articles warning the hop growers not to expect high prices forever and to be economical in every possible way. Over a five year period ending in 1882, the price paid for hops in New York hammered home the point that 1882 was an

An 1888 hop kiln in Fall City, Washington, part of the old Snoqualmie Hop Farm.
P. Ziobron photograph

aberration, not the norm. In 1878, the top price per pound was 14 cents; in 1879, 30 cents; 1880, 21 cents; 1881, 26 cents; and in 1882 a staggering $1.10.[19] It was suggested that if the hop growers didn't mend their ways bankruptcy loomed. The advice fell on deaf ears.

In late August 1883, the *Tacoma Daily News* reported on a telegram "just received from N.Y. by E. Meeker & Co., Puyallup," with the "latest reliable information" on the hop market. "Weather very favorable for the growth of the vine. The market is quiet but steady. The lice are increasing in New York, and the weather is favorable for a still further increase of vermin. The next few days must determine the prospects of the crop."[20]

SUMMER'S END

By the end of the 1883 harvest year E. Meeker & Co. had ten drying kilns operating in Puyallup and five kilns operating in the White
River Valley together capable of drying 12,500 pounds of hops in a
twenty-four-hour period. Ezra had been at the business now for eighteen years and in 1883 his two hundred acres were yielding an average
of two thousand pounds of hops per acre. His expenses over the eighteen years averaged eight cents per pound and he sold his hops at an
average price of twenty cents per pound. Assuming 1883 was an average
year, the hop yards of E. Meeker & Co. would have produced $80,000
in gross income and the company would have realized a net profit of
$48,000. Ezra and Eliza Jane Meeker paid $259.04 in taxes in 1883. E.
Meeker & Co. paid $784.10.[21]

That fall Meeker sent seven bales of hops to the London market on
a trial basis. This experiment opened a whole new chapter in the story
of the Hop King.

CHAPTER 9

The London Hop Trade

The seven bales of hops E. Meeker & Co. sent to London at the end of the 1883 hop season were a testing of the waters. For years the company had been sending its hops to Portland, San Francisco, and New York. For the past several years, a few Puyallup Valley growers had been shipping some of their hops abroad, mostly to Australia. Meeker had confined his trade to the continent. This initial entry into the London market would, over the next decade, lead to a showering of unimaginable riches upon the hop growers of the Puyallup Valley. Eventually E. Meeker & Co. would ship eleven thousand bales (nearly two million pounds) of hops a year to the London markets. In the process the company became the largest exporter of hops in the United States with a trade over ten years amounting to three million contemporary dollars.[1] One online inflation calculator adjusts the amount of Meeker's London hop trade to seventy million in today's dollars. But this trans-Atlantic trade had a rocky start.

CIF—CLEAR OF INSURANCE AND FREIGHT

The initial small, seven-bale shipment was very well received, and at the end of the 1884 harvest E. Meeker & Co. received a cable from his London broker agreeing to a larger purchase of hops.

The cable authorized Meeker to ship five hundred bales of hops at "four pounds sterling" or about twenty dollars per bale "CIF"—clear of insurance and freight.[2] Meeker was not familiar with the term and was surprised to receive word from his bank that he owed another $2,000 to cover the freight charges. Meeker was incensed and in two days was on the way to London. The *Ledger* simply stated, "Ezra Meeker has sold his store to his son, M. J. Meeker. He leaves for New York this week and Mrs. Meeker for California where she will spend the winter."[3]

Meeker wrote a series of letters while on this first trip to Europe, published periodically in the *Ledger*. In this way he kept his promise to many friends that he would write often. It took him four days to travel from Portland to Omaha and he marveled at the comfort of the train.

He could not help but contrast the luxury he was riding in with the service the Northern Pacific offered locally. "I have in mind our own little trip from Puyallup to Tacoma, where the very highest fare is charged, and where the car is nearly always full—why is it that we sit on hard boards, in a dirty car?"

The final leg of the trip, on the New York Central Railroad, brought Meeker to New York City on Christmas Eve. He checked into the Grand Union Hotel and over the next few days took in two plays, walked through the hop market and found it "demoralized," and dined at the famous Delmonico's restaurant on Broad Street.[4]

On December 31 at 5 a.m. the *Aurania* sailed for Liverpool. The Atlantic passage usually took eight or nine days, and for once Meeker didn't get seasick, as he was prone to do whenever he set himself upon the water. He decried the gambling, poker, and wagering that seemed to dominate the activities of the passengers. The *Aurania* arrived in Liverpool on January 9, 1885.

London

The next morning Meeker arrived in London and took a cab two miles from the train depot to the Charing Cross Railroad Station Hotel. The city was shrouded in "one of those dismal fogs that so often settle over that great city. I afterwards experienced the fog so dense (mixed with smoke) that I could not see my own hand at arms length; as the old saying goes as 'dark as a stack of black cats.'"[5]

The hotel was not far from the hop market and Meeker could get there each morning by paying a two-cent fare to ride the omnibus, a double-deck, horse-drawn bus.[6]

A five-minute walk away was the Lyceum Theater featuring Shake-speare's *Romeo and Juliet*. Shakespeare was not a favorite of Meeker, but this production featured the American actress Mary Anderson as Juliet. Eager to see Miss Anderson, Meeker decided to attend that first evening in London. He noted that, "The crowd was fairly well dressed, decent, intelligent looking people—the middle classes of London."[7] He had a very good seat, just back of what he described as an "elite company." However, it did not take London long to offend his sensibilities. The lady in front of him drew his immediate attention.

> I do not intend to describe the costume, but rather the "undress" so to speak, in this particular case. Prentice said, during the furor of the Bloomer fashion, that, "he was in favor of it," as he "did not have much time with the women, and that fashion gave him the opportunity of seeing a great deal of them in a very short time;" that is now nearly forty years ago, but if our witty journalist had been here, he could have been satisfied, though his favorite bloomer fashion had been discarded, yet the bloomer dress was yet worn, it was simply short at the other end...to my eyes in very bad taste.[8]

Despite writing that the fog often made it so dark it was difficult to study hop samples at the hop market, Meeker was able to attend to business. His first act was to transfer his business to another brokerage house, a step that he claimed laid the foundation for three million dollars worth of business over the next decade. He went on to say this could have only been done by personal contact and "all brought about by my blunder of not understanding the meaning of CIF."[9]

Meeker spent two months in the "Borough," the Hop Exchange, studying "the prejudices and learning the wants of the English hop market." He studied samples of more than one hundred thousand bales of hops from countries around the globe with local experts. With these experts he examined the samples from his thousand bales and found that his hops were selling from two to four pounds more than California hops.[10] These two months laid the foundation for a future transatlantic trade that helped bring the name Washington Territory to the front pages of the business sections of the U.S. and international newspapers. The territory would no longer be a remote backwater noted simply for its large trees, mountains, and rain. The moneymen of the world would hereafter not need an atlas to locate Puyallup or Washington Territory.

As he traveled across Europe, Meeker became a rather enthusiastic tourist. He visited Westminster Abbey and walked over the graves of Darwin, Newton, and Major Andre of Revolutionary War fame. He commented that a bust of Longfellow was the only sign of anyone of

American lineage in the Abbey. He also visited the South Kensington Museum, the British Museum, Trafalgar Square with Lord Nelson's statue, and the Pall Mall district containing its fifty exclusive private clubs. He stopped at Madame Tussaud's famous wax museum, and a concert at the Royale Theater impressed him greatly, as did the fist-fight that broke out in the audience during a performance.[11]

GERMANY

On February 9, 1885, Meeker left London for Germany with a Mr. Wilfred Twinch, a young Englishman "who expects to cast his fortunes in America and with the beet sugar industry in Washington Territory. Our mission here is to investigate the beet sugar industry in Germany, with all its influence and effect upon this great empire, and if possible, by comparison ascertain if it is feasible to undertake the manufacture of beet sugar in Washington territory."[12] They took a night boat to Flushing, Holland, and arrived at dawn. Four hours by train brought them to Halle, a major center of the sugar beet industry. There they visited factories and "collected a mass of statistics."[13] At the conclusion of their research Mr. Twinch was to go into an apprenticeship at one of the factories visited.

February 14 found Meeker in a Berlin hotel on Linden Street opposite the emperor's residence. On his first day in the capital Meeker amazingly bumped into Emperor Wilhelm I while visiting a nearby city park. They passed on the street. Mr. Twinch lifted his hat and received an acknowledgment. Meeker simply stared.[14]

Twinch and Meeker spent nearly two weeks touring Germany's beet sugar factories. In the evenings Mr. Twinch translated his notes into English. And Meeker fantasized about starting beet factories in Puyallup, Chehalis, or LaConner, duplicating what he had seen. He had long since "caught the beet sugar fever" and his visit to Germany made it worse.[15] It took a leap of faith to see the cities mentioned above becoming major beet sugar centers, but Meeker would one day try.

FRANCE

Everyone had told Meeker that his European trip would not be complete without a visit to Paris. So at the conclusion of his two-week stay in Germany, he said good-bye to his friend and took the train to France, stopping in Cologne along the way to see its great cathedral. He wryly mentioned that, "My guide told me it was 2400 years old. He had evidently forgotten when Christ was born, but he didn't forget to charge me double price for the lies he told me."[16]

Meeker arrived in Paris around February 21 and made his way to the American Exchange, where he received directions to a suitable hotel. Meeker's Paris stay included visits to the Catacombs, the Jardin des Plantes, the cathedral of Notre Dame, the great opera house, and Montmartre, which provided him with a panoramic view of the city. The Tuilleries Palace where French kings and Napoleon once dwelt, the Champs Élysées, and the Arc de Triomphe were also on his itinerary. Meeker toured the streets with their miles of booths, shops, and sideshows and marveled at the commerce and beauty of the city. As to the mores of Parisian society he had little good to say. Paris proved a bit too racy for staid Mr. Meeker. He had been told the "Eden" theater must be seen, so he went. He marveled at its physical appearance but walked out on the play commenting, "This Eden was simply a huge brothel. There now, friends do not ask me to tell you more of Parisian society. I hope I have seen the worst; if not may the good Lord have mercy on the best."[17]

Around February 28 Meeker returned to London for one last round of hop business. On March 8, 1885, he boarded the steamer *Germania* of the White Star line at Liverpool and began his journey home. He stayed away from the gambling parlors and spent much time in his room reading *Ivanhoe*, *Vanity Fair*, and a two-hundred-page classic titled *Sugar Bounties, an Official Account of the Beet Sugar Industry*, printed by the British government. He wrote that the volume was covered with pencil notations and earmarks by the time he arrived back in New York. A Tacoma newspaper noted his return. "Mr. Ezra Meeker landed in New York City from London on the 16th inst. He will go to San Francisco, where he will be met by Mrs. Meeker and return to this city on about April 15th."[18]

London Hop Exchange. *London Illustrated News, 1867*

THE LONDON HOP EXCHANGE

The London Hop Exchange, or Borough as Meeker called it, opened in 1867 or 1868 in the London Borough of Southwark a short distance from the River Thames and the London Bridge. Its purpose was to create a single market place for dealers in hops. It was a magnificent, multistoried building modeled somewhat after the Roman Coliseum. Its main feature was a large trading floor underneath a huge glass ceiling enabling traders to view samples under natural light. In a stroke of irony the samples were normally viewed in February and March, two of London's more gloomy months. Its location, on the main south road from the Kent hop-growing district, allowed hops to be brought in by rail from Kent to London Bridge Station or by boat up the River Thames, where they were stored in the many warehouses in the area. Outside of London proper, it also avoided much of that city's regulations. The merchants, whose offices were on the upper floors overlooking the trading floor, usually worked for brewers who would contract with them to make their hop purchases. This was done almost entirely through the use of samples.

Samples were one-pound sections of a 180-pound hop bale. Thick brown paper was folded around each cutout section, which was secured with brass nails. Samples from individual growers were then strung together with waxed hemp for examination by potential buyers. Accounts were usually settled in April.

In 1920 a fire destroyed the building's upper two stories and the glass roof, which were never replaced, and the exchange was converted to offices. The building suffered significant damage during World War II. It has been restored somewhat, but far short of its original grandeur.

CHAPTER 10

Diversification

A Short Career in Oil

Early in the summer of 1885 Cutler Salmon was drilling a water well on his farm in Elhi in the Puyallup Valley about a mile east of Alderton and a few miles southeast of today's Puyallup. At a depth of 1,250 feet the drillers struck water at a temperature of eighty degrees, and intermingled with the water was a considerable quantity of natural gas. Being an enterprising soul, Mr. Salmon piped the gas to his house, affording heat and light. Further exploration in the area found oil seeping out of the ground in several places.

This discovery triggered an oil and gas uproar that swept the entire county throughout the summer of 1885. It seemed that oil and natural gas were everywhere. In Tacoma workers thought they detected the odor of petroleum in a well they were completing for John Hess at South 11th and K Streets. Tacoma businessmen became so excited they formed the Tacoma Oil Company. Mayor Jacob Weisbach immediately formed a competing company called the Mutual Oil Company. Steilacoom also claimed to find signs of oil. All this was too much for the "Hop King" to ignore, so Ezra Meeker followed suit and incorporated the New Standard Oil Company. Lands were leased, oil stock was bought freely, and all were confident of riches.

The *Ledger* fed the excitement, stating "Everyone is confident that we have a rich oil field here. The indications are abundant. Oil is found running out of the ground at other places than Elhi." The start-up of new companies was touted as well as a commentary on residents leasing their land for exploration but prudently holding on to their royalty rights. "The discovery of oil and gas here will bring wealth to the owners of land, and stimulate many industries that are unthought of now."[1]

The Van Bibber farm, also in Elhi, became the focus of attention. The Tacoma Oil Company began construction of a derrick on June 11 in front of a small crowd that had gathered to hear speeches by company executives. By the end of August the derrick was complete and machinery was in place to begin drilling. Accordingly, a larger and more formal ceremony was held. Several hundred people from miles around attended. Governor Watson C. Squire and Mayor Weisbach made speeches. The governor must have been delighted to find his remarks printed on the front page of the *Ledger*. The newspaper even offered advice on how to get to the site.

> A good, speedy and cheap means of visiting the scene of the first boring for oil on the Pacific coast north of San Francisco is to take the 6 o'clock morning train, step off at Alderton and walk one mile and a half to the new derrick. The derrick and power machinery are on the ridge or hillside bounding the northern side of the Puyallup valley, being on a bench say seventy feet above the valley and within a stone's throw of the old Van Bibber mill, which cut the first lumber in that part of the valley.[2]

On September 8 the drilling had reached a depth of seventy-five feet, but the workers were having a difficult time. The rope powering the drill kept breaking. It was hoped that one of stronger material and fully 1,500 feet in length would arrive soon. Spectators came to gawk daily. The Northern Pacific Railroad offered special rates for those interested in the trip out to Elhi. Fortunes were just around the corner. On September 29 the *Ledger* breathlessly reported a new discovery just three miles distant.

> Gas was discovered on the farm of L. F. Thompson, at Sumner, this evening. That gentleman was prospecting for coal oil, and came to a shallow slough covered with water. Noticing bubbles upon the surface of the water, he touched a match to one and found that there was a flash of flame. Further investigation by probing the soft ground with a pole brought the gas to the surface in such quantities that the surface of the water was covered with a flame, resembling in color the flame of burning alcohol, that would rise above the surface of the water in a number of places.[3]

By mid-October the boom had played out. The Van Bibber well came up dry, the various oil companies folded and their stock became worthless. Meeker was back to growing and selling hops. Hunt in his *History of Tacoma* summed it all up quite succinctly. "There seems to be nothing like an oil excitement to separate fools and their money."[4]

Sugar Beet Fever

For years Meeker had dreamed of introducing a sugar beet industry into Washington Territory. As early as 1880 he had tentatively made plans to do so with his brother John Meeker and other prominent Puyallup Valley businessmen but held off. On his first business trip to Europe in 1884 Meeker noted that German farmers were selling beet sugar for four cents a pound and still presumably making a profit.

Meeker took his enthusiasm home. The following spring (1885) Meeker planted two acres of sugar beets on one of his farms near Kent, Washington. Thomas Alvord, a friend and Kent neighbor, also planted two acres. Meeker harvested forty-seven tons from his two acres that year and at different times during the year sent a dozen samples or more to the beet sugar factory at Alvarado, California, to be tested.

> The report came back highly favorable—rich and pure, and if figures would not lie, here was a field better than hops—better than any crop any of the farmers were raising at the time. So Mr. Alvord and myself organized a beet sugar company, and the next year increased our acreage to further test the cost of raising and of their sugar producing qualities. I raised over a hundred tons that year, and we sent ten tons to the Alvarado factory to extract the sugar—meanwhile had sent about a hundred samples at different times, to be tested.[5]

This crop yielded about half a ton of sugar, probably the first ever made from Washington-grown beets, and it was exhibited at the New Orleans exposition held during the winter of 1885–86.[6]

On August 1, 1885, the *Ledger* printed a rather long letter from Meeker in which he figuratively stood on the pulpit and shouted out the prospects for growing beet sugar, noting that imports had grown from 2,500 tons to 85,000 tons in five years. "Every man, woman and child in these United States has consumed, and will consume, at least one pound of sugar a week, on average or fifty pounds a year…Competent authorities estimate that by the year 1895 we will consume fully two million, five hundred thousand tons."

Fred Meeker was sent to the Alvarado, California, factory to learn the sugar beet business and report on the quality of the beets being sent from Puget Sound.[7] The news was bad. It seemed that first growth beets "were exceedingly rich and pure" but that the second growth crops "were worthless for producing sugar." Washington's moist autumn weather destroyed the quality of the second growth crop making it "extremely hazardous to enter into the business and so the whole matter was dropped as well as $2,500.00 of expenses incurred."[8] Years later the business was successfully established in the drier climate of eastern Washington and Oregon, but Meeker's hopes and dreams for the crop had finally died.

Hops

While oil was turning the heads of the locals that year, and Meeker was dallying with beets, the Puyallup Valley hop fields became a tourist attraction for out-of-staters. In June a number of visitors from

An 1884 view of Ezra Meeker's Puyallup hop yards. Fourteen-year-old Olive Meeker in the black dress and white hat; Lon Jeffery, Meeker's field boss, holding a book; Mrs. Mary Summerfield and her daughter May holding hops beside the hop box. *Courtesy John Berry collection, Puyallup Historical Society at the Meeker Mansion*

Iowa traveled to the Northwest via excursion train. They arrived in Tacoma on the evening of June 15 and took a steamboat cruise up the sound to Seattle where they were treated to a clambake. The following afternoon they returned to Tacoma just in time to attend the Third Annual Reunion of the Pioneers of Washington Territory at the county courthouse. Meeker, with the approval of General Sprague, tendered an invitation to all 339 pioneers and the Iowa excursionists to take a train ride to look over the many prosperous hop farms that now dotted the valley. Most accepted and upon their return they were treated to a grand banquet at the Opera House followed by an evening of speeches.[9]

In September hop-pickers—white, Indian, and Chinese—made their way to the valley from all points of the compass. A wilder element also appeared among them this year as the newspaper reported, "A lot of the roughest and dirtiest looking men that has ever been in the valley…Some have scarred faces, some black eyes, scarcely perceptible through the dirt…These rough men stay mostly around town so the white families who are here for picking are not disturbed any, as they are out in their camps at the farms." Two special marshals, John Martin and William Jeffery, were hired and put on watch at night to keep the "Scarred faces" in check. It was also noted that a lot of bread and cake stands were being erected.[10]

The larger portion of the harvest that fall was shipped directly to England, while brokers from around the country prowled the Puyallup Valley.

> This year the wholesale houses of Phillip Wolf & Co. and Phillip Neis & Co. of San Francisco, Hanson & Co. of Milwaukee, Corbitt & MacCleay of Portland, and our local buyers Isaac Pincus of Tacoma, and Schwabacher of Seattle, have had agents here buying for them; and George W. Elkins of Philadelphia has been here for a month. The growers that shipped to England received $10 a bale in advance, and will likely realize 10 cents a pound [profit] on them."[11]

Meeker, who had begun experimenting with Humphrey hops in 1885, sold that portion of his crop to a Milwaukee, Wisconsin, brewer named Blatz for twelve and a half cents per pound. The *Daily News* said, "The Humphrey hop is fully eight to ten days earlier than the common cluster hop and is the best hop grown in the United States, and probably the world; and this product of Mr. Meeker's is pronounced equal to any ever used by Mr. Blatz."[12] The year 1885 was a very good one for hops.

CHAPTER 11

The Chinese Expulsion

…Give me your tired, your poor,
Your huddled masses yearning to breathe free,
The wretched refuse of your teeming shore.
Send these, the homeless, tempest-tossed to me,
I lift my lamp beside the golden door!

From the poem *"The New Colossus"* by Emma Lazarus, inscribed on the Statue of
Liberty, dedicated October 28, 1886

America has had great difficulty living up to the welcoming inscription
on its statue in New York Harbor. In the 1850s two groups of "huddled
masses" flooded into the United States. A new wave of Irish and German immigrants arrived on the East Coast, while Chinese immigrants
arrived in the West. Neither group was welcomed. Catholic Irish and
German immigrants were met by waves of hostility that often turned
violent. Their presence spawned the ironically named Native American Party, renamed in 1855 as the American Party, but more commonly
referred to as the Know Nothings. Its goal was to "purify" American
politics by limiting or ending the influence of Irish and German Catholics and other immigrants who, it claimed, were controlled by the
Roman pope and "corrupting" the country. "Irish Need Not Apply"
signs became a fixture over the eastern half of the United States. In
1854 the Know Nothings won a large number of electoral victories,
sweeping to power in states such as Massachusetts. Secret societies
were formed to fight the "Catholic Menace" and, when questioned,
claimed to "know nothing" about any violence.

The Chinese met even more hostility. The first wave of Chinese
immigrants came in the early 1850s and flocked to the California gold
fields. To protect themselves they often worked in large teams, hoping strength in numbers would keep them safe. They often worked
areas regarded by white gold seekers as unproductive. Their success

93

only created envy and more hostility. The California legislature levied a monthly head tax on "foreign miners" and the state supreme court ruled in 1854 that the Chinese were not allowed to testify as witnesses before the court in California against white citizens, including those accused of murder. In *The People of California v. George W. Hall*, the court called the Chinese "a race of people whom nature has marked as inferior, and who are incapable of progress or intellectual development beyond a certain point… differing in language, opinions, color, and physical conformation; between whom and ourselves nature has placed an impassable difference and as such have no right to swear away the life of a citizen or participate with us in administering the affairs of our Government."

Laws were passed preventing the marriage of Chinese to white Americans. Chinese immigrants were stereotyped as degraded, exotic, and dangerous. Many claimed that the Chinese could never assimilate into "civilized" western culture. Nevertheless some 17,000 Chinese workers were hired to help build the transcontinental railroad in the 1860s. By 1871, 63,000 Chinese immigrants lived and worked in various parts of the United States. The hostility continued into the 1870s when Denis Kearney founded the Workingmen's Party of California. It took aim at the Chinese laborers who Kearney described as dangerous foreigners who took jobs from hardworking Americans. The party's slogan was "The Chinese Must Go!"

With the completion of the transcontinental railroad in 1869, Chinese scattered around the West searching for jobs. A contingent came to Washington Territory where they helped the Northern Pacific Railroad build a line from Kalama to Tacoma. Growers, desperate for labor in the 1870s, brought them to their hop yards, but the Northwest was no kinder than California.

In 1882 the U.S. Congress passed the Chinese Exclusion Act, touting it as a patriotic endeavor that would enhance national security and improve the greater health of the country. It was the first law ever to exclude a specific ethnic group. Signed by President Chester Arthur, it stopped the entry of further Chinese under penalty of imprisonment and deportation, and prohibited the Chinese who were already in the United States from becoming citizens. (It was repealed in 1943, two years after China became an ally in World War II.)

By the mid-1880s, citizens of Washington were echoing the cry of Denis Kearney: "The Chinese must go!" Ezra Meeker disagreed.[1]

The Chinese Must Go!

Beginning in early 1885 Jack Comerford, the editor of the *Tacoma Daily Ledger*, began publishing anti-Chinese stories and soon began calling for a Chinese expulsion from Tacoma. At a February 21, 1885, meeting attended by some nine hundred citizens, several hours were devoted to haranguing on the topic. By the end of summer the agitation had caused many of Tacoma's Chinese to flee to less hostile climes. However, some remained. The editor of the *Ledger* and his supporters, rallying around the battle cry "The Chinese Must Go," set a date of November 1, 1885, for the expulsion of those who remained. The agitation quickly spread beyond Tacoma to neighboring communities.[2]

On October 5, as tensions rose, Ezra Meeker wrote a long letter to the editor of the *Ledger*. He denounced the hysteria and warned "the better part of the community [that] so long as we keep silence, and neither by word or action, say or do aught to counteract the pernicious effects certain to follow in the wake of this agitation, our silence will properly be construed as an endorsement of the cry, 'The Chinese Must Go.'"[3] Meeker also warned the mayor that his actions tended to incite lawlessness, rioting, and bloodshed.

Two days later Meeker addressed the members of the Chamber of Commerce and urged them to obey the law.

> Among you I know I have many friends. You all know that I spring from and am of the labor class; that my sympathies are with them; that my every action has been to favor our own people. Yesterday I had 750 people in my employ, out of which 28 only were Chinamen, and these only in an out of the way place where it was not easy to get others to go.
>
> I am not in favor of the Chinese coming. I am in favor of the restriction act, but that is a very different question from that which you propose, a very different matter from saying in an unlawful manner, "You must go" to a person who is here under our laws, entitled to the protection of our laws, entitled to the rights guaranteed to all living under our laws. I say this intimidation movement is a very different question as to whether any of us favor the Chinamen coming among us.

Many of you will live to see the day that you will look back upon our actions with amazement and wonder, and regret that the recollection of this period should not be forgotten under the pressure of a busy life. I say, let us respect our laws, enforce their provisions, make them better if they are not good enough, deprecate lawlessness, place ourselves aright in the eyes of our nation and the civilized world, and we need not fear the result.[4]

Meeker moved that the Chamber set up an investigating committee to determine how many Chinese might be in Tacoma illegally, at the same time "condemning the popular cry that the Chinese Must Go" as "revolutionary in character, unlawful in intent, and if persisted in certain to lead to bloodshed and riot."[5]

Meeker wasn't speaking in a vacuum. On September 2, 1885, in Rock Springs, Wyoming, over two dozen Chinese mine workers were attacked and murdered. Six days later the *Seattle Post-Intelligencer* came to the defense of the white miners, putting blame for the killing on "the company which imported the Mongolians." Murder came to Washington Territory on September 7 at the Wold family hop farm near Issaquah when assailants made a night attack upon the camp of thirty-seven Chinese hop pickers, killing three and wounding four.[6]

Meeker's motion concluded with a call for the "enforcement of the law to protect every individual in his rights under the law."[7] The resolution was rejected. His stand was not well met in Tacoma. At an October 18 meeting, the featured speaker was the editor of the *Ledger,* John A. Comerford. He spoke to a packed house on the question of "the exodus of the Chinese."

Near the end of his speech Comerford verbally attacked Meeker.

And they will go unless the moral encouragement of some Pharisaical people and the promised assistance of some white Chinese [meaning those like Meeker] restrain the yellow ones. Ezra Meeker of Puyallup is one of that kind. He issued a letter against the popular will… He then read the same letter as a sort of speech to the Chamber of Commerce and then changed it around a little and had it printed in a newspaper. There ought to be a dead letter office specially for that letter (prolonged applause). Mr. Meeker asks, "What are you going to do if the Chinese don't go?" and says that we either mean violence or are bullies. On and after November 1st Mr. Meeker will find us upholding the law, while he and his kind will be hiding in cellars afraid to add to our influence.[8]

In Puyallup the Chinese were quartered in tents and in a building near the railroad depot where they were continually harassed. At times shots were fired into the building as a way of encouraging them to leave town. The harassment stopped when Alexander Farquharson armed his Chinese workers. He and Meeker were united, for once, in their stand against the mob.

The Knights of Labor held a "statewide congress" in Seattle in September and passed a resolution asking all employers to dismiss their Chinese employees immediately. Most of the hotels and factories in Tacoma complied. The newly christened Anti-Chinese League issued an order that Puyallup get rid of its Chinese servants, factory workers, and field hands. Veiled threats were made that Farquharson's barrel factory and other businesses might be burned down if the citizens of Puyallup did not comply. Meeker, Farquharson, and many of the town's businessmen did not take the threats lightly. Accordingly, thirty-six hop growers and business owners had themselves sworn in to serve as deputy sheriffs charged with protecting Puyallup and its citizens. The underlying message was that the Chinese would not be driven out of Puyallup. Among the list of deputies were Meeker himself, six of his relatives, and his business competitors, Farquharson, Thompson, and Meade.[9]

Puyallup quickly divided into two camps, with feelings running very high. "Saturday afternoon two prominent citizens of Puyallup had some harsh words [over expelling the Chinese] ending in one of the would-be combatants picking up a chair for the purpose of striking the other, when Constable Jeffries interfered and separated them."[10]

The swearing in of deputies enraged anti-Chinese leaders, and a meeting featuring the leaders of the Tacoma agitators was scheduled for Puyallup. The *Tacoma Daily News* covered the meeting and relished in Meeker's supposed discomfort. The article uniquely titled "At Puyallup, An Enthusiastic Demonstration among a Law Abiding People," reeked with the righteousness of the editor's cause and poured scorn on Meeker and those who opposed the Chinese expulsion.

On October 21, a "most enthusiastic outpouring" of Puyallup residents vented their spleens against "the evils of Chinese occupation... manacling as the years roll on this whole country with a beastly overflow of the seepings of barbaric Asia," reported the *News*. The crowd was particularly incensed at the hiring of the thirty-six deputy sheriffs "to preserve a peace, which has never been violated much less threatened." The *News* further editorialized that Meeker sat in the audience and listened silently to the attacks "with blanched cheek, as he felt the scourge or looked through the pillory at his irate fellow citizens."[11]

Expulsion and Aftermath

On the third of November 1885, some three hundred Tacoma citizens trooped to Chinatown and began rounding up the two hundred Chinese who had remained in the city despite the harassment, and marched them south to the Lakeview station where they were put on trains bound for Portland. Shortly thereafter the homes of the Tacoma Chinese were put to the torch.

The village of Sumner also expelled their Chinese that day. During the daylight hours, some fifty white men from Sumner and Puyallup went to the Chinese houses and ordered them to pack. This was hurriedly done and the thirteen Chinese were escorted to Tacoma where they arrived about eight p.m. They were placed in an empty house for the night and put on a train for Portland in the morning.[12]

One additional incidence of violence occurred in Puyallup when Thomas Smith assaulted John Meeker, an offense for which Sheriff Lewis Byrd promptly arrested Smith. His grievance was that Meeker had represented a Chinese man who had brought suit against him to collect money that was due.[13] Puyallup's Chinese, under the protection of its thirty-six deputy sheriffs, escaped expulsion.

A frightened Tacoma Chinese businessman named Goon Gau fled to the safety of Puyallup where he wired Governor Squire. "I am notified that at three P.M. tomorrow, a mob will remove me and destroy my goods. I want protection. Can I have it?"[14] Assistant U.S. Attorney Cornelius H. Hanford wired the governor, "Chinese houses here burning...do something quick." Mayor Henry Yesler, of Seattle, asked the governor for troops. Telegrams went to Washington, DC, and, upon orders from President Grover Cleveland, ten companies of troops from Vancouver Barracks arrived in Seattle on November 6 to protect the Chinese of that city. That evening the good citizens of Tacoma held a celebration ball.

Events moved quickly. On Wednesday, November 5, William H. White, United States attorney for the territory, asked Judge John P. Hoyt to immediately impanel a grand jury to investigate the expulsion. Jesse W. George, United States Marshal for Washington Territory, was dispatched to Pierce County with instructions to secure the names of witnesses to the expulsion. Marshal George arrived that afternoon with a number of prepared subpoenas, lacking only the names to be filled in. George issued Meeker and fourteen other county citizens subpoenas and was back home in Vancouver that evening. The witnesses traveled to Vancouver on November 6 and 7, where they testified to the grand jury that the Chinese had not left Tacoma voluntarily. The Grand Jury indicted twenty-seven conspirators, including the mayor, two city councilmen, the probate judge, and the president of the YMCA. On November 9 four companies of the United States Army occupied Tacoma. The indicted were arrested, taken by train to Vancouver, and formally charged. Bail was set at $5,000 each. They were home by November 13 after making bail, where they were greeted with a hero's welcome and a parade.[15] None ever served a day of jail time. Murray Morgan wrote that it was fifteen years before anyone who had opposed the forcible removal of the Chinese was elected to a local office.

Meeker never looked back. Shortly after testifying in Vancouver he left for New Orleans with his wife and youngest child, Olive, where he served as the state commissioner for the North, Central and South American Exposition, which opened November 10, 1885. Hop operations and the family business were turned over to his youngest son, Fred, who had just returned from California.[16] Meeker would not return to Puyallup for seven months.

Murray Morgan succinctly concluded that Ezra Meeker was correct when he told the Chamber, "Many of you will live to see the day that you will look back upon these actions with amazement and wonder, and regret that the recollection of this period should not be forgotten." On November 30, 1993, the Tacoma City Council chose to remember these events by passing Resolution No. 32415 authorizing the creation of a Chinese Reconciliation Park. Its purpose was "to reconcile the historic tragedy of the Chinese expulsion in 1885." In cooperation with the Chinese Reconciliation Project Foundation a stunning four-acre park was built at 1741 North Schuster Parkway on the Tacoma waterfront. Meeker's prediction had come to pass.

Tacoma's Reconciliation Park contains a number of interpretive panels telling the story of these events, a pavilion gifted from the sister city of Fuzhou, China, a waterfront walking path, and a number of impressive art pieces such as this depicting the Chinese expulsion from Tacoma. *P. Ziobron photograph*

CHAPTER 12

The American Exhibition at New Orleans

MR. COMMISSIONER/LADY COMMISSIONER

His Excellency Watson C. Squire, Governor of Washington Territory, on August 1, 1885, appointed Ezra Meeker to the position of Commissioner, representing the territory at the upcoming American Exposition at New Orleans.[1] The territory was offered a fine building and good location on the exposition grounds, and many public officials saw

Ezra, Eliza Jane, and Olive Meeker seated at the Washington exhibit at the 1886 New Orleans Exhibition. *Author's collection*

this as a golden opportunity to show the nation that the territory had the "right stuff" to become a state. Ezra Meeker was put in charge of collecting materials for the exhibit, shipping them to New Orleans, and setting up and running the exhibit. The decision to participate at the exposition came late, and Meeker at first was a little concerned that there would not be enough time to do all that needed to be done. He was especially concerned that much of the fruit, some of the vegetables, and various other products were out of season and could not be obtained. However, a legislative appropriation of $2,500 to help defray expenses and the Governor's appointment of Eliza Jane Meeker as Lady Commissioner on September 21 went a long way towards relieving Meeker's anxiety. His youngest daughter, sixteen-year-old Olive Meeker, is listed as Assistant Lady Commissioner in the exposition program, and she accompanied her parents to New Orleans. Ezra Meeker would again be promoting Washington Territory to the nation as he did in 1870 with Horace Greeley and Jay Cooke. He also managed in the process to introduce the territory to England.

Meeker called on his fellow citizens to "donate or loan all such articles as may be useful to illustrate our boundless resources, our famous scenery, our progress in art and manufacture, our mild climate; in a word to transfer a miniature Washington territory—the beautiful, the curious and the useful—to the ample space accorded the territory in the exposition buildings."[2]

Samples were requested of everything that grew in Washington territory: grains, fruit, grass, and vegetables. Oregon was sending 10,000 small sacks of wheat to distribute, prompting Meeker to ask, "Why can we not send more than 10,000?" California was sending a "magnificent showing of pears…Why can we not send better?…Nebraska, at the last exhibition, constructed a great arch with letters of corn that read, 'Corn is King.' We wish to construct an arch of letters, of timothy [hay] heads, a foot long each that will read that 'Grass is King.'"

Meeker exhorted owners of coal mines and lands to contribute "not less than one hundred pounds of coal from each vein…to construct a pyramid that shall show the world what boundless stores of coal we have. In a word friends, send samples of every kind, and in good quantities, of that which you have, and we promise yes that Washington territory shall be heard from at the coming exhibition."[3]

The Commissioner toured the territory collecting materials to exhibit. The first week of October found Meeker at the County Fair in Chehalis. Here he helped organize a committee to gather the products of the county. Ed Smith, a local resident, stepped forward and agreed to furnish thirty varieties of potatoes. The committee also agreed to furnish a section of a Lincoln Creek fir tree thirty-nine feet in circumference.

The Lady Commissioner was busy as well. Eliza Jane's interest in art guided this part of the exhibit. She collected an oil painting from the governor's wife, some good-sized painted clamshells from Pamela Hale, the Thurston County School Superintendent, and a wooden plate painted with apple blossoms, a painting on velvet, a moss wreath, and several other items from a Mrs. Barnes. Mrs. Hale fretted that she could not "make a better showing" and went on to say, "We are ashamed, Mrs. Barnes and I, to send our small 'exhibit' but we hope every town has sent a few things and altogether these may be even a drop in the bucket."[4]

Instructions went out to the exhibitors shipping from Kalama north to Puget Sound to forward their articles, free of freight charges, on the Northern Pacific Railroad, addressed to E. Meeker, Commissioner for New Orleans Exposition, Tacoma, W. T. Exhibitors living in the east part of the territory, Vancouver, or in coastal communities could ship free of charge over either the lines of the Oregon Railroad and Navigation Company or Northern Pacific Railroad.

All articles were to be received at either Portland or Tacoma, on or before the tenth day of October. The first railroad car was to ship out from Puyallup station on October 15 and go direct to the exhibition buildings in New Orleans. A supplemental shipment was to be made about November 1.

Hundreds answered the call to contribute. So much material arrived in Portland that a D. Prettyman, of Salem, Oregon, was employed for fourteen days in packing eighty-five packages, to forward to Mr. Meeker in New Orleans. Among the goods mentioned were forty-pound cabbages, the cut of a tree twelve feet in diameter, and a halibut weighing 207 pounds. Also shipped to New Orleans were twenty-one varieties of wheat, thirteen varieties of oats, ten of corn, five of barley, and two of hay.

There were ninety-four contributions of fruit, comprising nearly two hundred varieties of apples, pears, peaches, grapes, prunes, cherries, currants, blackberries, strawberries, raspberries, cranberries, and many other wild berries. Meeker proudly reported that the display contested "victoriously with older states and territories for preeminence in fruit and carrying off no less than seventeen prizes. Our fruit tables elicited unstinted praise, attracted universal attention and second to none in the exhibition as to quality, size and beauty of varieties displayed."[5]

One product Meeker exhibited with special pride was the "pounds of beautiful white sugar which was the wonder of many and the admiration of all."[6] Meeker had been experimenting with growing sugar beets and refining the sugar for several years, and now he had a good display of his results to show the nation. His disillusion with Washington's potential to produce quality beet sugar did not come until after the exposition.

Altogether thirty-three states and territories participated in the exposition. And even though it was a financial failure as a whole, Meeker called it a great success.[7]

Wrapping Up

Toward the end of the exposition the Meekers hosted a luncheon for the commissioners of the various states and territories. The *Ledger* described the Washington Territory exhibit as "effective, beautiful and instructive. Many novel features may be found here that will alone repay a visit to the exposition; such as the Snoqualmie Falls, a miniature reproduction of the great cascade mountain scene; a hop garden in full growth and a model hop house; a superb collection of pictures; a fruit display unequaled in the whole show."

Ezra Meeker spoke to the gathered crowd about his 1852 journey across the Rocky Mountains and his early experiences on Puget Sound.[8] At the close of the exposition on March 31, Meeker mailed the editor of the *Ledger* one of the badges issued at the reception and a copy of the photograph taken on the occasion.[9] A portion of the exhibit was then shipped from New Orleans to London for showing at Reading and Maidstone, England, to be part of the Colonial and Indian Exposition. Meeker contemplated the advisability of transferring the whole exhibit to display at the upcoming London-American exhibition in 1887, but settled for the time being to ship and display a sample of what was shown at New Orleans.[10]

All of the exhibit items not shipped to London, or not perishable, were stored at St. Paul, Minnesota, for future use. A permanent exposition was to open there on August 23, 1886.[11] Once home, Meeker made an attempt to raise funds by contribution to enable him to add to and maintain the exhibit at the London exposition, but after several days canvassing he found it was impracticable to raise the required amount ($2,000), and so he abandoned the attempt. Meeker had some hope that the Northern Pacific Railroad Company would utilize the exhibit in a collection for the great Northwest, and so he finally placed the exhibit of Washington Territory at their disposal for that purpose.[12]

Meeker included with his report a set of photographs of the exhibits, and a catalogue listing the various articles displayed. A copy of this catalogue may be found at the Washington State University Library in Pullman, Washington.[13]

On April 17 Eliza Jane and Olive Meeker returned to Tacoma on the evening train from Portland. They had come direct from New Orleans. The strain of the long absence from home and the stress of the return journey must have taken a toll as Eliza Jane spent the next two weeks ill, confined to her house.[14]

CHAPTER 13

Hop Tramping

After Ezra said good-bye to Eliza Jane and Olive in mid-April he went east to New York and then on to London. The 1885 hop crop had not been profitable. Meeker even called it disastrous for many. Hops that cost eight cents a pound to produce sold for as little as five cents on some markets. Meeker determined to visit the English and New York hop yards, draw from the experience, and make 1886 a better year. He was once again, as in 1882–83, absent from Puyallup for eight months.

Meeker reached London around April 25. Upon his arrival, he set up his display of Washington Territory exhibits at the Colonial and Indian Exposition. The New Orleans grain was shown again at the corn exchange at London. These activities kept him busy through the first week of May.

Field Work: England and New York

Meeker spent the rest of the month in the "Borough," London's hop district, doing hop business. At the beginning of June he went on a three-day, 150-mile tramp through the Kent hop district. It was his first visit to a foreign hop yard and he wanted to mingle with local growers and compare methods. Meeker found the winding English roads, usually bordered by a wall or hedge, pleasant to drive or walk on. He described the Kent district as "one vast hop and fruit garden" with the hop rows "straight as an arrow" and "everything giving the appearance of wealth, comfort and contentment." Upon closer examination however he found just the opposite. The farmers were losing serious money and wages were severely depressed. Meeker learned that the Puyallup growers could produce and deliver to London three pounds of hops at the same cost as the Kent growers could produce and ship two pounds. Half of the Kent growers had abandoned their yards and the rest were just hanging on, hoping "that the conditions will change and that we of America will cease to send them hops in such large quantities and that the extra tythe on hop land may be abolished."[1]

After a six-week stay in England Meeker returned to New York City arriving on June 15. He immediately went to the upstate New York hop district where he spent four or five whirlwind days assessing conditions there firsthand, visiting thousands of acres of hops from Albany to Cooperstown, Richfield Springs, Waterville, and Utica.[2] He examined twenty hop fields carefully and found hop lice in all, and expected to see the New York yield reduced by 15 percent. He felt "In New York, if the price remains low for the incoming crop, many thousand acres will be destroyed."[3]

Meeker, who had been absent since November, returned to Puyallup on the June 25 evening train from Portland.[4] "Home again, and glad enough I am," he wrote. "What with the notes of improvement all round about, the hearty welcome of relatives and neighbors, the kind greetings of friends everywhere, I feel that keen relish incident to return after long absence, that makes me feel almost young again and quite boisterous."[5]

1886 Prospects

The portents for the 1886 crop were good. In a July interview with the *Ledger* Meeker reported the New York yards were inundated with lice and that Germany would produce just half a crop. The *Waterville (NY) Times* of July 2 said, "Hop growers sit up nights to see that the lice do not carry off the poles and when they see one moving they anchor it with a log chain."[6] Each day's news brought fresh reports of the New York crop failure. Accordingly, Meeker refused offers of thirty cents per pound for his remaining 1885 crop. Some five hundred bales of 1885 hops held in storage in London were returned to New York to take advantage of the rising prices there.[7] By late July large areas of the New York fields were covered with black blight caused by lice and were beyond recovery. It became evident that there would not be enough hops raised in the United States to supply the demand and that importations from Europe must follow.[8] This meant, of course, that prices would rise dramatically. The *Ledger*, perhaps unintentionally, also called to the attention of its readers the ugly events of last year: "Numerous Indians are arriving daily to seek work in the hop fields and finding ready employment. Quite different from last season when John Chinamen held sway here."[9]

Late that summer Meeker sold 126 acres of hop fields near the railroad depot to his son Marion for $12,600.[10]

A New Home

In October 1886 an item appeared in the *Ledger* that would have caught the attention of the citizens of Puyallup. The Meekers were building a new home—the future "Meeker Mansion." The architects were Farrell & Danner and the excavation had begun. It would take the Meekers four years from groundbreaking to completion, but at long last they would move out of their log cabin.[11] No doubt it seemed odd to many that one of the wealthiest families in Washington Territory continued to live and entertain all manner of friends, relatives, neighbors, hop merchants, bankers, politicians, and businessmen from around the world in a humble twenty-five-year-old log cabin. It is doubtful that Meeker noticed or cared. He may have promoted opportunity, progress, and development for both the city and territory at every turn, but his cabin apparently was another matter. It was comfortable, and it was home.

The mansion was Eliza Jane's project. Meeker affirmed that the house was built from her plans and with her own funds (from a life insurance policy and with investments made from the sale of her half of the Fern Hill Donation Land Claim), at a cost of $26,000. That being said, one can hear the pride of place as Ezra many years later described the outcome of his wife's ambition, giving her all the credit as the "builder," but leaving no doubt of his own hand in the project.

Years later, in a tribute to his wife, Meeker wrote "the taste manifested in the planning and oversight in the building is indeed a marvel of completeness."[12]

CHAPTER 14

Meeker for Congress

RUNNING FOR OFFICE

Always active in civic affairs, Ezra Meeker in 1886 decided to run for the territorial seat in Congress representing the Republican Party. The political steps to accomplish this differed greatly from our process today. There was no primary election. In order to be placed on the ballot, a candidate first had to battle his way through the party's county convention, get a slate of delegates pledged to him, then move on to the state convention. There the candidate had to secure the votes of two-thirds of the delegates to get the party's endorsement. From the state convention, the chosen candidate then went directly onto the general election ballot.

Alexander Farquharson, whose feud with Meeker was chronicled in Chapter 7, wrote that in the fall of 1886, when returning from the Grand Army of the Republic Encampment in San Francisco, he encountered a number of delegates from eastern Washington on their way to the Republican convention in Tacoma. He stated that he informed the delegates of Meeker's "true character" and upon his arrival went immediately to the Tacoma Hotel where he met with the Democratic candidate Charles Voorhees.[1] He told Voorhees that he had given evidence of serious wrong doings on Meeker's part to the editor of the *Tacoma Times* to publish far and wide if Meeker was nominated. He thus assured Voorhees that he had nothing to fear from a Meeker candidacy, that in addition to tarnishing him in the press he would hound Meeker at each and every campaign appearance with his damning evidence. To reward him for these supposed actions Voorhees, upon being elected, arranged with President Cleveland for the appointment of a Farquharson supporter as Puyallup's postmaster. Farquharson went on to claim that his postmaster friend was a

Republican and that his appointment by a Democrat caused quite a stir in that city. The damning evidence was supposedly court testimony from the Maplewood Spring water dispute between Farquharson and Meeker from a decade previous. Farquharson also wrote that shortly after informing Meeker of his intentions, someone broke into his house looking for his copy of the trial notes and that the burglars were unsuccessful since the notes were safely stored in Frank Clark's office safe. Farquharson then claimed that consequently Meeker withdrew from the race, and a "Mr. Bradshaw" of Port Townsend was nominated in his place.[2]

This version of events was repeated virtually verbatim in Herbert Hunt's 1916 *History of Tacoma*, and Edgar T. Short's *Tacoma Times* articles, both of whom apparently did not actually research the election. Once in print, the story became accepted history even though it is wrong.

THE BACK STORY

To understand Farquharson's alleged threat to derail Meeker's run for office, one needs to recall the dispute over water rights that found both parties in court in 1879. The ubiquitous Frank Clark represented Farquharson and John B. Allen represented Meeker. Supposedly, both Farquharson and Meeker served as secretaries at the trial, keeping their own notes, each recording their versions of the day's testimony. These were the notes that Farquharson claimed burglars tried to steal.

In writing about that court contest, Farquharson said he called sixteen witnesses and ten of them testified that they would not believe Meeker under oath in a case wherein he was financially interested, and one testified of a past perjury on Meeker's part in a case in Steilacoom. This was the damaging testimony Farquharson said he threatened Meeker with in 1886.

A number of items in this account are suspect. A list of the 748 delegates and officers who attended the G.A.R. Encampment was published in the *San Francisco Call* newspaper. Farquharson's name does not appear on the list, calling into question whether he was even at the encampment, much less meeting with eastern Washington convention delegates on his way home.[3] Furthermore, no contemporary account of a burglary at his home has been found. Indeed, the court record is not in either Meeker's or Farquharson's handwriting, suggesting that there was a clerk at the trial. And what Farquharson didn't recall, apparently, was that he lost the case. The court sided with Meeker. And the supposed testimony of those sixteen witnesses is not in the court record. Only Farquharson's foreman Louis Sohus, John Meeker, and Sheriff Byron Young testified beyond the attorney's opening statements. Finally, in writing his version of the 1886 election, Farquharson also failed to recall that Meeker, in fact, did not drop out of the race.

The Convention

The 1886 Pierce County Republican Convention was held in Tacoma on August 4. It was a one-day event with 104 delegates attending. Puyallup was allowed only four delegates, but the leaders of the two competing slates, Ezra Meeker and James Stewart, were both from that city. Meeker's slate carried the day by a vote of 58-46; thus Meeker advanced to the state Republican convention, also held in Tacoma. The *Ledger* offered a preview of the candidates. Meeker seemed to be the early frontrunner, but several competitors emerged. Among them were Thomas Brents of Walla Walla, Governor Watson C. Squire, and Colonel J. C. Haines, Speaker of the House of Representatives. The *Ledger,* quoting the *Seattle Star,* wrote "Puget Sound, indeed the entire territory, has nowhere a better friend than the hop king of Puyallup… To him may be credited the hop fields of Puget Sound. There is no reason to believe that he would not make a faithful, conscientious and most indefatigable delegate."[4]

On September 8, 1886, the convention assembled in the Tacoma Opera House. Charles M. Bradshaw of Port Townsend was voted chairman. The four o'clock session adopted a platform and heard the nominations for the delegate to Congress and for various territorial offices. It wasn't until the evening session that the actual balloting began. The *Seattle Post-Intelligencer* gave a detailed account.[5] The vote for Congress was long, going through nine ballots as the delegates found it difficult to reach the two-thirds threshold required for nomination. Through six ballots the voting held steady for the top three candidates—Governor Squire, Mr. Brents of Walla Walla, and Ezra

Meeker. Squire held a large lead over Brents and Meeker on each ballot. On the seventh and eight ballots Squire's support began to collapse and Mr. Haines of King County sprinted to the lead. What happened next is in dispute. The *Post-Intelligencer* reported that on the ninth ballot King County changed its votes to convention chairman Bradshaw and a stampede followed, eventually making the nomination unanimous.[6] Others said it was "the stentorian voice of Colonel Jim Steel which rang out at the call of Pierce County—Twenty-two votes for Bradshaw!" which started the boom for Bradshaw.[7]

Charles M. Bradshaw had resided thirty years on Puget Sound. He had been the mayor of Port Townsend, a member of the legislature, a prosecuting attorney, a staunch railroad man, and a lawyer. He lost in the November election.[8]

POSTSCRIPT

Fact: Meeker was defeated in the voting at the state convention; he did not withdraw from the campaign under duress. It wasn't in his character to run from a fight. As for Farquharson, his only contribution to the campaign seems to be a made-up version of it in his manuscript.

The *Ledger* on June 21, 1886, reported, "A. S. Farquharson will soon remove to Seattle with his family. Mr. F., in conjunction with some other parties, intends to lease the barrel factory in that town. The stave factory has finished the last contract and shut down. Its closing is a heavy loss to the town."[9]

At the time this notice was published, Meeker had been absent from the Territory since November 1885, first as Washington Territory Commissioner to the New Orleans Exposition and then traveling to London. He did not return to Puyallup until June 25, 1886, four days after the *Ledger* reported Farquharson's impending departure. The two men had not crossed paths for at least eight months, and Farquharson's subsequent move to Seattle seems to have provided enough space for these two forceful men to finally get out of each other's way. Written well after the events took place, Farquharson's election "story" was his final jab.

CHAPTER 15

Farm and Home

NEWSPAPERMAN

Ever ready to take on a new opportunity, in 1887 Meeker became the agricultural editor of the *Seattle Post-Intelligencer*. His first article on January 2 was about his favorite subject—hops. As always, he waxed eloquent about the soil and growing possibilities in the Puget Sound basin. He went on to say that Washington had never had a crop failure due to any cause. He further said the only thing holding the territory back from driving New York and Europe from the field of competition was the Northwest's small population that could not supply the needed labor force for a major expansion of acreage. But he predicted that with immigration, production would soon be "multiplied five and perhaps ten, times over."

"Farm and Home" was a weekly feature that filled nearly a page in the Sunday newspaper. The column began with a section titled "Familiar Talk." For some unknown reason Meeker numbered these "Talks," beginning with "Familiar Talk No. 50." Talks one through forty-nine did not exist, at least in the newspaper. The unusual numbering system continued throughout the year. The column ran until April 5, 1888, when Meeker departed for an extended stay in New York.

Meeker kept his column interesting by introducing the reader to various family members and friends, using them to make his point. Thus the reader learned that "Aunt Hope used to run for the broom when she saw company coming and fall to sweeping with all her might." And that "Uncle Simon was fond of company; he would chat by the hour on the front porch." But they never let a visitor near their back yard as it was not fit for company. This led to a discussion of backyard cesspools breeding disease and the proper disposal of kitchen waste. The impetus for this discussion was the fact that the Puyallup city council had been discussing the sewage question for their city.[1]

115

Uncle Usual Meeker and Aunt Sally brought the reader information about fattening hogs. Thomas Alvord, of Kent, Washington, made regular appearances in the column. Meeker would visit his thousand-acre farm and tell the reader how to hay with modern machinery, or grow sugar beets. James Stewart of Puyallup wrote a letter to the editor describing how to grow peppermint. This led to a discussion that filled nearly a quarter of a page. Meeker's fourteen-year-old grandson, Fred Templeton, made an appearance, writing about farming in Halsey, Oregon. Eliza Jane was also a regular: "Jane 'slipped up' to the desk and quietly placed a nice bouquet upon the corner, as we were writing…The house seemed a little more cheerful, the home more pleasant, because of the quiet act."[2]

Meeker traveled around the Northwest gathering material for his column. In February he visited the cities of La Conner and Mount Vernon to look at Holstein cows. This was reported in the next issue. In March he visited dairy farms in the Portland area and wrote about milk production and dairy cows. His topics were wide and varied. One learned about rutabaga cultivation, how to buy a horse, how to feed poultry, the power of oats, picking pears, raising turkeys, and handling a bull. He also visited the Kittitas Fair. When visitors from Iowa came to Puyallup the topic turned to corn.

Meeker wrote the April 3 column on the train as he traveled to New York on hop business. The April 17 issue of "Farm and Home" was datelined New York. Meeker noted that the ground was still frozen and that he had spent two weeks in the interior of the state among hop farmers and dairymen. He visited Little Falls, the center of the New York dairy district, and attended market day. He described for his readers his trip home on the Canadian Pacific Railroad through the Canadian Rockies and the Selkirk Mountains. The article continued with a discussion of the many avalanches that plagued the line and how a thousand men were kept at work clearing the tracks.

Many columns discussed his Junction Farm, a property near the railroad depot.[3] The corn plowing started on May 12. Newborn calves arrived by May 31. On June 24 readers learned of his experiment in preserving butter in brine, arguing that it was the best way to preserve butter.[4]

That summer the column returned to a discussion of hops, and in particular the need for pickers. It was pointed out that the grower "knows that if the pickers do not come, he is 'done for' for the season, and his labor already bestowed upon the hops is lost." He stated that despite the worry, with one exception, the Native Americans pickers always came "in their canoes even from the confines of Alaska and all through British Columbia—the more hops we have, the more pickers come." He went on to argue that the public school term should be changed to a later date, claiming there were more than financial reasons for doing so and went on to describe the benefits the community would gain by the change.[5]

MEEKER'S MANY HATS

Meeker's energy never seemed to flag. Besides running his vast hop business and writing for the *Post-Intelligencer*, he took on other large responsibilities. In February 1887 he formed the Northwestern Fire Insurance Company of Puyallup, raised $78,000 of capital stock and subscribed another $22,000. He served as vice-president of the company and was a member of the board of directors. John Meeker was appointed secretary. On June 10 Meeker attended the annual meeting of the Washington Pioneers in Port Townsend where he was elected president of the association. In September he filed articles of incorporation for the Puyallup Water and Light Company, raised $30,000 in capital stock and became one of the trustees of the company along with his son Fred and his brother John. This tactic of filling the offices of his various enterprises with family members would become standard for Meeker in the next few years. Overseeing the construction of the new Meeker home was, of course, an ongoing concern.

The year's big event, however, was the completion of the Northern Pacific Railroad's direct line from the East Coast. Meeker did everything he could to make sure the main line went through Puyallup. He became the contractor for clearing and building the grade, and he tore down a portion of his warehouse to make room for the track. In July Meeker rejoiced in the fact that this last railroad link finally freed the valley growers from dependence upon San Francisco as their market and transportation hub. He wrote:

Now the market is transferred from California to within our own borders…As an illustration of what modern facilities will accomplish, how the telegraph and rail will annihilate time and speed, I would refer to a transaction of a few months ago at Puyallup, where a cable-gram was sent to London at 8 o'clock at night, an answer received before breakfast of next day, a thousand bales of hops disposed of through rail and steamer, bills of lading signed within a week, and bills of exchange passed through the banks of this city and bought at the same rate as wheat bills—coin, at once. How different this, when the hops needed to be hauled in wagons to tidewater, sometimes dumped into scows, sometimes waiting weeks for steamer freight room, then arriving sea damaged, heated and bedaubed with the filth of docks.[6]

HOPS

Despite the diversions, the final measure of a year was the success or failure of the hop crop. Meeker said, "It costs 18 cents per pound to produce hops in England, 14 cents in New York, and under 9 cents in Washington…At 15 cents per pound we may fairly count the profit upon an acre of hops at $90 a year, at 25 cents $250."[7]

By November 1887 the Puyallup Valley growers had shipped only 1,222 bales of hops, and orders were being filled at the rate of fourteen cents per pound. The low price led to calls to form a hop growers union as a counterweight to the combination of brewers and dealers who were holding out on purchasing to keep the price low. Meeker advised growers to hold on as prices were sure to go up.[8] It seemed that a profit of ninety dollars per acre was no longer acceptable.

CHAPTER 16

A Woman's Right to Vote

Suffrage in the Territory

In the winter of 1886 Ezra, and most likely Eliza Jane and Olive Meeker, took a break from their duties at the New Orleans Exposition and journeyed to Washington, DC, to attend the Eighteenth National Woman's Suffrage Convention being held February 17-19. Here Meeker said he first saw Susan B. Anthony in action, and had the pleasure of making her acquaintance.[1] A week later they were back in Louisiana. No mention of their convention attendance appeared in the contemporary press. On March 2, many of the suffrage conventioneers joined the 20,000 people who attended Woman's Day at the New Orleans Exposition. This was the first documented involvement of the Meekers in the suffrage movement, but as later events demonstrated, it is quite likely they had long supported the cause.

As the decade closed, the dominant topic of the day in Washington Territory was the question of statehood. A subtext to this issue was the question of women's suffrage. Efforts to give Washington women the right to vote started with the birth of the territory. In 1854 Arthur Denny of Seattle introduced a bill in the territorial legislature granting women suffrage. It failed by one vote. In 1867 women began using the argument that the law that created the territory gave the right to vote to "all white citizens over the age of 21." On that basis, fifteen women succeeded in voting in Thurston County in 1870, arguing that they were indeed citizens. Efforts elsewhere around the territory using this argument were not so successful. There matters rested until October 1871 when Abigail Scott Duniway, Laura de Force Gordon, and Susan B. Anthony paid a visit to the Northwest. They traveled around Puget Sound for about a month lecturing and organizing in such towns as Seattle, Port Townsend, and Olympia. At the conclusion of their tour they held a woman's suffrage convention in Olympia, attended by approximately three hundred men and women.[2] The entire non-Indian population of Puget Sound at that time was about five thousand, so this was a rather large turnout, especially considering the difficulty of travel. (Meeker had returned from his East Coast trip by this time, but it is not known if he or Eliza Jane attended the convention.) Following the convention, an attempt was made to move the territorial legislature to grant women suffrage. It failed. Despite the lack of initial success, Anthony and Duniway left behind the seeds of future success, for the convention created the Washington Equal Suffrage Association. The members of this organization lobbied Olympia time and again over the next decade.

In 1878 the territory sent a memorial to the U.S. Congress requesting that they grant Washington the right of statehood. A call was made for a constitutional convention. On February 12 the Pierce County commissioners appointed Ezra Meeker to help run the election that would choose the Pierce County delegate to the convention. On April 9 each county chose a delegate, 15 in total, to meet in Walla Walla that summer to write a state constitution. On June 11 the convention convened. On the third day the question of women's suffrage was brought to the floor, and on June 17 delegate Benjamin F. Dennison from Clark County presented a petition from Abigail Scott Duniway containing the signatures of nearly six hundred men and women, asking that the convention grant women the right to vote.[3] Mrs. Duniway addressed the convention and urged the delegates to make Washington the first state to grant women's suffrage. The convention voted it down 7–8. The new constitution, minus any provision for woman's suffrage, was then put to a vote of the people and passed 6,537 to 3,236. Unfortunately, the entire effort turned out to be an exercise in futility as the statehood-enabling act failed to pass out of committee in the other Washington.

In 1881 a suffrage bill passed the Territorial House of Representatives 13–11, but failed in the Council 5–7.

In late March 1883 Duniway was back in the territory pressuring the legislature yet again. She spent three days in Puyallup where she lectured to what was described as fair-sized audiences in a local church on Sunday evening and in Gimel's Hall on Monday and Tuesday evenings. This time her campaign was successful and on November 13 Governor William Newell signed the bill making Washington the third territory behind Wyoming and Utah to grant women the right to vote. Then the hammer dropped.

In 1887 a gambler was indicted by a grand jury that included several women. He appealed to the State Supreme Court. That body declared the indictment null. The court said the law granting women suffrage, and by extension, their right to serve on juries, was invalid due to a technicality in the writing of the legislation. The territorial legislature corrected the error in its next session. The court then countered by ruling that the United States Congress had intended to put the word "male" before the word "citizen" in the 1853 Washington Territory Organic Act that established voter qualifications for the territory, thus closing the door completely on women's suffrage. (How, exactly, they deduced this intent from a Congress that met a quarter of a century earlier is anyone's guess.) This ruling also had the effect of excluding women from the convention that was to write the 1889 state constitution. The seventy-nine delegates chosen to draft this new state constitution were to meet in July in Ellensburg. If women's suffrage was to become a reality in Washington, mountains needed to be moved, and quickly.

Organizing began almost immediately. Clara B. Colby, the editor of the *Women's Tribune*, the nation's leading pro-suffrage newspaper, arrived in the territory in April 1889. She began organizing chapters of the National Woman's Suffrage Association in city after city. An early stop was Puyallup. Colby was known to the Meekers as they subscribed to her newspaper. Indeed, among the Meeker Papers is a bound scrapbook containing articles cut from the *Women's Tribune*. On April 18 the *Daily Ledger* announced Colby's arrival and stated that the women of Puyallup were moving for suffrage in the yet-to-be-written State Constitution. After a well-attended lecture by Colby, the *Ledger* reported that a branch of the NWSA was formed with the following officers: "Mrs. N. J. Ross,[4] president; Mrs. E Meeker, Mrs. E. P. Spinning,[5] vice-presidents, Miss [Ella] Crounse,[6] secretary; Mrs. T. S. Hubbard,[7] treasurer."[8]

Clara Colby left her own account of her efforts in Puyallup, praising the work of Elizabeth Spinning, who "obtained the use of a church, had dodgers [handbills] printed, and attended personally to their distribution, placing them in the stores and sending them out to the distant houses and neighboring ranches."

The women of Puyallup formed committees and planned for other talks, including one in Orting by Laura De Force Gordon. Colby praised the leading men of Puyallup who supported suffrage for women, with special words for Ezra Meeker, "the largest hop grower in the valley, and a man of influence, [who] helped the meeting greatly by his presence and earnest participation. Mr. Meeker has done much for the Territory, having been its Commissioner during the second season of the New Orleans Exposition, and he believes not only in woman suffrage as a right, but that the establishment will do more for the state than anything else."[9]

The all-male convention that drafted the new state constitution placed it on the ballot on October 1, 1889, along with two amendments. The constitution readily passed (40,152 to 11,879). The two amendments, prohibition and woman's suffrage, were defeated, the latter by a vote of 35,527 to 16,613. Only Asotin, Clallam, San Juan, and Whitman counties voted yes. Years later Meeker wrote that he felt a major reason for the failure was that suffrage had become entwined in the minds of too many male voters with the temperance movement, a pairing that was reinforced by the efforts of some women's organizations to ban alcohol during the brief time when women in the territory had the right to vote.[10] It was probably no accident that the ballot was presented to the male voters of the new state with these two issues as amendments. On November 11, 1889, President Harrison issued a proclamation declaring Washington's constitution approved, with no provision for woman's suffrage. For the suffrage movement, this defeat was but one battle lost in a long campaign. For the Meekers it provided impetus to focus on the national campaign.

ELIZA JANE'S JOURNAL

How active were the Meekers in the national suffrage movement? The answer is hinted at in a small, spare journal that Eliza Jane Meeker kept of her activities in the winter and spring of 1889-1890. This journal remains the only instance of Eliza Jane's writing to survive to this day.

From the journal we learn the Meekers and their youngest daughter Olive, then twenty years old, left Puyallup on December 12, 1889, heading east. Their first stop was the nation's capital where they stayed just long enough for Ezra to lobby for a transportation corridor through the Puyallup Indian Reservation for a light rail line he was building. The family visited the Smithsonian and attended a session of Congress before moving on to Baltimore, Philadelphia, and New York City. The remainder of December was spent touring such places as Independence Hall and the Statue of Liberty, where Ezra and Olive went to the top of the torch and admired the view while Eliza Jane stayed below.

On January 6 the Meekers returned to Washington, DC, where they rented an apartment and settled in for a long stay. Almost immediately Mrs. Meeker began receiving two women callers on a regular basis. Eliza Jane identifies them simply as Miss Burns and Mrs. Cleveland. No first names were given. The identity of Mrs. Cleveland remains a mystery, but Miss Burns may have been Lucy Burns, a noted suffragist. Between social functions with her lady friends and doing the wash Eliza laconically records that she attended Mrs. Harrison's first public entertainment at the White House on the afternoon of Saturday, January 25. Mrs. Harrison was the First Lady of the United States.

On Tuesday, February 18, the Meekers attended the opening session of the National American Woman Suffrage Convention. Eliza Jane noted that they heard Elizabeth Cady Stanton deliver her farewell address.

This was a notable moment in the national suffrage movement. There had been, until 1890, two competing organizations, the National Woman Suffrage Association and the American Woman Suffrage Association. The two organizations merged into one at this convention and became the National American Woman Suffrage Association (NAWSA). Upon combining, the following officers were elected: President, Elizabeth Cady Stanton; vice-president at large, Susan B. Anthony; recording secretary, Alice Stone Blackwell; treasurer, Jane H. Spofford; and chairman of the executive committee, Lucy Stone.

Eliza Jane noted that on the evening of February 19 they heard addresses from Mrs. Ormiston Chant of London, a leading British suffragist, and others.

On February 20 Eliza Jane "listened to the reports of the delegates from the different states...and [s]peaking from Mrs. Beecher Hooker and others." Mrs. Isabella Beecher Hooker was the sister of Henry Ward Beecher, who gained notoriety with his Beecher's bibles—rifles that were handed out to anti-slavery agitators.

That evening Susan B. Anthony took her turn at the podium to announce the campaign in South Dakota as the next battleground for the movement, and she asked for donations. Sixteen attendees donated the equivalent in today's currency of between two and three thousand dollars each. The honorable Ezra Meeker was the fourth name on the list of donors.[11]

On Saturday, February 22, Eliza Jane wrote that she "went to Riggs house to business meeting of woman suffragists." The Riggs House was a Washington, DC, hotel that served for years as headquarters for the National Woman Suffrage Association headed by Elizabeth Cady Stanton and Susan B. Anthony. Jane H. Spofford was treasurer of the organization and her husband was the proprietor of the hotel. On Wednesday, February 26, Eliza Jane attended a chapter meeting in the forenoon. On March 19 she cryptically wrote, "Am going to white house at 1 o'clock." On March 21 she wrote, "Drove to Riggs house to see Mrs. Spofford and Miss Anthony or in other words Susan B. Anthony."

The implications of these meetings are remarkable. The Meekers' familiarity with these national suffrage leaders and the donation of money suggest more than a cursory interest in the movement. Attending the business meeting makes an even stronger case for a deeper involvement. Unfortunately for historians, the trail left by the Meekers is obscure. The full extent of their involvement cannot be known without more evidence.[12]

At the close of the convention the family made their way to Boston where they left Olive with friends. Then they started a leisurely trip home, stopping at Niagara Falls, Indianapolis, Elkhorn, and Eau Claire, Wisconsin.[13]

A year later Meeker, with Eliza Jane by his side, reciprocated the hosting duties when President Benjamin Harrison and the First Lady of the United States came calling. They visited Puyallup on May 6, 1891, and the entire town, of course, turned out to greet them. President

Harrison gave a speech that evening at the railroad station. The subject of that speech: opening a transportation right of way through the Puyallup Indian Reservation. Indeed, President Harrison said, "Its opening would be one of the first matters to receive his attention on returning to Washington."[14] The Meekers had made their mark on the other Washington.

THE VOTE AT LAST

The public suffrage movement in Washington faltered after the vote for statehood, and a long period of inactivity ensued. The cause occasioned little attention in the media. It was an exception to read in the *Tacoma Daily News* on July 22, 1891, that "Mrs. Concheta Ferris Lutz, State lecturer of the Minnesota Woman's Suffrage Association, will give a free open air lecture Thursday evening in front of the Park Hotel [in Puyallup]...This will be her first appearance on the Sound. She is said to be a fine speaker and soloist."[15]

In 1896, in his capacity as the editor of the agricultural page of the *Tacoma Daily Ledger*, Meeker penned some thoughts on the suffrage movement's failure to hold on to women's votes in Washington.

> Not long ago I met a lady, a casual acquaintance and ventured to say something in favor of woman's suffrage and for awhile felt like I had gotten into an awkward scrape. "No business to be bothering about politics; let that be for the men to attend to, a pretty sight to see women march up to the polls with a crowd of men to vote; I am not going to do it," and so with the toss of the head that meant to say, 'that settles it,' she relapsed into silence. Breaking out again, "What is the difference whether the women vote or not," said she, "they rule the nation anyway; for they rule the men." I think some men will resent that idea and some women will think that is not according to their experience. It would seem to me that the direct vote would be better. But we must possess our patience. This enfranchisement of women means a mighty revolution. This generation may not see it fully accomplished.[16]

The same year, 1896, Susan B. Anthony returned to tour Washington State, giving speeches and tirelessly campaigning for the vote. It is highly likely she visited Elizabeth Spinning who was still active in the national organization at that time. Spinning carried on the fight to final victory in 1910. Just before that vote she wrote: "I have been a fighting woman ever since I was old enough to sustain an argument, and I am not going to surrender my right to live in this world while the injustice under which woman is living in Washington exists. When the people enact that women shall vote and remove the reproach to the state and the insult to our sex, I will be perfectly willing to close my eyes and go down into my grave, but not until then."[17]

By 1906 Eliza Jane Meeker was drifting into dementia. She died in 1909, one year before the women of Washington finally won, and kept, the right to vote.

CHAPTER 17

Society News and Real Estate

On March 25, 1888, the *Seattle Post-Intelligencer* announced, "On the 5th of April the editor of this [agricultural] department of the *Post-Intelligencer* will depart for the Eastern states to be gone for two months or more traveling to Ohio, New York, Illinois, and Indiana." Since New York was a focal point of the hop industry and the Midwest was filled with Meeker relatives, one assumes the trip mixed business and pleasure for Ezra and Eliza Jane. Fred and Marion Meeker most likely handled the family businesses during their absence.

The Meekers were back home and entertaining in their cabin by late May and June. Their names appeared frequently in the society news of the *Tacoma Daily Ledger*. Music, recitations, and the use of a phonograph highlighted one gathering.[1] Others involved friends from the Oregon Trail days.

"Mr. and Mrs. Meeker have today been entertaining Mr. and Mrs. M. D. Ballard of Seattle, Mr. and Mrs. Dayton Ballard, of Lincoln, Neb., and friends from Tacoma. M. D. Ballard and E. Meeker came over the plains together, and they are greatly enjoying this reunion after forty years."[2]

In August another old friend came calling. "William Buck, of California, visited E. Meeker last Sunday [August 3]. Buck came across the plains with Mr. Meeker and had not seen him or the Sound Country for thirty years. He finds the change in this country past all belief."[3]

Even Mrs. Meeker's health was considered newsworthy. It was duly reported that she took ill and was confined to bed for over two weeks, and that her daughter Carrie Osborne traveled down from Seattle on June 26 to care for her. By mid-July the *Ledger* reported, "Mrs. E. Meeker is much improved, although not yet able to sit up."[4]

REAL ESTATE

Over the years Meeker acquired much valley land beyond the original 160 acres of his Puyallup homestead claim. The details of these purchases are scattered. However, records at the Meeker Mansion tell us that on November 13, 1876, Meeker purchased 126.1 acres of what had been part of the Romulus Nix donation land claim from Henry and Elizabeth Temple for $2,000. This land formed a portion of what eventually became known as the Junction Farm. Sometime prior to 1884, Meeker acquired sixty acres in the White River Valley and put that land into hop production. It is estimated that by 1888 Meeker owned over 1,000 acres, and early that year he advertised in a Tacoma newspaper that a significant portion of this land was for sale.

> For Sale at Puyallup, 322 acres of land and the Puyallup Water works. This property includes a large number of town lots, four houses, barn, hop kilns and warehouses, orchard, 65 acres of hops, four miles of water mains and abundant water supply. More than 100 acres suitably located for division into town lots.
>
> Price $53,000. Particulars furnished on application to parties meaning business.
>
> I will also sell the Junction Farm one mile from Puyallup, 326 acres for $115 per acre.
>
> E. Meeker, Puyallup, W.T.[5]

By March Meeker had subdivided some of his land into 120 town lots under the title Meeker's First Addition to Puyallup and suddenly found himself one of the larger real estate agents in the valley. The lots were sold at prices ranging from one hundred to four hundred dollars. He advertised Puyallup as a "thriving town of some seven hundred inhabitants" with "a commodious school house, three churches, several good hotels, a number of stores carrying large stocks of goods, a good system of water works and a thrifty and enterprising population."[6]

Land that had been in cultivation as hop fields the year before was turned into home sites. It was reported that: "E. Meeker has sold the lot on which his office now stands to Wingate C. Gibbs for $6,000. Mr. Meeker bought this same place in 1877 for $35."[7] Then there was this news. "E. Meeker has sold $20,000 worth of lots in the last thirty days."[8]

What was driving Meeker's need for cash? He was involved in two large building projects in 1888—his grand new house and the Park Hotel.[9] Both were devouring money. The Park Hotel was eating up an estimated $1,000 a month, and the mansion would eventually cost $26,000 before it was completed in 1890. However, a brief notice in the Tacoma *Daily Ledger* described the birth of a project that was the main culprit in this need for liquidity: "The trustees of the Puyallup valley railroad company held their first meeting yesterday and organized by electing E. Meeker President, L. F. Thompson Vice President, and George W. McAllister Secretary."[10]

Meeker declared plans to build a light railroad line from Puyallup to Tacoma to better serve the community. It would mean going head to head in competition with the Northern Pacific Railroad Company, and it would be enormously expensive. It was a project of immense scale for a city of just seven hundred people. It would consume much of Meeker's income over the next few years, cause a family rift, and ultimately become a major factor in his financial collapse. But all that was still in the future.

HOPS

Hops still provided the foundation upon which the Meekers' lifestyle flourished. In 1881, with the formation of Meeker, Osborne & Co., Ezra Meeker entered the hop brokerage business. Over the years he continually expanded this side of his hop business. Sons Marion and Fred Meeker, nephew Joseph Pence Meeker, and son-in-law William Templeton[11] traveled to the hop yards of Oregon and Washington each fall, obtaining samples, signing contracts, and buying and shipping hops. E. Meeker & Co. had semi-permanent offices in the Willamette Valley and seasonal ones elsewhere, scattered from southwest Washington to Grants Pass, Oregon. All hops purchased were sent to Puyallup where they were consolidated into large trains and shipped east with banners attached to their sides advertising the company. Meeker even began arranging financing for the Northwest growers, advancing them money on their future crops, a practice that allowed him to get his start in the industry, but would eventually cost him dearly. By the end of the 1880s Meeker had become the Northwest's largest hop broker and this part of the business had actually outgrown his own hop growing activities.[12]

At the end of the 1888 season, a Meeker hop circular stated that 50,000 bales were grown in the territory that year,[13] but a scarcity of pickers resulted in some 8,000 bales not being harvested. However, the quality of those picked was high, because they were allowed to ripen on the vine longer than normal, thus producing a very fine berry. His monthly circular on September 7, 1889, announced the opening of the hop-buying season—a sale of one bale of hops by J. V. Meeker to E. Meeker & Co. for fifteen cents a pound.

On September 6, 1889, the *Ledger* reported the status of the harvest and suggested that Meeker journeyed far up the British Columbia coast to recruit Indian hop-pickers. The article offered insight into the details of picking and attitudes toward the Native workers.

> One hundred and fifty Indians from Fort Roper [British Columbia][14] are at the mouth of the Puyallup river, on the way to Campbell & Meeker's hop field.[15] Mr. Meeker has also returned and reports he had no trouble in securing these Indians. From what he could see and hear this last week, there are many more Indians who have not yet secured work. In fact he had to refuse to take any more. It is an unwritten law that a band of Indians must not be broken up, and they are very unwilling to be separated. Indians are quicker to take in the situation than they are credited for, and these times when picking is scarce, they will try and crowd in as many as they can, claiming that they belong to the band. Mr. Meeker's efforts had to be exerted to keep the number as low as possible, and finally he drew the line at 150.
>
> E. Meeker & Co.'s Indians have arrived and commenced today on A. J. Spencer's yard. Some small growers who have no drying house, take advantage of their neighbors' kilns and pickers and thus get through very easily. Meeker's band of 150 Indians have two or three small yards to pick this week and will, on Monday, begin on the forty acre tract at the junction.[16]

In mid-December 1889 E. Meeker & Co. shipped a trainload of hops, consisting of eleven hundred bales, to London and contracted for five hundred more.[17] Meeker supplied these statistics to the July 13, 1890, issue of the *Daily Alta Californian*: "The hop crop of the two States, Oregon and Washington, for the year 1890 will load 1000 cars of seventy bales each. It will take 500,000 pounds of sulphur to cure this crop and more than 300,000 yards of cloth to bale it. It will take an army of nearly 20,000 people twenty days to pick the crop. It will cost over $750,000 to harvest the crop."

A visitor to the Puyallup Valley that year reported that the Northern Pacific carried 180 tons of hops to Baltimore for shipment to London, with a profit realized of more than 1.5 million dollars (more than 42 million in today's currency).[18]

Clearly these kinds of profits were transforming not only the Puyallup Valley but the entire Puget Sound basin. In 1890 Meeker's Kent farms alone earned a profit of $30,268 or $771,000 in today's currency. His Puyallup farms did equally as well, as did his brokerage business.

JAPAN

In 1887 Meeker began a multi-year effort to open a market for Puyallup Valley hops in Japan. Meeker wrote in his "Farm and Home" column, "For many years the Japanese have consumed large quantities of strongly alcoholic beverages called 'sake' made from rice. With the arrival of large numbers of Englishmen, Germans, and Americans in Japan came a demand for beers of the European type, and the light bottom fermentation beers brewed in Germany were preferred to the heavier and more alcoholic English beers. The taste for these beers spread from the European residents to the natives."[19]

Unfortunately, the Japanese brewers found their climate unsuitable for the growing of hops. Accordingly they had imported hops from England and San Francisco. Meeker advised the Japanese buyers to import directly from Puget Sound.[20] In the fall of 1887 Meeker sent several samples of Washington hops to Japan and received a trial order of twenty bales.[21] The next year Meeker sent more samples, which resulted in an order that amounted to a ton of hops, or eleven bales. These bales were scattered to eleven different breweries and were so well received the Japanese ordered an additional railroad carload of hops. Unfortunately the order arrived at the close of the season and was not sent.[22] In September 1889 E. Meeker & Company received another order for a ton of hops, which was immediately sent by steamer from Vancouver, BC.[23] The Tacoma newspaper trumpeted the potential of the Japanese market:

We are geographically well situated to supply the orient with many staples, now that the nation is adopting European civilization. In this connection it would probably be of interest to state that an order recently came from Japan for 15 cows, some pigs, sheep and chickens, and the firm ordering them instructed Meeker & Co. to hire a suitable man to take charge of them and bring the entire lot to Japan, saying that they would pay all the expenses. The money was deposited in Tacoma, but by and for some unexplained reason the steamship company running between Yokohama and Victoria refused to accept the stock, and the sale fell through. This is a new enterprise, shipping direct to Japanese brewers by a Washington Territory firm. So it will be seen that the Puyallup valley is not an unknown section but is favorably known throughout the world, from the occident to the orient, as it were.[24]

Ultimately this market failed to materialize despite the efforts of Meeker and the local press, but the dream died hard. In 1895, while on a steamer crossing the Atlantic, Meeker wrote Eliza Jane, "[If] we only can make that trip to Japan this next summer I will expect a season of enjoyment better than any outing of mountain climbing, camping or hunting—you and I 'by our lone' we two and no more."[25]

THE MANSION AND THE PARK HOTEL

Construction of the mansion had been ongoing for nearly four years since the contract was let to build the stone foundation in October 1886. Clara Meeker,[26] Fred's wife, wrote in March 1890: "Your new house looks fine now, that is the outside of it—I went out on the roof once but I don't think you will ever get me out again. Fred had a pair of nice field glasses and we wanted to try them so went on top of the house but I was so frightened I don't think I saw anything. If I did I forgot it before I reached the ground."[27]

Although the outside was mostly completed, there was still work being done on the inside and on the grounds. John C. Plummer and John Byrns McIntosh, a future Meeker-in-law, did the plastering. The Tacoma Manufacturing Company did the inside finishing at a cost of something over $4,000.[28] Landscaping required one hundred loads of earth to be hauled in for grading around the house and for a half-acre garden, which was surrounded by a "neat picket fence."[29]

By summer, construction of the Park Hotel had progressed enough that its restaurant was open for entertaining. A dinner was given in honor of Frank Meeker's cousins, Jabish and Ada Clement, who had come up from San Francisco for an extended visit.[30] On October 16, 1890, both unfinished buildings became the scene of a unique dual celebration—a wedding and a birthday:

> One of the most enjoyable events of the year occurred at the residence of Mayor Meeker[31] at Puyallup yesterday. The occasion was the celebration of Mrs. Meeker's birthday and the marriage of their daughter Ollie to Roderick McDonald.[32] The marriage took place shortly after 2 o'clock in the beautiful home which has for so long been in process of construction…The ceremony was performed by Rev. Dr. Gunn of the Presbyterian Church in an impressive manner. The bride was lovely, and of course, the attraction for all eyes, attired in a white silk faille, lace and ribbons, white veil, kid slippers and gloves. The groom bore himself becomingly, and the ceremonies throughout passed off in the happiest manner. At the close, the mansion being not yet finished, the company adjourned to the Park Hotel restaurant…As only relatives were present a true, old-fashioned family reunion here took place. In all forty-four sat down to the table, among them Mayor Meeker's fourteen grandchildren. When the company had assembled, the worthy mayor, on behalf of the children and grandchildren, presented Mrs. Meeker, upon the occasion of her fifty-eighth birthday, a very fine and artistic etching, entitled "The Old Connecticut Road." Mr. Meeker has not heretofore been considered an orator, but as he dwelt upon the time of his marriage and told the children present of "the early days" and the struggles of that time, in making his presentation speech, a suspicious brightness was noticed in many eyes. Evidently the memories of youth took strong hold upon him as they did upon his hearers.[33]

The couple received a wedding gift of $2,500 from the Meekers and later, in 1892, Ezra also gave his daughter Olive G. McDonald a Warranty Deed to lots 1, 2, & 3 in block 5 in Meeker's Second Addition, property on which Olive and Roderick built a house.

The *Ledger* reported in December, "The Meeker mansion is nearing completion. Mrs. Meeker said she will cook their first meal there today."[34] The lights were fully on by February 1891. "The elegant E. Meeker residence presented a very gay appearance Monday night when every room and window in the edifice was illuminated with electric lights."[35] The Park Hotel, however, was another matter. Construction was going slowly and a meeting of the stockholders was called for the purpose of doubling the capital. It was hoped by April to have the east wing finished for the accommodation of visitors.[36]

The Park Hotel. This south side view faced Ezra Meeker's first hop-drying kiln. *Washington State Historical Society 2015.0.298*

CHAPTER 18

"Inclined to be Pugnacious"

First Mayor

Ezra Meeker is credited by most historians and by the City of Puyallup with being the town's first mayor. In truth, he was the town's first "legal" mayor. The city had incorporated in the summer of 1888, or at least it thought it had, under the direction of a board of trustees. James Stewart was chosen chairman of the board. Over the next year city officers were appointed, ordinances passed, and Alexander Campbell became mayor. However, a problem developed. The trustees had created a valid corporation but had not put the issue of incorporating the city up to a vote. A farmer who did not want to be part of the city sued. In February 1890 the Washington State Supreme Court declared the incorporation of Puyallup illegal. The town council met and decided that until they actually received instructions from the court they would continue to operate as usual and that they would re-incorporate as soon as the legislature passed a pending bill that gave more power to towns than the law they originally incorporated under. James Stewart was sent to Olympia to investigate the matter of the pending bill.[1]

John Meeker, who had a reputation for fairness, was authorized by the court to employ Judge Galusha Parsons of Tacoma to help with the new incorporation process. On July 11, 1890, Judge Parsons requested that the county commissioners hold a special session to consider a petition filed by seventy-one Puyallup citizens requesting incorporation.[2] An election was ordered for August 16.

There were 350 eligible voters for the August 16, 1890, election in Puyallup. The final tally was 199 for incorporation and 75 against. For mayor, the vote was Ezra Meeker, 171, and James Stewart, 137.[3]

The city of Puyallup officially came into existence on August 19, 1890, when the incorporation papers and election results were filed in

Olympia. Ezra Meeker became the new city's first legal mayor just in time for its first official crisis. Newly incorporated Puyallup joined a long parade of western cities in suffering a major inferno. On September 17, 1890, just days after Meeker's inauguration, a large section of downtown Puyallup was destroyed by fire.[4]

HAVE A DRINK AND VOTE FOR ME

Meeker's first term as mayor was quite brief. He was elected in August 1890 and by the end of the year was facing reelection. The normal term of mayor had been set for one year, but the complications of incorporation delayed the first election. Meeker faced James Knox in his second run for mayor in December 1890. At some point in the campaign Knox supposedly put a barrel of beer in front of one of the town's saloons with a note attached to it reading, "Have a drink and vote for me. Signed E. Meeker." Knox later claimed that the sign was a joke put up by one of his more avid supporters. But the damage was done, ironically, to teetotaler Meeker. At a time when temperance was a hot-button issue of the day, the non-drinking voters gave the nod to Knox, who won by a handful of votes. Knox served from January to December 1891 as Puyallup's second legal mayor.[5]

In 1891 Meeker again announced his intention to run for mayor. Three candidates faced off in the election: James Knox headed the Citizens Party; Chauncey Potter headed the People's Reform Party; and Ezra Meeker headed the Party of Economy and Progress. On December 8, 1891 Puyallup held its third mayoral election.[6]

According to the *Tacoma News*, Meeker won with 206 votes to Knox's 204. Potter came in a distant third with 70 votes.[7] But there was a back-story that once again demonstrated Meeker's pugnacious nature. The *News* also reported that after losing to Knox in the city's second election Meeker began grazing his cattle in Pioneer Park, on land that he had recently donated to the city. Knox then instructed the town marshal to remove the cattle. Meeker retaliated by locking the gate with the cattle inside and filing suit against Knox and the city for violating the terms of his gift. Meeker asked the court to void the gift of the Pioneer Park as it was made when the city was not legally incorporated and thus not legally entitled to accept such a gift. He asked the court to allow him to resume legal control over the property.

With this controversy simmering, Knox refused to accept his two-vote defeat. He contested the election on grounds of fraud and bribery. He claimed that men were offered various sums of money in payment for their votes and that some were not even residents of the precinct in which they voted. The charges failed to adhere, however, and Meeker became Puyallup's third mayor. However, by virtue of being elected, Meeker found himself in the unique position of being both plaintiff and defendant in his lawsuit against the city—private citizen Ezra Meeker was suing the city that he now led. Logic would argue that the case be dropped, but private citizen Meeker fought Mayor Meeker all the way to the state Supreme Court.

The suit was not resolved until after Loyal Hill defeated Joseph N. Fernandez, John Meeker's son-in-law, by 42 votes out of a total of 515 ballots cast, in Puyallup's fourth mayoral election.[8] On February 13, 1893, in *Meeker vs. the City of Puyallup*, the court ruled for the city.[9] Pioneer Park remained under city control. In a fit of stubbornness, Meeker appeared at the city council meeting following the court decision and made one last pointless effort to stall the inevitable. A resolution was introduced to authorize the town marshal to remove Meeker's barriers and take possession of the park. Meeker argued long and loud that the city could not act while the injunction that he had obtained was in force, which, said Meeker, would not be until thirty days after the Supreme Court ruling. The council did not agree. The vote was unanimous.[10] It would be two decades before Meeker again ventured into the political arena, where he lost yet again. Politics was not his forte.

The Chicago World's Fair

Ezra Meeker's experience at the 1885 American Exposition in New Orleans made him a logical choice to lead Washington State's participation in the 1893 World Exposition, also known as the Chicago World's Fair. Early in 1891, the Washington State World's Fair Association Committee was formed to plan Washington's participation in the event. Thirty-nine committee members, one from each county, would be headed by an executive commissioner to be appointed at a meeting to be held on May 20 in Ellensburg. The plan was for each county to have an exhibit and thus create a spirit of competition among the counties with the overall coordination of exhibits controlled by the executive commissioner.[11] On March 27 the *Tacoma Ledger* reported that Edmond Meany, the King County committeeman, state legislator, and press agent for the association said, "Mr. Meeker would have been elected had the vote been taken any time during the day yesterday."[12]

The committee, meeting in Ellensburg in May, made Meany's prediction official by electing Ezra Meeker executive commissioner. He immediately went to work making "arrangements to commence taking photographs of buildings and scenes for the world's fair."[13] Notice was sent out to architects to submit plans and cost estimates for the state building "to be built as nearly as possible from the materials found within the state."[14] In July Meeker took the train to Chicago where he looked over the grounds and potential locations for the Washington building.[15]

Shortly after his appointment, Meeker and Meany clashed over the financial control of the organization. Meeker publicly accused Meany and the other commissioners of financial impropriety. The dispute became personal, bitter, and was played out in the state's newspapers. At an August meeting held in Olympia, the committee abruptly removed Meeker as executive commissioner. He was replaced with Dr. Nelson G. Blalock of Walla Walla. The Yakima newspaper offered the following: "Ezra Meeker, the late executive commissioner of the world's fair commission, spent Sunday and Monday in this city. He is inclined to be pugnacious, and if Dr. Blalock or any of his late ejectors want to go him a few rounds, Marquis of Hosbury rules, they can have 'em at the drop of a hat."[16] The *Chicago Tribune* ran the story of Meeker's removal on August 22 giving the dispute national play. The job seemed to be ill fated, for Dr. Blalock resigned in December 1893. The *Yakima Herald* opined that Meany forced the resignation and that he was the political autocrat of the board, while nominally only its secretary.[17] After Blalock's ouster Edmond Meany became the third and final executive commissioner.

Meeker's accusations of financial impropriety by the commissioners and Meany played out in the pages of the *Daily Ledger* and resulted in public hearings by a joint committee of the state legislature. At these hearings Meeker grudgingly rescinded the accusations against Meany, while letting the others stand. Eventually all were exonerated.[18] The two men would clash again in the press in 1905 with the publication of Meeker's *Pioneer Reminiscences*. Again the dispute became bitter and personal. But that is a story for another time.

Frank Meeker's college photograph. *Courtesy of Division of Rare and Manuscript Collections, Cornell University, Carl A. Kroch Library, RMC2009_0150*

CHAPTER 19

Railroads, Swindles, and the Troubled Life of Frank Meeker

Francis Oliver Meeker was born on May 3, 1855, in Steilacoom, Washington Territory to Amanda and Oliver Meeker. After Oliver's tragic death in the 1860 wreck of the *Northerner*, Ezra and Eliza Jane took Amanda and Frank into their household. When Amanda married a local man, Benjamin Franklin Spinning, in 1867 and moved to Steilacoom,[1] Frank stayed with the Meekers. He was twelve years old. The valley hop industry was in its infancy at this time, and there was as yet no hint of Ezra and Eliza Jane's future prosperity. The Meekers simply kept Frank and continued to raise him as one of their own.

CORNELL UNIVERSITY

In September of 1872 Frank, age eighteen, and Marion Meeker, twenty, left together for Cornell University in Ithaca, New York, an event that was probably set in motion by Ezra when he was back east in the winter of 1870–71.[2] Admission was contingent on passing the entrance examination administered at the university. The journey from Puyallup to New York was exhausting. It involved a sea voyage from Puget Sound to San Francisco, followed by a transcontinental train ride of nearly a week in duration in conditions that Ezra, who had traveled the route just a year earlier, described as uncomfortable in the extreme. Passengers slept sitting upright in rigid seats with only cold food to eat, as dining cars had yet to make an appearance on this route. At the end of the journey the hopeful students-to-be faced the exam.

It cannot be overstated how remarkable it was for two home-schooled and country-educated boys from the raw edge of a fledgling territory to compete favorably with the children of the East Coast elite for admission to an Ivy League School. According to the December 5, 1872, Steilacoom *Puget Sound Express* only thirty-seven claimants lived in the entire Puyallup Valley, with a meager 1,360 acres under cultivation. The Northern Pacific was building a railroad line from Kalama to Commencement Bay. Its terminus, the future city of Tacoma, was a small collection of cabins and a single wharf. The town of Puyallup did not yet exist. The non-Indian population of the entire territory was just 23,955 according to the 1870 U.S. Census. The valley hop industry, while making money for a handful of growers, was not yet the money machine that it would become in future years.

The responsibility for financing Frank's education was likely assumed by his Uncle Ezra. After Oliver's death in 1860, Amanda Clement Meeker inherited title to his donation land claim in the Midland area of Tacoma. Six years later, in 1866, she deeded that claim to her brother-in-law, Ezra Meeker, "in trust for Frank" who was a minor. (Amanda retained her own claim.) Ezra was given the right to derive income from the land and he mortgaged it during his term of ownership, perhaps to pay Frank's college costs.[3] When Frank came of age in May 1876, Ezra deeded the land back to him in accordance with Amanda's wishes.

When Frank and Marion arrived in Ithaca, New York, they were required to pass an entrance examination before they could actually be enrolled. The Cornell University examination schedule was three days in length and very difficult. Whether he failed the entrance examination or simply became homesick, Marion soon returned to Puyallup. Frank remained at Cornell, and sample questions in the *1877-78 Cornell University Register* suggest that he was well-taught during his growing up years in Steilacoom, Fern Hill, and Franklin.[4]

Cornell University opened on October 7, 1868, with an enrollment of 412 men.[5] The university started admitting women in 1870 and Sage Hall, a woman's dorm, was opened in 1872, just before Frank arrived. Frank was in the university's sixth class. Tuition, room, board, lights, and fuel were $315 a term. Depending on the definition of "term" (either one or two per school year), Frank's education would have cost between $1,500 and $3,000.

In his senior year Frank competed for the University's prestigious Woodford Prize for English oration and was one of six finalists. He graduated in the spring of 1878 and returned to Puget Sound with a Bachelor of Science and Letters degree—and a bride.[6]

In 1878, Frank married Ettella Wells, a native of Ithaca. The newly-weds took the railroad to Puyallup shortly after Frank's graduation and, according to the 1880 census records, made their home with Ezra and Eliza Jane in the Meeker cabin.

Frank practiced law in Puyallup and Tacoma, grew hops with his uncle, and became involved in a number of financial dealings. Ettella gave birth to two children—Oliver Wells Meeker born in 1888 in The Dalles, Oregon, and Felix Waldo Meeker born in 1890 in Tacoma, Washington.[7]

Real Estate and Randolph Radebaugh

On May 10, 1887, Frank Meeker, now 32 years old, took a three-year lease on 343 acres of timber and farmland located between Tacoma and Puyallup on the south side of the river. He and his mother had sold their Midland acreage to Charles H. Spinning (not related to Amanda's second husband Benjamin Spinning) in 1884 for $5,500, and Frank probably used a portion of his share to purchase the lease.[8]

Most of the property was valley land with a small segment going up the hill to the south. This area would become known in all future legal documents as Maplewood. The property belonged to the widow Louise Ackerson. Louise's husband had been one of the founders of the Hansen/Ackerson and Company sawmill in Tacoma. Profits from the sawmill and wise real estate investments had made the Ackersons quite wealthy. In the 1870s and early 1880s the Ackersons bought several parcels of property in the Puyallup area and became social friends with Ezra and Eliza Jane Meeker.[9] A year and a half into the lease, on January 24, 1889, Frank bought a full 350 acres for $55,000; he put $11,000 down and took out a $44,000 mortgage with Mrs. Ackerson, making himself and his wife Ettella responsible for the payments.

At the time Frank was working in several capacities. He was an attorney working out of an office in Tacoma. He was an unofficial partner in Ezra Meeker's various farming enterprises and he was often put in charge of the hop business when Ezra and his sons were away from Puyallup. Frank was also an editor on the staff of the *Tacoma*

Daily Ledger, owned by Randolph Radebaugh. These two men were partners in a number of businesses. Radebaugh was the president of the Puyallup Water & Light Company, the Tacoma & Fern Hill Street Railroad Company, the Park Hotel Company, the South Side Street Railroad Company, and the Puyallup Lumber Company. Frank Meeker was the vice-president or treasurer in all of these enterprises.

Two weeks after taking out his mortgage, Frank sold one half of the Maplewood property to Mr. Radebaugh and his wife for $36,400. He did not use this money to pay down the mortgage. By the end of the year the original balance of $44,000 stood unchanged. It is doubtful that Mr. Radebaugh gave Frank any money at all. More likely he simply secured half of the Maplewood property with a promissory note. Time and events would make the reasons for this clear.

BUILDING A RAILROAD

Ezra Meeker had been frustrated since 1877 by the lack of a convenient, comfortable transportation link between Puyallup and Tacoma. The carriage road along the river was terrible, mostly mud and stumps, and virtually unusable in the winter. In June 1877 the Northern Pacific Railroad Company built a line from Tacoma, through Puyallup, to the coalfields at nearby Wilkeson. They proudly called it the Cascade Division. It served the valley hop growers for years. Instead of hauling their hops overland to Tacoma, they could now load them at the Puyallup depot. Passenger service, however, was another matter. Hop buyers and sellers were constantly arriving in Puyallup. To get there they either had to take the carriage road or the railroad. Almost all opted for the railroad. Meeker frequently made trips to Tacoma and Seattle on this railroad. He described the trip to Tacoma as distinctly unpleasant. Service was twice a day in unheated, closed boxcars with simple wooden benches. Passengers crowded in shoulder to shoulder. Meeker said the summer heat in these closed cars and the physical closeness of the passengers resulted in a profusion of unpleasant odors.

As the new decade approached Meeker made plans to improve transportation between the two cities, and, as always, he hoped to make some money in the process. His plan had several components. He would build a competing narrow gauge railroad from Puyallup to Tacoma. It would run through mostly rural areas, where in his mind, he saw thousands of homes being built, turning the parts of the Puyallup Valley not under cultivation into a giant bedroom community for Tacoma. The Tacoma-Puyallup Railroad would run many times a day. The rush hour runs would carry workers to and from their new valley homes. Midday and evening runs would carry the produce of the valley to Tacoma for sale the next day. Fresh fruit, fresh vegetables, and fresh dairy products would flood the markets of the "City of Destiny." And all of it would travel on Meeker's new railroad. Coincidentally, money could also be made selling the lots on which all these new homes would be built. Finally, a huge hotel called the Park, to include a fancy restaurant, was to be built on Meeker land on the southwest corner of today's Pioneer and Meridian, giving hop buyers and tourists a first class place to stay and spend their money while in town.

On April 1, 1888, the trustees of the Puyallup Valley Railroad Company held their first meeting. Meeker was elected president, Levant F. Thompson vice-president and treasurer, and George W. McAllister, secretary.[10]

Major hurdles stood in their way. The proposed route of the railroad followed the valley along the south side of the Puyallup River. It was a direct, level route to Tacoma and would require a minimum number of expensive bridges, but this proposed route would cross the Puyallup Indian Reservation. The company needed the tribal council's permission for a right-of-way, and, in addition, legislative approval to resolve a host of other issues and legal matters. Apparently not much forethought was given to how the Northern Pacific Railroad might respond to competition. The answer came quickly. The NPRR moved aggressively to block Meeker at every turn. It was a no-holds-barred fight. The Meeker camp resorted to bribery, not too successfully as it turned out, in an attempt to secure tribal approval.

Facing accusations of wrong-doing, Frank Meeker, representing the railroad company, asked for an investigation.[11] He likely regretted making the request. The *Oregonian* reported, "Agent [Edwin] Eells called up twelve Indians and charged them with receiving bribes from George J. Dougherty, agent of the Puyallup Valley R.R. One and all confessed." Agent Eells questioned Dougherty in front of the local press and Ezra. Dougherty testified that under instructions from his superiors, he paid a considerable sum of money to the Indians as an inducement for the tribe to give their consent to the right-of-way for the railroad.[12] We never learn who issued those instructions. In any case, it seemed not to matter. In an interesting double standard, Agent Eells declined to charge the railroad company with offering bribes, but charged the Indians with accepting them.[13]

Bribery failed to secure the upstart railroad a route through the Indian reservation. The tribe denied Meeker his needed right-of-way. One can only speculate that the NPRR was playing the same game at the same time, but with the benefit of deeper pockets and a subtler touch since they did not get caught. Bills were introduced in the legislature, backed by the NPRR, throwing up further roadblocks. The preferred route was abandoned in the face of these obstacles, and a new route was devised that would follow the grade up South Hill in order to skirt the reservation. A number of trestles would be needed across steep ravines. By dramatically increasing the cost of the proposed railroad, the NPRR executives hoped to kill the project. Nevertheless, Meeker persevered.

Just before Meeker left for a tour of the East Coast with his wife and youngest daughter, the railroad company reorganized and renamed itself. On October 16, 1889, articles of incorporation were filed for the Tacoma Puyallup Railroad Company.[14] Capital stock was to be $100,000, and 1,000 shares valued at $100 each were issued. Tacoma was listed as the principal place of business and a new set of officers was announced: Randolph F. Radebaugh, President; Frank O. Meeker, Vice-President and Treasurer; and George W. McAllister, Secretary. A board of directors was also created, and Ezra made sure the family was represented there as well. A seat was given to Clarence O. Bean, a Tacoma City Engineer who was married to Ezra's niece.

Meeker left for the East Coast in December 1889 confident in Frank's ability to oversee railroad construction in his absence. In Washington, DC, Meeker, having relinquished an official role in the company, still lobbied for last-ditch help from U.S. government officials in securing a right-of-way through reservation land. In this quest he failed.[15] While traveling he received a letter from George McAllister informing him that Mr. Bean had been replaced with a Mr. Woodruff.[16] At the time the change seemed innocent enough. Meeker did not return home until spring of 1890.

By May 5, 1890, seven and one-half miles of track had been laid from the Tacoma depot at Twenty-Sixth Street and Pacific Avenue to Midland, and two miles of track had been laid from Puyallup towards Midland. The intervening stretch had been graded and was ready for the rails that arrived from San Francisco and were being unloaded on the Tacoma docks. Trains were actually running from the Tacoma depot to Midland with cars that were described as "after the style of the standard passenger coach, two rows of upholstered seats with an aisle through the center of the car, and finished in fine style."[17]

Plans were in the works to build an extension of the line to south Ninth Street in Tacoma. This required a bridge several hundred feet in length to be built across the gulch at the south end of C Street, and it was hoped the city would "unite with the company in constructing a bridge of sufficient width to accommodate both wagon and railway traffic."

In mid-June the *Ledger* gave a progress report. Rails enough to finish the line had arrived and there was just one more small bridge to build.[18] By the end of the month the news was encouraging. There were just 2,000 feet of rails to lay on the Tacoma end, and with good weather to allow the grade to settle, ten trains daily could be running within two weeks.[19]

The *Ledger* was a major booster of the project. It reported the same vision as Meeker's—thousands of suburban homes and the produce of the Puyallup Valley coming daily to Tacoma.[20]

The *Ledger* raved about how special trains would, besides supplying Tacoma with daily fresh fruit, allow valley residents to enjoy that city's cultural offerings such as an evening at the theater. It also suggested that valley residents might want to send their children to Tacoma's superior schools via Meeker's railroad. Commuter rates would be made available to the regular traveler. And it was hoped that this line would connect with other lines that were opening up new suburban areas for development, such as Wapato Lake, creating a transportation network covering much of the county. (Frank Meeker moved to Wapato Lake in Tacoma around 1890 and incidentally became a neighbor of Randolph Radebaugh.)

Meeker returned from his long trip east in early May, in plenty of time to witness the completion of his railroad. The *Ledger* reported that on June 29,

> "Frank O. Meeker, with a smile of satisfaction on his face and a good-sized sledge in his hands, dealt the stalwart blows which sent home the last spike on the Tacoma & Puyallup railroad, which connects Tacoma with her charming and rapidly growing suburb. ...The projectors and managers of the road promised to have it in operation on July 1, and they have kept their promise, with some forty-eight hours to spare. Quite a little group of workmen, and others interested in the completion of the road, including Ezra Meeker of Puyallup, saw the spike sink into the solid sleeper. Then they shook each other heartily by the hand, smiled in a satisfied, I-told-you-so sort of a way, and the thing was done.[21]

Meeker's railroad got off to a good start with the *Ledger* reporting that during a Sunday in mid-July, the train was filled to capacity on nine round trips from Tacoma to Puyallup. The seventy-five-cent fare included dinner at the Park Restaurant, across the street from the planned Park Hotel.[22]

Ken Keigley, grandson of Puyallup city engineer Clarence O. Bean, recalled that his mother told him how "she rode the train to Puyallup several times to visit Ezra and Eliza Jane and that the engine was a wood burning steam engine and that they usually made a stop at a wood lot on the right of way to load wood."[23]

THE PARK HOTEL

The Park Hotel was expected to open for occupancy about March 1, 1890. Designed by architects Daniels and Cook, it was to be six stories high. A stock company composed of Tacoma and Puyallup investors financed it. The 1889 Tacoma city directory listed the officers of the Park Hotel Company: President, Randolph F. Radebaugh; Secretary, Charles H. Ross; and Treasurer, Frank O. Meeker. But behind the scenes keeping watch from Washington, DC, was Ezra Meeker.

On April 5, 1890, Fred Meeker wrote his father in Washington, DC, "Work on the Hotel is progressing fine. Cook was up yesterday evening and says it's all O.K."[24] But in fact, construction was far behind schedule. By the planned opening date of March 1, little more had been done than clearing the ground. On May 7, the day after Meeker returned home from the east coast, the major stockholders of the Park Hotel Company met and selected new officers. Meeker was named president. Ex-mayor Alexander Campbell, co-owner of a large valley farm with Meeker, was selected as vice-president. Charles Ross and Frank Meeker retained their positions as secretary and treasurer, respectively.

It was clear to Meeker that the railroad would be finished well before the hotel could open. He speeded up construction, pouring roughly a thousand dollars a month of his own money into the building. By early June the framing was complete and by late June a contract was signed with the Sumner Lumber Company to do the outside finishing.

Across the street from the now-rising Park Hotel was a restaurant. The marketing plan for the railroad included a meal in Puyallup with the purchase of a railroad ticket. As the hotel restaurant would not be finished before the railroad was operational, the Park Hotel Company leased the aptly named "Park Restaurant" and quickly painted and redecorated it.

With the revitalized hotel project back on course, Ezra and Eliza Jane Meeker formally signed over to the Park Hotel Company the warranty deed to the land on which the hotel was being built. It was September 26, 1890, and the future looked bright.

THE SWINDLE

Recall that Frank Meeker purchased 350 acres of land called Maplewood from Louise Ackerson in January 1889. Frank put $11,000 down, and took out a mortgage with Mrs. Ackerson for the $44,000 balance. Two weeks later he sold half of those acres to Randolph Radebaugh, ignoring the fact that there was a $44,000 lien on the property. Through a series of complex and no doubt illegal financial maneuvers the two men soon turned Frank Meeker's initial investment of $11,000 into a potential profit for themselves of well over a quarter of a million dollars. In their wake they bilked Mrs. Ackerson, the stockholders who financed the building of the railroad, the Mason Mortgage Loan Company, and did serious financial and emotional damage to Ezra and Eliza Jane Meeker. The swindle was complex and aided, in part, by Ezra's complete trust in Frank. It was done quietly and smoothly, and it took some time before Ezra realized what his nephew was doing.

Five days after Meeker departed for New York in December 1889, Frank and Randolph Radebaugh sold their combined Maplewood acres to the Tacoma & Puyallup Railroad Company that, as officers, they controlled. The selling price was $246,200. Land Frank had purchased in January for $55,000 was now sold in December (at least on paper) for a quarter of a million dollars. The fledging railroad obviously had no assets as yet to pay this enormous sum. Mrs. Ackerson still held a lien on the property until her mortgage was paid. The investors who had committed $100,000 to construction of a railroad were now obligated to pay Frank Meeker and Randolph Radebaugh much, much more.

When Meeker returned from his long trip east in May 1890, many projects demanded his attention. His new home (the Meeker mansion) was nearing completion, as was the railroad line. The Park Hotel needed serious attention. Meeker's pattern had always been to initiate and fund projects, then turn them over to others to manage. In the case of the railroad, that proved to be a serious error.

On August 13, Radebaugh mortgaged all the properties of the Tacoma & Puyallup Railroad Company for $100,000 with the Mason Mortgage Loan Company as trustee. The signers of this mortgage were Randolph F. Radebaugh, President, and George Watson McAllister, Secretary. (Although still treasurer, Frank O. Meeker's name does not appear on this document.) The bank apparently did not run title searches on the Maplewood property to verify the deeds of ownership involved. Was the $100,000 used for legitimate railroad expenses or did it line someone's pocket?

The final phase of their grand plan called for subdividing the Maplewood property and selling it off as individual building lots. This began in May 1890 with a series of small advertisements, followed in June with a full-page advertisement that ran multiple times in the *Tacoma Ledger*. The advertisement was flamboyant in the extreme, and it lied. Frank and Radebaugh falsely advertised themselves as sellers of land they no longer owned. They had already sold it, secretly, to the railroad.[25]

In October the Tacoma & Puyallup Railroad Company platted 136.32 acres of the remaining property that was known thereafter as the Third Maplewood Addition. Again Frank kept his name off the document. With this plat it became public knowledge that the lots were being sold by the railroad, not by Frank and Radebaugh as individuals. It was not public knowledge that Frank and Radebaugh had mortgaged the Maplewood property twice, once with Mrs. Ackerson and again with the Mason Mortgage Loan Company. More to the point, it is obvious Ezra did not know of the second mortgage because he stepped into a legal quagmire. On December 10 he assumed the Ackerson mortgage, paid it off, and gave the railroad $24,411.29 in return for title to the Third Maplewood Addition. Meeker then exacted a pound of flesh for his bailout. For each and every lot the TPRR sold in the rest of Maplewood, he was to receive a payment between $175 and $250, or around half the sale price. No doubt Meeker saw his action as extracting his widowed friend, Mrs. Ackerson, from a potential mess, while at the same time making a point with his nephew that there was a financial cost for not being above board in business matters. But with an undisclosed second mortgage complicating ownership, Meeker, in fact, did not get clear title to anything. Meeker's mistake was in not realizing how deeply his purchasing the Third Maplewood Addition would entangle him in his nephew's shenanigans.

Frank's fraudulent business dealings with Radebaugh had cost Meeker nearly $70,000 to this point ($44,000 to Mrs. Ackerson and $24,411 to the TPRR), not including his original investment in the railroad company stock. They would cost much more by the time the dust cleared. Ezra's reputation was damaged as well, tarnished by association. The lawsuits and court actions came fast. Meeker found himself embroiled in cases that dragged on until 1899. The railroad (and/or Frank and Radebaugh) had sold many lots before Meeker stepped in, and the purchasers were rightly upset to learn they had no clear title to their land. The first lawsuit was *A. C. Utterback, et. al, against Ezra Meeker*. Fifty families living in the Maplewood Third Addition sued in an attempt to clear up their titles. The court ruled that Meeker could not give a satisfactory account as to the tangle between himself, the Tacoma & Puyallup Railroad Company and Mrs. Ackerson's mortgage, involving the land he had purchased. It ordered him to

grant clear title to the plaintiffs.[26] More suits followed. Eventually the
Mason Mortgage Company joined the parade and they cast their net
wide, suing Radebaugh, Frank, Ezra, and several others.[27] The financial
drain was enormous and Meeker's bailout proved not nearly enough
to save the railroad. On February 27, 1892, the Tacoma & Puyallup
Railroad went into receivership, just twenty months after it opened
for business.

On November 15 the residents of Fern Hill, who had purchased
lots and built houses along the railroad in what was then a very rural
area, held a mass meeting to complain about the lack of promised service and the constant breakdown of the locomotives. On November
20 a committee of Fern Hill residents appeared before Judge Frank
Allyn in Pierce County Superior Court asking for judicial relief as the
court was now in charge of the railroad.[28] Instead of relief the court
assigned Otis Sprague of Tacoma as receiver with instructions to sell
the railroad, its property and assets, including all of the Third Maplewood Addition, at auction for the benefit of the creditors of the railroad company.[29] Frank Meeker actually signed this court document.
One can only imagine Meeker's reaction and the feelings engendered
toward the nephew he had raised as a son.

On January 9, 1894, the *Tacoma Daily News* announced the sale in
a front-page story. The Tacoma & Puyallup Railroad was sold to W. N.
Coler & Company of Chicago for $85,000. The Maplewood property
was sold to the same company for $15,000. Apparently Coler & Com-
pany at first attempted to keep the railroad operating, as it was reported
in October that the railroad was building cars to haul hops to Tacoma
for shipment east on the Great Northern Railroad.[30] The Tacoma Puyallup Railroad appears in the 1893–1894 Tacoma City Directory with
"Otis Sprague Receiver, Ninth and Railroad to Puyallup."[31] By 1895
and 1896 the railroad had disappeared from city directories.

Legal proceedings dragged on for a number of years in efforts to
clear up titles for the unsuspecting buyers who had purchased Maplewood lots in good faith. Finally on March 1, 1898, the banks foreclosed
on any property in Maplewood still owned by Frank O. and Ettella W.
Meeker; the Tacoma & Puyallup Railroad Company; Otis Sprague, as
assignee of the Tacoma & Puyallup Railroad Company; Ezra M. and
Eliza J. Meeker; and Roderick and Olive McDonald.[32] It was a clean

sweep. On October 13, 1899, at a sheriff's auction, the London and San Francisco Bank purchased the Maplewood property for $12,500. Meeker's investment in the Park Hotel was also lost as collateral damage in all this. It was never completed and was eventually torn down for scrap.

Mr. Radebaugh lived out his days in Tacoma and seems to have suffered no ill consequences from his role in this affair beyond losing both the Puyallup railroad and his Point Defiance railroad as well. In 1907 he founded the *Tacoma News Tribune*. By 1922 he was retired.[33] Frank continued to practice law until he found another even more dramatic way of aggravating and aggrieving his uncle.

LOUISA BANNSE DEWITT

Within a few years of his return from Cornell University, Frank began a long-term involvement with Louisa Bannse DeWitt, an affair that eventually burst onto the front pages of newspapers from Seattle to San Francisco and led to a final estrangement between uncle and nephew.

Louisa Bannse was the eldest daughter of Margaret Bergman and Herman Bannse.[34] She was born in either 1861 or 1863 depending upon which record one accepts.[35] She grew up in Bucoda, Washington, married young, and was widowed at age twenty. Her husband Frank DeWitt was shot and killed in Tacoma, Washington, on September 29, 1881, as a result of a political argument about President Garfield.[36] Louisa gave birth to Frances Louisa DeWitt ten months and a week after her husband's death. One year after the birth Frank O. Meeker and Ettella W. Meeker adopted Frances Louisa DeWitt and legally changed her name to Grace Meeker. How Frank became acquainted with Louisa is not known. Perhaps they met on one of Frank's visits to his Bucoda relatives (Eliza Jane Meeker's family lived there), or perhaps they met on the streets of Tacoma where Louisa's husband worked as an agent for the Wheeler & Wilson Company, near where Frank had his law office.

Louisa was very young, widowed, financially destitute, and facing social scandal with the birth of a child ten months after her husband's death. In the adoption proceedings, the court noted that Louisa had given the care of her child over to Frank and Ettella some months earlier.[37]

Was Frank Meeker the biological father of this infant girl? The circumstantial evidence is strong. The probate court judge who handled the adoption seemed to have his doubts that Ettella was entering into this arrangement willingly. He brought her into his chambers and questioned her privately. The judge then entered into the court record a statement that Ettella "acknowledged to me that she signed the same freely and voluntarily and with [no] fear of or coercion by anyone."[38] The fact that Frank apparently supported Louisa financially for years after the adoption also suggests his paternity. For the next decade, Frank's dalliances remained hidden from public view. Then, in 1892, he was caught "under compromising circumstances with Anna Knox, Ezra Meeker's bookkeeper." Anna Knox was discharged from her position and went to Portland, but this was not the end of her association with the Meeker family.[39]

The Knox family came over the Oregon Trail in 1852, settled on Sauvie Island, just north of Portland, Oregon, and eventually took a donation land claim at today's Ridgefield, Washington. The couple had four daughters, all of whom would play a role in Puyallup's history: Sarepta born 1851, Emma 1859, Letty 1864, and Anna 1868.[40]

Emma, a Portland school teacher, was the first to move to Puyallup. She came as a bride in August 1883 after marrying Charles Ross, a long-time friend and business associate of Meeker. Letty came next, after marrying William M. Seeman in October 1884. William became the Puyallup City Clerk and served in that office through Meeker's terms as Puyallup's mayor in the early 1890s. Sarepta, the oldest sister, followed in 1889 with her husband, John B. McIntosh, who helped build the Meeker mansion and who traveled with Fred and Marion Meeker to Cook Inlet, Alaska, in 1896 and to the silver mines of British Columbia with Ezra in 1897.

Anna, the youngest daughter, taught art in a Portland high school.[41] Anna most likely first saw Puyallup in 1885 when she came north to visit her sisters.[42] She came back four years later and made preparations to stay.[43] In 1890 she made the move permanent. "Miss Anna Knox has returned from Portland and will hereafter, with her mother, reside in Puyallup."[44]

Anna probably replaced Roderick McDonald as Ezra Meeker's book-keeper. She settled in Puyallup just three months before Roderick married Ezra's youngest daughter, gave up his former position as bookkeeper, and became a partner in Ezra's business affairs. Unmarried Anna needed a job. Her sisters and their husbands, all Meeker friends and associates, no doubt supplied good references. Anna was twenty-four years old in 1892 and very attractive. Not too long after she went to work for Ezra, she and Frank were discovered together, which led to Anna being fired and sent away.

Frank was at the same time continuing his affair with Louisa M. DeWitt, whom a Tacoma newspaper

Anna Knox. *Courtesy Puyallup Historical Society at the Meeker Mansion*

described as "a rather comely widow woman of medium height, with a well-rounded form...and beautiful brown eyes that look through a pair of spectacles."[45] Frank was now juggling at least three women at the same time. Louisa, however, again became pregnant. She gave birth at St. Luke's Hospital in San Francisco, and Frank was there when his son Paul DeWitt was born on October 23, 1893.

In November 1894 Louisa, the new baby, and, strangely enough, her now thirteen-year-old daughter Grace—or Frances as she appears in some records—who had been raised until then by Frank and Ettella, moved into an apartment in Tacoma. When and how Grace came to be living once again with her mother is unknown. The *Tacoma Daily News* breathlessly described the stunning events of the evening of December 13, 1894.

> [Frank] Meeker had visited Mrs. De Witt at her residence at 2116 E. street, and according to his story he had called for the purpose of securing a letter, which the woman had in her possession and which he says belonged to him, and related to some business affairs. They

quarreled and he left the house. The woman ran after him and drew a revolver. He attempted to take it away from her, and during the scuffle was shot in the lower part of the abdomen, the bullet taking a slanting course and making a wound about 16 inches long. The woman fainted when the pistol exploded. Meeker picked the smoking revolver up, tried to carry the woman to her home, but fell by weakness caused by his wound. Several men rushed to the scene and picked up the prostrate form of Mrs. DeWitt and carried her into her house. Meeker called to an expressman, climbed into the wagon and asked to be driven to the office of Drs. Misner & Munson in the Tacoma National Bank building. There his wound was dressed and he was removed to the Fife hotel, where apartments were secured for him. At his request a messenger was sent to Wapato Lake for his wife…The woman was arrested by Detective Evans and taken to the city jail. Mrs. DeWitt was permitted to take her two children with her, when arrested, but as there are no accommodations at the jail, she was persuaded to permit her 13-year-old daughter to be given to the care of Mrs. Metcalf, who resides at the corner of Twelfth and A streets, close to the jail. The other child is about eleven months old and it is said that Meeker is the father of it.[46]

The story continued with an interview with Louisa, who stated that the child was Frank's and that she knew he was married; and Frank's conversation with the Chief of Police about whether he wished to see Louisa prosecuted. "I am physically and mentally unable at present to decide what I shall do," said Frank.

Louisa DeWitt was released on a $500 bond at her own recognizance as she was unlikely to leave the city with a baby in tow.[47]

While at home recovering from his wounds Frank wrote to Ezra.

When I was in bed Fred [Meeker] told me you would come to see me. My inconsiderateness in getting well perhaps checked your impulse to come and see me or perhaps it was more on Ettella's account than mine that you had in mind to come. In so far as your unfriendliness to me is grounded on my ill treatment of Ettella in my reckless conduct I fully acknowledge its justice, but as to the Maplewood misfortune you have judged me too harshly. I do not wish to perpetuate animosities. I came to see you two weeks ago to say as much, but you were not at home.[48]

There is no further correspondence between the two men in the Meeker papers. The breach seems to have been permanent.

On January 3, the *Tacoma Daily News* confirmed that Frank still had no interest in prosecuting Louisa. "It is possible, though not considered probable, that Mrs. L. DeWitt may be prosecuted for shooting a few ounces of lead in the body of Frank O. Meeker on the evening of December 13 last...It is understood that he [Meeker] is still not desirous of prosecuting the woman. Mrs. DeWitt is said to be still in the city."[49]

Sometime later, apparently uncharged, Louisa DeWitt moved back to Bucoda with her daughter Frances (Grace Meeker) and her son Paul, where they sought shelter with Louisa's parents. According to the 1900 Census the three DeWitts were living in Bucoda in the home of Louisa's mother, Margaret Bannse.

Grace married nine years after her mother shot Frank Meeker, raised her young brother, and sent him to college. Paul grew up to become a naval officer and helped found the naval aviation corps. He later became a contractor and inventor in San Diego. After her mother's death in 1902 Louisa wandered from city to city, usually finding work as a domestic. She died in 1939 in San Francisco.

EXILE

Frank disappeared from the Tacoma city directories after 1896. His last mention in a Tacoma newspaper came on November 25, 1896, in an article in the *Tacoma Daily News* that cited a report he gave to a local judge as the receiver of an estate. After that, he drifted from state to state and occupation to occupation, seemingly uprooted by the scandals that cut him off from part of his family and the life he should have led. Frank, Ettella, their sons Oliver and Felix, and Frank's mother Amanda, next appeared in Colorado, living in both Greeley and Fort Morgan. Ettella died on March 22, 1905, at age forty-two in St. Anthony's hospital in Denver after a long illness and was buried in Fort Morgan.[50]

Less than three years after Ettella's death, and sixteen years after Anna Knox left Puyallup, Frank and Anna were married on November 27, 1907, in Union, Oregon, a small town located in the northeast corner of the state. How Ezra found out about the marriage and his reaction to the news is interesting. He was in Indiana with his ox team and covered wagon on the first Old Oregon Trail Monument Expedition when he received the news from his daughter, Carrie Meeker Osborne, on January 5, 1908.

Ezra replied on January 5, 1908. "I did not open my mail this morning until I got on the train and when I came to that short paragraph in your letter 'Frank Meeker lately married Anne Knox' I impulsively said in [an] audible voice, 'My God,' and I expect the people who heard me may think I was about half crazy. Like you however, I have no comment to make."[51]

The newlyweds settled near Grants Pass in the southwestern corner of Oregon. While Ezra severed ties with Frank, his daughter Carrie did not. She carried on a correspondence with the cousin she knew as a brother, and at times attempted to work out a reconciliation between the two men.[52] Through her we learn that Anna gave birth to her only child, Ruth Knox Meeker, four years after her marriage and that the child lived barely a month. Carrie also wrote about her Aunt Amanda fracturing her hip and of her death on New Year's Day 1917.[53] The following year Frank and Anna were living in Los Angeles where Frank operated an auto repair garage. Anna Knox Meeker, age fifty-eight, died on September 22, 1926. Francis Oliver Meeker died March 25, 1946, six weeks before his ninety-first birthday, in Los Angeles, California.

CHAPTER 20

Hop Lice

INVASION

Meeker's office, on Meridian Street in today's downtown Puyallup, was the heart of the valley's hop business. It was about to become the epicenter of a catastrophe. Charles Hood, a longtime friend of the Meekers, described the building as he remembered it.

> It was then the busiest place imaginable. At the left front was the office of Mr. Meeker. Following through a passageway at the right side, one came into a big skylighted room with large flat tables in the center and labeled filing cases around the four walls. In these files were placed two samples of hops from every ranch and of every variety grown in the valley. Buyers from England and other countries gathered to inspect the samples and sign contracts. Large companies maintained resident agents, while scores came and went during marketing season. Two samples were needed because some buyers would take one back to their companies for inspection. Seven or eight stenographers were needed to take care of the land-office business at the season's height.[1]

E. Meeker & Company's June 24, 1890, *Hop Circular* was full of optimism. "Unless all the usual signs fail we will grow as large a crop as that in 1888, and our neighbors in Oregon will turn out twenty thousand bales or more, so that with no unforeseen event the two states will grow fully seventy thousand bales of hops the present year."[2]

One evening, near the end of the month, Meeker stepped out of his office and looked over his Puyallup hop fields. He noticed that the foliage seemed "off color...not natural."[3] He walked the quarter mile to his fields and discovered to his horror that his hop plants were alive with thousands and thousands of pale green aphids—hop lice. The "unforeseen event" had arrived.

The vermin had tormented English hop growers for over fifty years and had also been a regular visitor to the New York hop yards. The West Coast hop industry had been spared the scourge and the cost of fighting the lice since its inception. This advantage was about to end. It is likely that *Phorodon humuli* made their way west on the very railroad cars that Ezra had sent east bedecked with banners advertising E. Meeker & Company. Meeker actually found hop lice hiding in empty railroad cars in a train he was traveling on in Montana in 1893, confirming their path west.

In the winter of 1889 the newly arrived lice settled on their winter hosts, a variety of plants and bushes such as damson, blackthorn, bird cherry, and plum. Here they thrived and multiplied. With the arrival of spring 1890 the aphids grew wings and in late June migrated to the Washington and Oregon hop yards. They multiplied on the hop plants going through seven generations, each with thirty to eighty offspring. Meeker's description was quite accurate. "The fly deposits the 1st generation of lice 'alive and kicking,' no bigger than the point of a pin, but these soon grow if left alone, and multiply very rapidly and are then much more difficult to destroy."

Meeker said, "It transpired that the attack of lice was simultaneous in Oregon, Washington and British Columbia, extending over a distance coastwise of more than 500 miles, and even inland up the Skagit River, where there was an isolated yard. It came like a clap of thunder out of a clear sky, so unexpected was it."[4]

The first generation developed in fourteen to eighteen days. The aphids gathered on the young leaves and ate their way to the flowers and cones at the top of the vines. They left behind a shiny sticky layer on the upper side of the leaves, which was referred to as sooty mould. In the process the hop plant and berry were much damaged. By the second half of September the females appeared and mated. In October they laid their eggs in protected areas between the buds and branches of the hop plant. With the coming of winter this final hatch grew wings and migrated back to the nearby woods and their winter hosts waiting for spring to repeat the cycle again.

Meeker wrote, "I sent my second son, Fred Meeker, to London to study the question and to get their methods of fighting the pest, and to import some spraying machinery."[5] This was Fred's second trip to

England, as the local papers placed him in there from late 1888 to early 1889.[6]

Fred gave his father power of attorney on November 14, 1890, witnessed by Roderick McDonald and John Meeker, and departed for New York and London shortly after. By November 27 he and his wife Clara were in New York where Fred conducted some hop business.[7]

Fred and Clara returned to Puyallup in mid-May 1891 with the formula for the insecticide the English were using to fight hop lice and an English spraying machine.[8] The machine was turned over to the Puyallup Hardware Company's machinists, who quickly turned out an improved version called the Puyallup Roller Hop Sprayer. Ezra immediately put into practice what Fred had learned about the English methods of fighting the hop lice.

THE DAMAGE

The 1890 crop came in at 42,746 bales, 84 percent of what was expected. *E. Meeker & Co.'s Hop Circular* of November 14, 1890, stated, "The crop year of 1890 has been one of surprises as well as of disappointment. Promising at first to be the heaviest on record, the yield was finally cut down to the usual average by the prolonged drouth and attack of vermin combined."[9]

The appearance of the hop lice also put an end to a traditional business practice—contracting at a set price for future delivery. Meeker was scathing in his condemnation of the practice.

> The disastrous results to both growers and dealers who scrupulously fulfilled all contracts, coupled with the threatened loss of a portion of the crop by vermin thus rendering the quality uncertain for future crops, has put a stop to the practice of contracting for future deliveries, and it is to be hoped never to be revived. Had the growers not contracted any of the crop of 1890 until in the bale, and then met the market, there would have been more than a million dollars more money in circulation in the two states of Washington and Oregon than now, and a "world" of litigation avoided that now crowds our court dockets. Hereafter this firm will make no contracts for hops until the same have matured and are ready for delivery.[10]

The 1891 hop season also began with high hopes. The *Tacoma Daily News* reported, "E. M. Pine, of Puyallup, is constructing 40 hop presses in anticipation of a busy season at picking time."[11]

In his June 1, 1891, circular Meeker listed the cost of producing a pound of hops in the various growing regions around the world— New York, fifteen cents; England, eighteen cents; and Washington, nine cents. Over the years Meeker and other Puyallup Valley growers had established a very lucrative trade in London. The English merchants could not get enough of Washington's "summer hops." They were of excellent quality and could be stored for a year without losing any of their flavor-producing qualities. The low cost of labor (Indian and Chinese) more than offset the cost of shipping and export duties. An average price of twenty-five cents a pound over the years, which at times spiked much higher, almost guaranteed healthy profits. Meeker expected a harvest for his Kent, Washington, fields (owned under the name "Puyallup Hop Company") to produce 115 tons of hops in 1891. E. Meeker & Co.'s Puyallup farms were expected to yield twice this amount. Almost as an aside Meeker mentioned in the circular that there were no vermin present in the state. On June 16 his agents told the *Tacoma News* that stories being sent abroad saying Meeker's hop fields were infested with lice were false and "there is no lice at the present time."[12] By the end of the month those statements proved false. A second season of dealing with hop lice was at hand.

Many of the growers simply panicked and harvested their crops before they were ripe, resulting in much financial loss. Everyone who could sprayed, and everyone had a different idea as to how it should be done.[13] Some growers adopted a coal oil emulsion spray recommended by USDA entomologist Charles Valentine Riley,[14] instead of using the quassia wash—made from a South American tree with insecticidal properties—favored by English growers.[15] Some like A. J. Query of Alderton invented their own sprays. Meeker, in his February 6, 1892, *Monthly Hop Circular* urged the adoption of the English method. Ingredients for the spray, quassia chips and whale oil soap, were purchased in huge quantities and shipped around Cape Horn. Plans were made to manufacture the quassia chips in Puyallup so as to reduce the cost, and some three hundred tons of quassia tree and bark were ordered. Meeker reported that he sprayed sixty-six acres eight times that year at a cost of $1,980. At first he used a cumbersome and inefficient English machine to do the work. It sent out wasteful solid streams of spray. The Puyallup Hardware Company produced a more efficient model that covered the plants with a fine mist. Five of these Puyallup spray rollers were put to use in Meeker's yards, with two men per roller, spraying five acres a day. Meeker credited the spraying with saving his crop. The sixty-six acres he described spraying in the circular matches exactly the size of his Farm A in Kent, Washington. Certainly Meeker would have made an effort to spray the remainder of his fields.

The 1893 edition of Meeker's *Hop Annual and Hand Book* had a large section dedicated to spraying for hop lice along with an advertisement for the "Puyallup Roller Hop Sprayer," available from the Puyallup Hardware Company.[16] The purchase price was two hundred dollars. The reader was advised to order sprayers and supplies well ahead of time, to use quassia shavings rather than chips, and that the quassia should be soaked in cold water rather than boiled, as was common practice.

One problem that soon became apparent was the height of the vines. They were growing on training poles over sixteen feet tall and all had a knot of flowers at the top. The sprayers could not reach that high,

Meeker's roller hop sprayer. *Author's collection*

Ezra Meeker on right with a hop sprayer, ca. 1891. *Courtesy of the Puyallup Historical Society at the Meeker Mansion*

giving the lice a safe haven in which to multiply. The obvious solution was to shorten the height of the poles. Then twine was tied around the top of these shortened vines cutting off the growth of the foliage at the top of the plant, eliminating the hiding place. Meeker experimented with spraying the shorter vines on a few of his acres and deemed it a success. He hoped that he could cut the number of sprayings needed in half and get the cost per acre down from the thirty dollars it cost him in 1891 to twenty dollars for the 1892 season. All that remained was to cut 100,000 poles and replant them for the 1892 season. It is doubtful that he factored the cost of this into his equation.

The damage the lice inflicted on the yield in 1891 was considerable, with significant declines from the previous year in the number of bales shipped (see chart below). Only Chehalis and Yakima saw an increase in hop production in 1891, and this was due entirely to a large increase in acreage planted at the start of the year. Everyone else suffered losses, and Meeker estimated the total loss for the state at over a million dollars. For public consumption he put on a happy face. He told the *Seattle Post-Intelligencer*, "[T]he crop is uninjured by lice and it is very large. We have demonstrated within the last three weeks that beyond question we can save the hop crop from pests that at one time threatened it, by practicing the usual diligence of the ordinary careful farmer."[17] The *Ledger* picked up on the theme reporting, "Picking is now underway in Oregon, and reports show that while there has been some damage from the pests, they agree it has been overestimated. Some yards in the western part of Polk County are much disfigured by mould and others by lice, but the general prospect for the state is more favorable."[18]

PARTIAL LIST OF BALES OF HOPS SHIPPED ON THE NORTHERN PACIFIC RAILROAD

	Sept.—Dec. 31, 1890[19]	Sept.—Dec. 1891[20]
Puyallup	8,618	5,999
Kent	3,153	2,524
Orilla	1,487	1,069
O'Brien	1,279	1,122
Orting	2,633	1,819
Buckley	1,325	1,175
Slaughter (Auburn)	4,761	4,041
Sumner	4,745	2,378
Snoqualmie	8,382	2,474
Chehalis	466	862
Alderton	1,490	1,251
N Yakima	1,872	2,710
Total for		
Washington	42,746	34,026
Oregon	25,000	14,420

Meeker stated that for the years 1886 to 1890, on a sixty-one acre farm (Farm A in Kent), he earned a net profit of $162.02 per acre, per year.[21] Meeker had five hundred acres in hops in 1891. Factoring in a 20 percent lice damage cost from his pre-lice yearly average gives Meeker a post-lice profit of around $130 per acre. Simple math tells us that his net profit from his five hundred acres of hops in 1892 was around $65,000 or, using an online inflation calculator, about $1,600,000 in today's dollars. He did not supply the numbers for the brokerage part of his business where his loses would have been substantial.

Meeker apparently brought the damage from the hop lice under control relatively quickly, at least in his own fields. He argued that by 1893 the hop growers had learned how to combat the lice and were doing so effectively. "The lice are not increasing in King county nor will they cut any figure in the quality of the crop in this locality and the reports from other localities show that the lice are not thriving. This may be attributed to an understanding of how to mix and apply the most improved spraying emulsions, which the growers have learned through the experience of the past three years and is, without doubt, also greatly due to the peculiar climatic condition of the season."[22]

The April 1893 edition of his *Monthly Hop Circular* described a declining price, down from a high of twenty-two cents per pound for the 1892 harvest to seventeen cents for advanced purchases on the 1893 crop. Meeker stated that the hop lice invasion had damaged the last three crops and estimated that Washington growers had lost half a million dollars on the 1892 crop due to improper spraying. It was advised that spraying early in the season was highly effective in controlling the hop lice. However, according to the circular, the decline in prices was caused by several factors that were outside the grower's control. Among them were: adverse legislation in Germany and England that caused many brewers to hesitate in making their usual advance purchases; a strike among the cotton workers in England that reduced demand for beer; and the circular suggested, that a cholera scare in the United States could have been a factor. Despite the gloomy news the circular estimated hop acreage would grow by 15 percent statewide in 1893.

BROKERING

Despite these large profits, Meeker's hop empire was in serious jeopardy as the year 1891 closed. His hop business stood on a two-part foundation—hops grown in his fields and hops purchased from other growers around the Northwest. Over the years Meeker had expanded the small hop brokerage business he started in 1881 with his son-in-law, Eben Osborne, under the title of Meeker, Osborne & Co. to a large multi-state operation. By the turn of the decade his sons, nephews, in-laws, and agents purchased hops throughout Oregon and

Washington on behalf of E. Meeker & Company. Each purchase was shipped to Puyallup where it was carefully logged into a ledger, and then put on trains for shipment, primarily to New York and to London.[23] Numerous notices appeared in the local press about Meeker's brokerage business in a single month in 1891. For example: "E. Meeker and Co. shipped yesterday 1100 bales of hops in a trainload to London, England. Over 3400 bales have left Baltimore in two ships also for London." (As seventy bales made up a train car, this train would have carried sixteen cars of hops.)[24] The Olympia *Washington Standard* said, "Two shiploads, of 3,417 bales, have just departed from Baltimore, Md., for London. This company estimates that they will ship this year somewhere near 10,000 bales."[25]

Those who harvested early or failed to spray produced an inferior hop, which Meeker found difficult to market. At the close of the season he admonished his fellow growers for their panic and offered much advice on how to grow and prepare a quality crop. The last circular of the year stated that 1892 was expected to be a very good year for the hop business.

By 1893 Meeker was not only purchasing hops, he was financing the growers from whom he made his purchases. He had assumed the role that wealthy men such as John Gale and Charles Prindle had played in the 1870s.[26] Meeker was now supplying the capital needed by the Northwest growers to harvest their crop. The amount of money loaned reached the $100,000 mark by 1896. This would be around $2.5 million in today's currency. It was more money than Meeker could manage by himself. Consequently he made pilgrimages to New York and other large eastern cities where he borrowed the money, using the future crop as collateral. The *Puyallup Citizen* reported in August 1893 that Meeker was in New York City attempting to raise funds to hire hop-pickers for the September harvest.[27] Later that month, the *Chicago Tribune* wrote, "Ezra Meeker, representing the growers, secured an advance of $15,000 [around $380,000 in today's currency] from the Milwaukee brewers and renewed negotiations with Lindsey, Bird & Co. of London." Meeker was risking much of his fortune on a successful hop-picking season, and with the appearance of the hop lice he had little control over the quality of the product put out by the individual growers. It was a recipe for trouble.

CHAPTER 21

Travels with Ezra

Finding Faith

As the New Year dawned, the Meeker family was unaware that 1893 was to be the apex of their personal prosperity. The "castles in the air" that Meeker had built over nearly thirty years were soon to come crashing down. But that was still in the future. The year was to be a good one, primarily filled with travel and entertainment, with a little work mixed in for good measure.

Meeker's first venture away from home came at the end of January when he attended a Unitarian Church conference in Portland, Oregon. Over the years Meeker contributed to the building fund of several local churches, including Methodist and Presbyterian, but he did not for a long while identify himself with a particular religion. It wasn't until Meeker discovered Unitarianism that he found a religious philosophy that he felt comfortable with. A conference reporter recounted a "heart-stirring" moment at the Portland gathering when Meeker had talked about his faith. "He had been thirty years a Unitarian without knowing that there was a fellowship such as the Unitarian denomination represents. There were tears in his voice, if not in his eyes, as he spoke of his past isolation and his present joy in fraternal fellowship. His words found quick and stirring response in the deeper feelings of many present."[1]

Meeker's brother John also attended the conference and delivered an address titled "Our Gospel and Mission."[2] Meeker attended a second conference in May 1895 in San Francisco where he was elected to the Board of Directors of the Pacific Unitarian Conference.[3]

Eliza Jane, whose religious faith initially leaned toward the Methodists, became a life-long member of the Unitarian church along with her husband.[4] Their daughters, however, were Presbyterians, as was a son-in-law who served actively as an elder and in other capacities in that church for over sixty years. One grandson became a Presbyterian minister and a granddaughter married a Presbyterian minister. With a family full of very active Presbyterians, Meeker was well aware that many of his relatives viewed his religious choice with skepticism or worse.[5] But he did note that "times change." In 1910 while in Baker City, Oregon, on his second Old Oregon Trail Monument Expedition, he attended a Presbyterian service. At the close of the sermon the minister recognized Meeker in the audience, introduced him to the congregation of some three hundred, and invited him to speak at the conclusion of the evening service. Meeker wrote, "A curious incident occurred just as the choir were closing, the minister asked me if I was a church member; I told him I was a Unitarian and in his introductory remarks mentioned my being a Unitarian. This is some different than what it would have been years ago, a Unitarian occupying a Presbyterian sermon—the world does move."[6]

Taking Care of Business

Stories of mining in the Cascade Mountains of eastern Snohomish County had appeared frequently in various Washington newspapers during the previous two years, so in March 1893, Meeker spent a week visiting the Monte Cristo mines.[7] Within three short years, after his hop empire collapsed, he would trade farming for mining as his new avocation. In the meantime, hops remained his main concern.

In early July Meeker left Puyallup bound for New York once again. At a stop in Butte, Montana, he got out of the train at the depot, picked some sweet fennel,[8] and discovered it was hosting a big hop louse. He wrote, "I do hope Fred will not risk too much in not spraying promptly for I consider now is the nick of time to act promptly."[9] As the journey continued he noted that nine of the seventeen people in the car knew him, and stated, "I find that it would be hard to get out of the country without detection, so I must resolve to walk straight as it appears that I am notorious even if not noted. I do often wish that I could be known by the public by some other distinguishing mark other than 'that hop man.' I would rather be known as a zealous Unitarian."[10]

The main purpose of this trip was to secure funding for picking the 1893 hop crop, and Meeker was less than successful. "It had been Mr. Meeker's desire to raise sufficient money where with to pick the entire Puget Sound crop but after seeking aid from every conceivable source he returns with but credit to do less than he had hoped to accomplish."[11]

On the way home, he stopped at Waterville, New York, to attend the hop-growers convention on Saturday, August 19.[12] Meeker was in Puyallup for the hop harvest and then off again on a five-month trip.[13]

ELIZA JANE TOURS EUROPE

The Chicago World's Fair was one of the 1890s must-do events and a production Eliza Jane Meeker was not about to miss. Her husband, probably still harboring bitter feelings over his dismissal as Washington's Executive Commissioner to the fair, had hop business to conduct and remained in Washington through October wrapping up that season's hop harvest. So Eliza Jane and her daughter, Olive Meeker McDonald, set off on their own in October 1892. Upon their arrival at Chicago four days later they checked into the exclusive Victoria Hotel. Here they met Mrs. Louise Ackerson. The three ladies spent a month enjoying the fair and Chicago. Olive celebrated her 24th birthday in the Windy City while her husband remained in Puyallup.

Ezra Meeker arrived in Chicago on November 6 and visited the exposition grounds with the three ladies.[14] That evening Olive started for home with Mrs. Ackerson. The following afternoon Ezra and Eliza Jane boarded an express train for New York. After more than twenty hours they arrived and settled in at the Grand Union Hotel. It was a brief but busy stay. In the afternoon Meeker met Mr. Robert C. Alexander, editor of the *New York Mail and Express*, to discuss a Puyallup land deal.[15] That evening Ezra and Eliza went to a flower show. Meeker spent much of the next day at the offices of hop brokers Fox & Searles discussing hop business and meeting again with Mr. Alexander. The next day the Meekers left the Grand Union Hotel and moved to the steamer *Luciana* on which they would cross the Atlantic Ocean. In the evening they indulged themselves with a trip to the theater where they saw *Becket*, and then returned to the steamer to sleep.

The *Luciana* sailed for England the following morning in fair weather. However, on the second day the ship encountered rough seas. Ezra reacted as he often did when at sea on a rolling ship. He got sick. Eliza Jane had no such problem. She went to dinner and left her husband in bed. A friend sent Ezra flowers, candy, and magazines. Eliza Jane improvised a vase and decorated the stateroom. The storm increased in intensity over the next two days and Eliza mostly stayed in the stateroom comforting her husband. Three days into the voyage, Meeker was finally able to eat a little and the couple decided to take an evening's entertainment in the ship's music room. Instead of entertainment, they found a mess. Staterooms were flooded and several people had been injured from the violent rolling of ship. As the storm continued, the casualty list grew. One evening a benefit concert for a hospital fund was held in the music hall. People slid off their seats as the ship lurched. Some of the gyrations of the ship were so violent that seats were wrenched from their fastenings. The Meekers were driven back to their cabin where they stayed for the remainder of the voyage, except for meals. On Sunday, November 19, at noon they landed at Liverpool. Meeker immediately cabled home that they had arrived safely. That evening they checked into the Royal Hotel in London.

It was Eliza Jane's turn to head for bed with a bad cold. She entertained herself by reading the newspaper accounts of the storm, which left some four hundred vessels lost or missing. Ezra spent a good deal of time at the Hop Exchange. Each Sunday they attended a different church. They visited St. Paul's Cathedral, and attended a Unitarian Social held at the Essex Hotel. Ezra said that 150 people were present and described the music as "splendid."

On December 21 the Meekers departed London, crossed the English Channel, and spent the Christmas holiday in Paris where they took rooms in the not-so-Parisian-sounding London and New York Hotel. Ezra had apparently forgotten or got over the feelings he evinced about a sinful Paris a decade earlier when he wrote, "I hope I have seen the worst; if not may the good Lord have mercy on the best."[16] Having Eliza Jane at his side surely made for a more pleasurable trip and likely tempered much of his initial negative reaction to the city. Another evening they went to the Grand Opera House to hear *Faust*.

On Christmas Eve day the Meekers took a cab to the Madeleine Church, which they were told was the most magnificent in Paris. Meeker made these observations: "a most magnificent altar & interior; good music, no chairs or seats for communicants, saw sacraments administered to several persons. Such bowing, kneeling, and crossing I never saw before."

Christmas Day found the Meekers back at the Madeleine. They could not obtain seats and stood for half an hour listening to the service that Meeker said was "founded on superstition." Afterward they continued their round of sightseeing, visiting the new church of Montmartre, the cemetery Pére Lachaise, and the Bastille.

It is not known how long the Meekers stayed in Paris, but a January 6, 1894, letter from Alfred Williams of the Atlantic Transport Line inviting them to dinner the following evening suggests that they were expected back in London shortly after the New Year. The Meekers remained in London until late February when they departed on the Atlantic Transport Line freighter *Mohawk*. The ship's manifest shows the Meekers, age 63 and age 61, occupying one of five mid-ship cabins with seven pieces of luggage in tow. Passage, no doubt, courtesy of Alfred Williams. This Atlantic crossing was shared with fifteen returning cattlemen with their stock. The manifest does not tell how many stock animals the ship was carrying or relate what the odor of the vessel must have been like, but on his fourth Atlantic crossing in 1895 Meeker gave a hint.

> Whatever may be said in praise of the ships in this line, and they certainly do deserve praise, one thing is sure and that is that no ship can carry livestock without discomfort to the passengers. Some days the smell from the cattle pens is as one lady put it "perfectly awful." We have about 1000 head of livestock on board and now towards the close of the passage we can almost begin to "feel it" at times and in some places on the ship.[17]

The *Mohawk* arrived in New York City on February 28, 1894. Around March 12 Ezra and Eliza Jane departed for San Francisco where they attended the midwinter fair. They arrived home in Puyallup on Saturday, March 23, after an absence of five months for Ezra and six months for Eliza Jane.

The Queen Victoria Myth

A commonly repeated myth in Meeker circles refers to an event that likely never happened, the presentation of Eliza Jane to Queen Victoria. This story first appeared in the writings of Charles Ross and became a part of the Meeker legend. It was repeated in Eliza Jane's obituary.[18] In 1960 Ezra Blaine Meeker (Marion's son) visited Puyallup and mentioned that in a trunk at his home was the gown in which his grandmother was presented to Queen Victoria. Ezra Blaine donated the gown to the Puyallup Public Library, and it eventually made its way into the possession of the Ezra Meeker Historical Society. The story of Eliza Jane, Queen Victoria, and the gown were enthusiastically incorporated into the established Meeker Mansion tour. However Box 11 of the Meeker Papers offers a different story. There Ken Keigley found a brief history of Mrs. Meeker's Parisian-designed dress, including a notation made by granddaughter Olive Osborne Jones (Carrie's daughter) that her grandmother was never presented to Queen Victoria.[19] Upon discovering this document Keigley contacted the Court of St. James in an unsuccessful search for a record of such an audience.

Olive was very close to her grandparents. Eliza and Ezra lived in the Osborne home in Seattle in 1904–05, and Olive also helped care for her grandmother during her final illness. Although her testimony is not to be taken lightly, there are a number of blank dates in Meeker's 1893-94 diary during which an audience with the queen could have been possible. However, the skeptics among us believe that if a dinner with Mr. Williams earned a notation in the diary, an introduction to Queen Victoria, had it happened, would absolutely be there as well. Realistically, it seems quite unlikely that the visiting wife of an American businessman would be selected for such an honor. Until definitive proof of her presentation can be found, the widely accepted story should be considered apocryphal.[20]

CHAPTER 22

The Siege of Puyallup

The Meekers arrived home from their European tour to find the country and Washington State in economic turmoil. The worst depression in American history to that point stalked the land. Some six hundred banks were shuttered. Seventy-four railroads had declared bankruptcy. And over 15,000 commercial businesses had collapsed. The *Tacoma Daily Ledger* interviewed Meeker a few days later. He apparently was not fully aware of just how bad things were in the United States. "You talk about hard times here, but if you want to see real, genuine hard times go over to Europe where we see farm laborers working for 48 cents and a half gallon of cider a day. England has 1,000,000 paupers and they increased last year 30,000."[1]

Coxey's Army

Over the winter, masses of the unemployed began to organize into groups that petitioned authorities for food and the railroads for transportation to places of potential work. These armies of unemployed moved from location to location en masse. Many citizens found this new phenomenon frightening. In the spring of 1894 battalions of the unemployed joined the call of Jacob Coxey to organize and march on Washington, DC, to force the United States Congress to do something meaningful to help them find work. A branch of that army was about to descend upon Puyallup and show that city what hard times looked like, up close and personal.

On April 8, 1894, some two hundred unemployed men gathered in a Seattle Skid Road hall where they elected Harry Shepard as the "general" to lead their part of the march across the continent to the nation's capital. Shepard urged the Seattle branch of Coxey's army to be orderly and disciplined, and set to making plans to gather food and funds for the journey east.

Tacoma's unemployed met on April 15 in the National Theater, where they elected Jumbo Cantwell, a saloon bouncer and occasional prize fighter, to be their general. The men organized into companies of sixty, marched in the morning, searched for food in the afternoon, and set up a commissary serving two meals daily.

Two railway lines going east from Puget Sound could have taken Coxey's army to Washington, DC, and the halls of Congress: the Great Northern and the Northern Pacific. The Great Northern was in the midst of a strike and workers had blockaded the tracks in several places in Montana and Idaho. In a major display of cynical opportunism, the Great Northern offered a ride to the "Industrials" or "Commonwealers," as these groups of the organized unemployed were called, if they would help clear the tracks on their way east—in effect turning them into strike breakers. The offer was declined. The head of the American Railways Union, William Adams, visited the Commonwealers and received a promise that they would in no way help the Great Northern open the line and break the strike. The Northern Pacific Railroad Company had gone bankrupt, had been placed in the hands of receivers, and was under the control of the federal courts. The last thing the federal government wanted was to expedite the shipment of thousands of unemployed men to Washington, DC.

So the dilemma generals Shepard and Cantwell faced was how to get their armies to the nation's capital. Eventually they settled upon a plan to meet in Puyallup, where they would pressure the Northern Pacific for a train ride east. While the discussion centered on cooperation, there was much talk of stealing a train. This sort of talk, and the fact that on April 21 a group of Commonwealers had commandeered a Northern Pacific train in Montana and were being pursued by federal troops, alarmed the authorities. U.S. Marshal James C. Drake began swearing in deputies at five dollars a day plus room and board. A dozen deputies were sent to guard the Puyallup train yards. Drake wanted no trains stolen in Washington State.

The very real possibility of having a thousand unemployed men descend upon their small city worried the citizens of Puyallup. The prospect for violence was palpable. The Commonwealers wanted a train ride and the Northern Pacific wasn't about to give them one. On April 25 Mayor Charles E. Hallenbeck called a city council meeting "to consider and take such action as is necessary regarding the coming of the 'Commonweal' army to the city." The council gave him the power to appoint special police "for the preservation of public order." It also asked the governor to send state troops if needed. Two responsible men were hired to guard the train depot located about a mile east of downtown at Meeker Junction.

Ezra Meeker also held a meeting of several of Puyallup's prominent citizens with the purpose of developing a plan of action. He proposed that the citizens form a counter organization to protect the city and wrote a letter to the governor outlining his proposal. On April 25 Governor McGraw answered, "The counter organization by the people would be unwise, and might precipitate trouble that we would otherwise escape." The governor also stated his opinion that such "industrial armies" were unlawful assemblies, but organized opposition was unnecessary. The governor was confident that these armies were not disposed to cause serious trouble.[2] The next day Meeker was in Olympia,[3] probably to see the governor.

On April 26 the Seattle Industrials, 650 strong, started their march to Puyallup. That night they camped six miles south at Maples.[4] In the morning they broke camp in a driving rainstorm and followed the train tracks to the Kent Driving Park, arriving at noon wet and muddy with blankets on their backs, canteen and plates at their sides, and knives and forks in their pockets. The *Ledger* said they presented "a novel sight, to say the least."[5] The men made campfires in sheds at the racetrack and in the exhibition building and spent the afternoon drying wet clothes. At 4:30 p.m., they received their dinner rations. In the evening, a Kent bakery baked a thousand loaves of bread for breakfast. The *Ledger* gleefully noted that Kent's mayor hid all the beef in his butcher shop in a back room, and when the Industrials arrived to purchase, the shelves were bare. However, other town residents supplied all the food that the army needed. The *Ledger* also noted that twenty-five deputy marshals armed with Winchester rifles were watching the army and that each passing train was guarded. One company of the Seattleites went out and foraged among the farmhouses and earned a reprimand from their leader. General Shepard ordered the men to cease "bumming" immediately.[6]

The camp at Kent was broken at 6:30 in the morning and the men followed the railroad tracks to Sumner. Waiting for them at Puyallup was the county sheriff.

County commissioners would not allow Sheriff Alexander G. Matthews to hire more deputy sheriffs, so instead, reported the *Daily News*, "He has selected fifty men whom he can trust and upon the first danger of real trouble he will swear them in as a posse comitatus and swear them in to regular duty. He has the power and right to do this without requesting permission from the county commissioners."[7]

A contingent of U.S. Marshals was waiting for the Seattleites at Meeker Junction, expecting them to come down the railroad tracks from the north. They had blocked the route into town from that direction, but the Seattleites took the county road from Sumner and were in town before the marshals became aware of their presence. Meeker's vacant restaurant at the Park Hotel was commandeered and became the kitchen and sleeping quarters for the 650-member-strong Seattle brigade. Contributions of meat and flour came from the town's citizens and helped fill the larder. The contributions were "voluntary" in a sense. Some gave freely. Louis Zimmerman of the Pacific Meat Company offered "just one day's meat for the army—1,000 pounds—on condition that they promise to keep off our premises. They readily accepted the conditions. We gave them the meat."[8]

An immediate confrontation was avoided.

JUMBO CANTWELL

The Tacoma army began their ten-mile trek to Puyallup in an afternoon drizzle, with a parade of some four hundred marchers singing and chanting their way through the streets. Jumbo Cantwell told his men, "We go to Puyallup and we don't walk from there."[9] The *Tacoma News* said by 6 p.m. 384 Industrials from Tacoma and 652 from Seattle were camped in Puyallup. By midnight the numbers had swelled to 695 from Tacoma and 900 from Seattle. After dinner a mass meeting was held in Robinson Hall, which the *Ledger* described as a tame affair.[10]

Just before the evening rally a United States marshal served Jumbo with a restraining order prohibiting interference with Northern Pacific trains. Jumbo looked it over and then put it in his pocket. The town was full of armed police: seventy U.S. marshals, fourteen deputy sheriffs, the town marshal, and three or four of his deputies. The numbers varied by newspaper and date.

Jumbo offered George W. Dickinson, assistant general superintendent of the railroad, one thousand dollars for furnishing his army with twenty cars and transporting them to St. Paul. His men would do any needed train work for free. Dickenson referred the matter to the traffic department, which refused to entertain it.

On Sunday, April 29 Mayor Hallenbeck swore in twenty-five special policemen.

The Industrials called for a mass meeting at the opera house Sunday night. The speakers were to be generals Shepard and Cantwell among others. Some of the men remained in their barracks, worn out from the marching and weather. But the townspeople turned out in large numbers to get a look at the leaders of the movement that had taken over their city.[11]

A hush came over the crowd as Jumbo took to the stage. He was a bit hoarse having spoken fourteen consecutive nights. The *News* said, "He was witty and said many things that were strikingly characteristic and original. He paid his compliments to Ezra Meeker for asking for protection from Governor McGraw. 'That man is paying 75 and 80 cents a day to men for working for him. Isn't he a nice guy?,' shouted Jumbo. 'He needn't be afraid. We won't touch him: we're a little particular what we touch. I'd sooner sleep in the Puyallup River than on his land. I wouldn't eat a piece of chicken stolen from him, and I like chicken too.'"[12]

Jumbo was wound up and the crowd cheered loudly. He ended by proposing to have a minister address the crowd. "I don't suppose some of you fellows have been in a church in twenty years, so it'll do you good to hear a minister. When I left Tacoma some of the good ladies of the W.C.T.U. and Gospel Temperance Union gave me this book," and he exhibited a small Testament. "I told them I'd take it to Washington and back, and I'm going to do it."[13] The entertainment ended with several other speeches, a song, "Remember the Tramp Has to Live," and a three-round boxing contest, after which the hat was passed. The minister had to wait for another time.

STALEMATE

Over the next two days there were meetings and much discussion but no movement on the question of a train ride. The *News* published a story that the management of the Northern Pacific was setting the stage for a strike. A conductor was interviewed and said, "Again, the sympathy of the railroad boys is to a very great extent with the poor devils who are out of employment, and we would like to give them a lift."[14]

Most of the citizens of Puyallup didn't really care how the Industrials left town; they just wanted them to leave. Two committees met with the generals Tuesday morning in Christian Hall.[15] A petition from the mayor and city council was also sent to Governor John McGraw.

> We, the undersigned citizens of Puyallup, beg to inform your Excellency that there are now and have been for more than four days past, congregated in our city about thirteen hundred citizens, mostly from the cities of Tacoma and Seattle, who came here with very little food or means for securing same, and are now short of rations, and if they remain here will soon be thrown upon the charities of this city. Already large quantities of food have been furnished them by our citizens. We are unable to feed and shelter them any longer. In fact we are barely able to properly care for our own citizens. This body of men is peaceable but show no disposition to move on unless transportation is furnished them by the Northern Pacific Railroad. They claim to have tendered the railroad company money for a "box car" transportation, which the road, so they say, has refused. Something must be done at once to relieve us. We most sincerely petition and pray that you come at once to our city to investigate the situation and by virtue of the authority of your position as chief executive of the state, take such steps as shall relieve this community from the charge thus unjustly thrust upon us, and either assist them in taking the journey eastward that they desire or cause them to be returned to the cities from whence they came.[16]

The governor arrived on the scene on May 2 on the 5 p.m. train, where he was met at the depot by John P. Hartman Jr., one of Meeker's attorneys,[17] an officer of the Puyallup National Bank and the head of the committee that requested him to come. The Puyallup Brass Band was in attendance as were most of the leading citizens of the city and three thousand spectators, including Jumbo and Shepard. A procession made their way to the opera house. John Hartman called the assemblage to order and explained the object of the meeting. A.E. Barrett was elected chairman. The governor was introduced to a silent audience; John Hartman and two others spoke but offered no solution to the impasse. The *Ledger* said, "Ezra Meeker realized the gravity of the situation, but he could not say he was in favor of sending these men away from here, over the railroad, and before he would be willing to say what he would favor, he would like to hear from the leaders of those people, an expression of what they wanted. Then any proposition they might make could be considered."[18]

Jumbo then took the stage and delivered his standard stump speech and requested a ride at least to Spokane. Next, someone suggested that a committee be appointed to confer with the Northern Pacific Railroad on the subject. The Governor then addressed the crowd, told them he sympathized with their plight, but informed them that it was pointless to confer with the railroad, that he had already done so, and they were adamant that they had no intention of helping the Commonwealers. McGraw continued, saying that they would not be welcomed in Washington, DC, and they would suffer much needless hardship attempting to get there. He said he would do all he could to find them employment, but he would tolerate no violence. This was greeted with catcalls, booing, and other raucous behavior. Despite the governor's words, a committee was named to confer with the Northern Pacific and the assembly was quickly adjourned. The governor returned to Olympia on the 11 p.m. train.

The morning of May 4 saw the army start to disperse. The 1,300 men each tried to find their own way to Spokane, by either walking or stealing rides on trains. The evening found Jumbo at the hot springs near Auburn and the Commonwealers scattered for miles along the tracks north from Puyallup. A number of the Industrials hopped a freight train that seemed to intentionally slow down as it went by, apparently without objection from the Northern Pacific. As the *News* reported, "The siege of Puyallup is over."[19]

That evening the city council met. Ezra Meeker proposed that the town furnish jobs to the Industrials who remained in Puyallup. The men would work on the town's streets under supervision of appointed foremen. The Meeker proposal passed.

Jumbo and a number of his followers worked their way east on a cross-country odyssey, a story in itself that has been well chronicled by Murray Morgan.[20] Coxey and several of his leaders were arrested for trespassing on the U.S. capitol grounds while Jumbo was still in Montana, taking much steam out of the movement. Nevertheless, he persevered and arrived at the nation's capital where he set up a small camp for the few remaining Puget Sounders who accompanied him. Joining with eight other generals, he helped draft a petition to Congress in support of the unemployed and proposed a work relief bill. A Kansas senator presented the petition to the Congress and introduced the work bill in the Senate, but it died in committee.

CHAPTER 23

Troubled Times

Despite Meeker's perennial optimism, he could see trouble ahead. In 1892 he and his son Marion spent a good deal of time looking over the Yakima hop yards, where the lice seemed less severe than in Puget Sound yards.[1] Meeker probably gave some thought to moving his hop growing operations to the Yakima Valley, as he made a purchase of 640 acres near Sunnyside.[2] With the onset of the national depression in 1893, local business failures began to take their toll. Meeker's Tacoma-Puyallup Railroad, the Park Hotel, and his Puyallup City Light Companies all went under within the next three years. Hop prices—which in 1892 held steady in the range of twenty-two to thirty-two cents a pound—declined in 1893. Nevertheless, Meeker appeared to carry on as if everything was normal and there was no national depression ravaging the country.

THE CARTEL

According to the Salem, Oregon, *Capital Journal,* New York hop brokers made an effort in the late summer of 1893 to use the financial situation to their advantage. The national depression made local banks unable to loan the growers funds to pick and market their crops. This situation forced the growers to turn to the brokers, who apparently had large cash reserves for financing. A cartel of New York brokers intended to offer contracts to the desperate Pacific Coast growers at ten to twelve cents per pound for their entire crop, knowing full well that a looming European shortage of hops would eventually drive the price up to perhaps as high as twenty-seven cents per pound. With the Pacific Coast hops securely in their possession, any rise in the market above twelve cents was pure profit.

Meeker, representing the Pacific Coast hop growers, went to New York to secure financing for the upcoming harvest and found no one willing to loan him money. He finally gave up and went to Milwaukee where he secured a $15,000 advance from the Milwaukee brewers. With this small sum in his pocket, he returned to New York and renewed negotiations with Lindsay, Bird & Co. of London. Shortly thereafter the company cabled Meeker that they had arranged for the cash to harvest the Northwest crop and pledged up to $1,200,000 in financing. The back of the broker's cartel was broken.[3]

Meeker used $250,000 in gold obtained from England to advance eleven cents per pound to Northwest growers to enable them to pick their crops.[4] He eventually made contracts for these same hops with London at seventeen to eighteen cents. What portion of the difference went into his pockets is not clear. Meeker also announced that a branch office of E. Meeker & Company would be set up in Salem, Oregon, under the direction of his son-in-law William Templeton with all the powers of the main Puyallup office.[5]

In late September Meeker told the editors of the *Puyallup Citizen* that the early samples from his yards were the best he had drawn in ten years. Two carloads of hops were shipped to London from his White River farms and 635 pickers were at work in his Puyallup yards, eventually sending three more carloads of hops to New York and London. He even put a crew of men to work clearing twenty-seven acres in the Maplewood Addition, which he intended to plant with hops the next season.[6] Meeker had used his skills and connections to stave off disaster for himself and his fellow Northwest growers for another season.

1894 Troubles

Hop troubles continued into 1894 and the situation looked grave. Meeker was interviewed by the *Tacoma Daily Ledger* on September 16. He claimed that only two-fifths of the Puget Sound crop would be picked and that a number of yards would not pick at all due to mold and lice. When asked the status of his crop of five hundred acres he responded, "With the exception of two or three acres they are as sound as a nut; in fact we have never had a better crop but they are ripening very late. We do not expect to lose but very few." He credited his spraying schedule with the health of the crop. He expected his five hundred acres would yield 4,500 bales and cost $30,000 to harvest and that hop pickers would be paid sixty-five cents a box rather than the traditional one dollar. Negotiations with the London brokers were very discouraging, he said. "They magnanimously offered to pay the freight and about 1 cent per pound besides, so we have leased warehouses and are putting our whole crop in warehouses here and at Kent." As for the future of the hop industry in Washington State, "Some growers will have to go out of the business, and in fact all should do so who do not make up their minds to spray their hops thoroughly and in season."[7]

The interview was telling. Meeker revealed that it would cost him $30,000 to harvest and bale his hops but the market was such that he could not sell them. He leased warehouses and stored the crop until the price improved. Meeker could afford to do this. Many of his fellow growers could not. At the end of the month the *Ledger* informed its readers that the hop harvest for 1894 in western Washington would be 20,000 bales, while the previous year's production was about 44,000 bales.[8] Damage from lice and the low prices were to blame.

The depression brought another change to the valley hop-growing scene. The time of Native American hop-picking was nearing its end. Both a dramatic increase in the Puget Sound white population and hard economic times sent large numbers of white pickers into the fields. The *Ledger* noted a change in traditional hiring practices. In years past hop growers sent agents out to meet with the various tribes and solicit pickers. Now, the roles were reversed. The tribes were sending out the agents to make agreements with the growers.[9]

In a December letter to an associate Meeker wrote that he had three clerks engaged full time in writing four to five hundred letters a week in search of U.S. markets. He ended with a note of optimism and a suggestion that he was thinking of moving his business away from hops.[10]

1895, A Sorry State of Affairs

Meeker's business correspondence for 1895 was sobering. The letters are primarily from people asking him to pay overdue bills:

"I wrote you about a month ago with reference to the little balance, $12.62, which is coming to me... but received no reply. When I left Puyallup you gave me to understand that I might look for a remittance of balance due me during the coming week. That was five months ago."[11]

"I was very disappointed in not receiving the past due interest upon your loan. I note what you say, that on the 20th of August you will pay this arrearage. We will expect this promptly when that time arrives. Please make a mental note of it and do not allow it to pass by."[12]

"You have apparently overlooked our request...asking for settlement of your Note and we must again remind you of it. We do not want to appear pressing in the matter but when we give credit we certainly expect our customers' obligations to be met when they come due."[13]

Troubles came from all directions. But Ezra Meeker maintained his sense of humor, as seen in this letter to the editor of the *Seattle Post-Intelligencer*.

> In this morning's report of the Methodist conference I notice under the heading "A Curse on the Hop Crop," that Preacher Hanson of Puyallup reported he had some good news from that great hop country—the hop crop, the main support of the people was a failure; the crop had been cursed by God. Whereupon Bishop Bowman said "Good" and from all over the room voices could be heard giving utterance to the fervent ejaculation, "Thank God."
>
> For the edification of the reverend fathers and fervent brethren I wish to publish to them and to the world that I have beat God, for I have 500 acres of hops at Puyallup and Kent that are free from lice and the "curse of God," and that I believe it was the work of an emulsion of whale oil soap and quassia sprayed on the vines that thwarted God's purpose to "curse" me and others who exterminated the lice...
>
> I want to recall to the memory of the Rev. Mr. Hanson that the church in which he has been preaching for a year past was built in great part by money contributed from gains of this business "cursed by God." For myself I can inform him that, as a citizen of Puyallup, I contributed $400 to buy the ground upon which that church edifice is built, every cent of which came from this same hop business "cursed by God." I would "thank God" if they would return the money and thus ease their guilty consciences.[14]

Ezra's letter earned him supporters among the newspaper's readers. Wrote one: "For over 5 years constant reading [of the *P-I*], I have never seen anything so cutting, so overwhelmingly stinging and uncontrovertibly just as your letter...And unless that reverend ass Hanson is totally devoid of manhood and decency—not to say of honor, he should settle up his affairs in your vicinity, hide his senseless carcass forever from the view of men and betake himself to some well guarded idiot asylum where he rightfully belongs."[15]

On March 1, 1895, Meeker incorporated the E. Meeker Company and declared it to be the successor to E. Meeker & Company, which was formed in 1867. The new masthead proclaimed "dealer in hops, lumber and shingles." Ezra, Fred Meeker, and John P. Hartman Jr. were named the officers. The capital of the new company consisted of 212 shares of stock at $1,000 per share. In addition Ezra split off his Kent properties and incorporated them separately as the "Puyallup Hop Company."[16] Perhaps he saw this as a way to somehow save the properties. Whatever he intended, with this slight change of name, a fixture in the business world of western Washington for twenty-eight years disappeared at the stroke of a pen.

Puyallup Hop Company letterhead from 1890s. *Author's collection.*

Seven Cents a Pound

Despite Meeker's bravado the *Tacoma Daily Ledger* headlines spoke more accurately to his chances of pulling out of the hole into which he was falling. In an article under the headline, "Outlook for Hops is

Gloomy," Meeker dodged a reporter's question about his opinion of the situation. "I have been too busy to pay much attention to other people's hop yards, and can only say that all of our hops, comprising about 525 acres, are in first class condition and will yield an average crop, similar to that grown in 1890." When asked if any growers made money from their 1894 crop Meeker responded, "Why yes, I sold without loss upon the whole cost, while others did not get their picking money back. Anybody, this year that picks green, immature or lousy hops will get left. That is all I care to say at present."[17] The 1895 hop crop sold for seven cents a pound.

The Puyallup First National Bank

The familiar version of Meeker's financial fall recounts that he went under when he mortgaged his hop farms and used the money to pay off the depositors of the failed Puyallup National Bank, of which he was president. The story involved secured creditors demanding their money, a fight, torn clothes, and an after-dark return of deposits by armed men to startled Puyallup Bank customers. Much of it was true, but the central point of the story, that it bankrupted Meeker, is in error. The *Ledger* printed two stories that bear on the subject, but as Meeker devoted a chapter of his 1916 book to the affair, an examination of this event should begin there. Here is his version.

> So one day when the deposits had run to a very low ebb, and the cash balance correspondingly low, and a threatening demand had been made by one of the secured banks it was evident that the bank must go into the hands of a receiver and what money was at hand to be frittered away in receiver's fees…It was impracticable to pay the depositors in part, or part of them in full…On my own responsibility I obtained enough, with the funds of the bank in hand, to pay the depositors in full. An attorney for one of the secured creditors of the bank suspected what was going on, and believing the money was on my person undertook to detain me in an office in Tacoma until papers could be gotten out and served. But he was too late, as A. R. Heilig, my attorney,[18] was already in Puyallup with the funds…The attempted hold up in Tacoma resulted in nothing more serious than a scuffle, the loss of a collar button or two, with plenty of threats, but no action. I took the train for Puyallup, went to bed at the usual hour, and slept soundly, as I always do.[19]

The *Ledger*'s version of the story had a less relaxed tone, describing a "stormy scene" with the Pierce County Treasurer John Hedges and his attorneys.[20]

According to the newspaper story, Meeker went to Tacoma, collected $2,400 in gold coin from his personal bank "intending to use it along with the remaining funds in his Puyallup bank to pay off some ninety depositors who were at risk of losing their savings." Carrying the money in a small sack, Meeker and his attorney, Alfred Heilig, met up with "Mr. Whitehouse," attorney for Hedges. Whitehouse "seemed to grow strangely urgent and excited" as they talked, but Meeker agreed to an appointment in Mr. Heilig's office. Meeker suspected Whitehouse was mainly interested in the money sack he was carrying and that the purpose of the meeting was to get him to hand it over to Treasurer Hedges. Apparently Hedges had deposited $4,725.44 of the county's money in the First National Bank of Puyallup under his own recognizance. Upon learning that the bank was going under he was understandably quite concerned, and forced the confrontation that led to the scene.

Meeker turned the money sack over to Heilig, who took the next electric car to Puyallup, and went on to the meeting with Treasurer Hedges, Whitehouse, and Mr. Shackleford, the assistant county attorney. According to the *Ledger*, "a spirited conversation took place." The attorneys insisted that Mr. Meeker settle with the treasurer in cash at once, and Meeker stated it was impossible. Harsh words were exchanged and Meeker ended the discussion. He got up as if to leave, only to find Mr. Shackleford blocking his way to the door. Meeker pushed past, tearing a button off his vest in the process, and made his way to the elevator. No further effort was made to prevent Meeker from going to the Puyallup train.

To be certain that they were not enjoined by a court order, Heilig and a small entourage of Meeker associates went around town by buggy and paid off the depositors.[21] As it was getting near dark they also took along a couple of armed men for protection. The *Ledger* wrote, "The peaceful people of Puyallup who were the depositors in the bank hardly knew what to make of it when called upon by such a party, but Mr. Heilig easily explained what was wanted." The next day Meeker retrieved his lost button, many of the Puyallup depositors opened new accounts in the E. Meeker Company's private banking office,[22] Pierce County was eventually repaid, and "peace reigned in Warsaw."[23]

A few days later a formal letter was mailed to all the involved parties informing them of a November 25, 1895, meeting to vote on the liquidation of the Puyallup First National Bank. The letter placed the blame for the bank's failure on the Panic of 1893 and the collapse of hop prices in 1894 and 1895, asserting the quality of the hops were not in question, but that offered prices barely met the cost of production.[24]

Mortgaging the Farms

Obviously $2,400 did not send the Meeker hop empire into ruin. Although Meeker did mortgage some part of his hop land to obtain it, the troubles of the Puyallup First National Bank were incidental to Meeker's much more extensive money problems. A look at the November 1, 1895, balance sheet of the E. Meeker Company gives a graphic illustration as to why the mortgage was necessary. The company was hemorrhaging money and had been for several years. It owed Lindsay Bird & Company $18,348; Fox & Searles $5,349.17; Arctic Oil Works $3,078.26; and the total bills payable were $151,101.73. The balance sheet showed that Meeker owed the Puyallup bank $212.84 and G. Hedges $3,252.43.[25] Cash on hand was listed as $1,373.54.

The bills were enormous and had to be paid. Meeker's prime asset was real estate held by E. Meeker Company valued at $80,316.50. A balance sheet for the Puyallup Hop Company has not been found, but it is likely to be similar. As a result, on November 6, 1895, Meeker went to the London and San Francisco Bank, Limited, in Tacoma and mortgaged his Puyallup properties. Probably he also did so with his Kent properties, but, again, those documents have not been found.

Two weeks after Meeker took out his mortgage, the *Ledger* reported that the county commissioners went to the treasurer's office and counted the cash on hand with several witnesses keeping a watch on the counters. The books balanced to the penny.[26] This affair and another financial impropriety the following year eventually cost Treasurer Hedges his job, but he stayed out of jail, which the *Ledger* had discussed as a distinct possibility. For Meeker, it was simply one more bill to pay.

CHAPTER 24

❧

The End of the Hop Empire

In a last-ditch attempt to save his hop empire, Ezra Meeker made his fourth and final voyage to England in the winter of 1895–96. He was absent for a little over three months. Meeker kept a journal of this trip, which he mailed to Eliza Jane in segments. Some eighty pages have survived, giving a complete accounting of his activities from Puyallup across the continent to New York City and across the Atlantic to London. The journal ends just before Christmas. The last two months telling of his stay and his voyage home are lost. The eighty-plus pages

Meeker's 1895 crop was probably stored in this fashion. *From the collection of the Schmidt House, Olympia Tumwater Foundation*

that have survived are much different from any of Meeker's previous writings. These pages contain personal information, much of which is new. His love for his wife is evident, but we learn for the first time that he struggled on occasion with what he called "the blues," and that his son Fred had a problem with alcohol. He titled the diary, "Journal of my trip from Puyallup to London, Written Expressly for My Dear Wife E. J. Meeker."[1]

LAST TRIP TO LONDON

Meeker left home November 29, 1895, on the Northern Pacific Railroad. The next day he reached Lincoln, Nebraska, where he met John Hartman, fellow officer of the E. Meeker Company, who accompanied him to Omaha. In Omaha they visited Mr. Holridge, the railroad superintendent, most likely to work out a favorable rate structure for shipping hops under Meeker's new plan to save his company. There was a three-hour layover in Omaha and then Meeker took a night train to Chicago. Hartman traveled with Meeker until 2 a.m. and then took a returning train to Omaha.

Meeker arrived in Chicago on December 3 and walked over to the office of Mr. John T. Sickels of the Atlantic Transport Line.[2] Sickels was in New York, but his brother William was at the Chicago office and sent one of the office boys to arrange Meeker's free transportation to New York, a perk he was often granted by his business acquaintances and one he actually needed in his present state of financial distress. He arrived "by this slow but comfortable train," on December 5 at 8:30 a.m. "just 30 minutes behind time and which by the way was the only time during the trip in which I was not precisely on time."

Meeker checked into his room at the St. Dennis Hotel and immediately took a streetcar to the offices of Fox & Searles. He had breakfast with Mr. Searles, the vice-president of the Puyallup Hop Company and a trustee of its Board of Directors, and arranged for free passage for himself to London and back.

Meeker spent his two-day stopover in New York conducting business, but made time to take in a show. He "accepted an invitation to go and hear Trilby. [A play based on the 1894 bestselling novel by George du Maurier, which introduced the character Svengali.]

The party consisted of Mr. Herman of San Francisco (who had invited us all to go with him) Mr. King of New York (a friend of Mr. Searles) Mr. Searles and myself, all hop men—'birds of feathers will flock together' etc. I did not fancy the novel; neither did like the play as well as the novel."

On the morning of Saturday, December 7, 1895, the steamer *Mobile* set sail for England. At 11 o'clock they rounded Sandy Hook and were cut off from all communication with the world. As usual Meeker got seasick. He ate lightly and read the novel *Jane Eyre*. He wrote that eighteen trips around the ship equaled a mile and that he visited a good deal with the ladies. Next Meeker read *In Darkest England, and the Way Out*, by William Booth, founder of the Salvation Army, and commented on the chapter titled "Deliverance for the Drunkard." He wrote, referring to his son Fred's problem with alcohol, "Still they do succeed in some cases, so we must not give up in despair." On December 15 Ezra went to bed with his spirits down, suffering from the "blues." He awoke refreshed and did his laps around the ship in a driving rainstorm.

Fred's drinking weighed heavily on Meeker's mind. Later during his voyage he wrote to Eliza Jane, "Fred's weakness is a constant thought of solicitude that will not disappear. Nevertheless I deem it to be a duty to ourselves not to let it 'wear' on us and I do hope and trust that you <u>will</u> bear up under it and keep of good cheer and good health. Such is, and has been my daily prayer since leaving home and will continue until I return."

The problem would persist. Later, in his letters from the Klondike, Ezra refers to Fred's drinking often. In one bitter letter he said Fred was doomed to "fill a drunkard's grave."[3] Fred would die of consumption in Dawson City, Yukon Territory, in 1901 with his wife Clara and sister Olive at his bedside.

A Plan to Save the Hop Empire

On December 17, Meeker wrote of his plan to save his hop empire. He hoped to arrange three-year contracts between local growers and himself for six cents a pound and half the expected rise in prices beyond that. Northwest hop growers who otherwise would have plowed under their hop yards might in this way hang on for another three years. He felt certain the price of hops would increase at least by the third year of the proposed contracts. If he could finance his plan in London it just might provide a way out of his troubles. He envisioned his son Marion spending the year in Oregon working the brokerage business there while he would be in London guiding that part of the business. "The only question in my mind as to the advisability to undertake it is the ability to carry it through; that is what I mean to work hard to accomplish. I would be willing to go to the extent of 5000 bales—building castles in the air I hear you say—well we will see; there is nothing like trying. I have been building castles in the air all along."

Meeker arrived at England on December 18 and wrote to his sons about his business plans.

> I think these letters outline a plan for the future that will enable us to recuperate—anyway it is well to canvass the plan closely. I admit that it is not without its element of danger, and that it involves a great deal of labor and watchful care, all of which I have canvassed in my mind, but so does any venture we may undertake let it be ever so void of anything bordering on speculation, but I am satisfied that if this is carried out that it is the way out of our embarrassment. I had something like this in my mind before leaving home but not the whole plan as now developed in my mind in thinking over it. This would involve our being in London for at least five months of the year so long as the contracts last.

Once in London it became obvious that Meeker faced an uphill climb in building his "castles."

> Tell Fred that Bird [of Lindsay, Bird & Co., Purchasers of Hops, which had for a number of years purchased Meeker's hops] says the bulk of the Patterson [another Puyallup farmer] crop had been sold at about 30 [shillings]...He says he never saw anything like it the way they were slaughtered [sold for a pittance]. He showed me some samples of them, which, however, I did not examine closely, but which looked to me to be as nice or in fact brighter than any of ours.

Bird and Collins told him their warehouses were full of unsold hops and that the English farmers were in a "horrible fix." The tenants were abandoning thousands of acres of hop yards and the landlords were equally in trouble. One bright spot was that certain Kent districts were faring a little better. Upon hearing this Meeker resolved to go to Maidstone, Kent, and "hear their tale of woe first hand."

Meeker spent nearly two months in London and was back in the United States by the end of February. He wrote Eliza Jane from the Hotel Walton in Philadelphia on February 26, 1896. He was still striving valiantly to save the business, but couldn't resist suggesting a side business that might make a few dollars.

> I wish you would quietly get a good lot of Skunk cabbage root dug before the leaf starts too much and spread it out to dry in the room adjoining the laundry. Get some one to dig for a day or two. I believe there is real virtue in that root and that we can turn it to profit...You mustn't laugh me out of this for I am really in earnest to believe it can be turned to profit and at the same time be a benefit to others.[4]
>
> I hope we are laying the foundation for something better later on. I am economizing even if I do stop at Palace hotels and am able to praise God every night that I am blessed with good health and strength, and every morning for refreshing restful sleep. This morning however I did not go to bed until after two o'clock, did not receive Fred's long telegram and Hartman's until nearly midnight and then after deciphering them[5] which was no small job for there was an aggregate of 100 words and going to the telegraph office for some corrections and writing two letters to London for this morning's 4 o'clock mail and one to Fred & short note to Hartman, no wonder that it was nearly three before I got to bed; but I caught up and got up as refreshed as ever.[6]

By the end of March Meeker was home, but the handwriting was on the wall as far as the hop industry was concerned. Prices remained at rock bottom with virtually no prospect of a reversal. His efforts in London had failed. Meeker was swimming in debt and could get no financing for his brokerage business. He had reverted to the old practice of mortgaging his hop properties to cover the cost of planting and harvesting his own fields, and now there was no prospect of paying off that mortgage with the sale of the 1896 crop. His sons gave up and left for Cook Inlet, Alaska, to prospect for gold and Meeker began to cast around for other ways to make money. On May 3, 1896, he became the Agricultural Editor of the *Daily Ledger* and ran a weekly page on Sundays (always on page 12) just as he had done nearly a decade earlier for the *Seattle Post-Intelligencer*. He called it "Farm, Field and

Fireside." On July 20 he was in Colfax, Washington, where he wrote a story about the populist movement in eastern Washington. On September 6 he wrote about a pioneer reunion held on Nancy Meeker's farm in Sumner with over 150 people in attendance. The pioneers were celebrating her seventy-first birthday. It was a moment of brightness in a gloomy year.

END OF THE ROAD

On October 31, 1896, Meeker received notification from the London & San Francisco Bank, with whom he had mortgaged his hop properties, that the sale of those properties would take place on November 11 at noon. Stapled to this notification was a listing of his company's assets, including: hops and baling cloth stored in the warehouse in the First National Bank Building in Puyallup, hops in a warehouse in Kent, hops in the warehouse of Chappell & Cox in North Yakima, and hops in the warehouse of Fred Pennington also in North Yakima—representing his entire 1895 crop. Meeker responded by telling the bank that he was expecting word from Lindsay, Bird & Co. in London with an offer to purchase Meeker's hops at a price higher than what the bank would get for them at auction. Meeker asked that the auction be delayed until final word could be received from London, probably in mid-December. The bank gave Meeker twelve days.

It was to no avail. London did not answer. On November 23, 1896, Meeker's property was sold at auction in two separate sales. David C. Stam was the auctioneer. Edward S. Alexander, along with a Mr. Holt and a Mr. Jackson of the bank supervised the sale. Meeker's entire hop crop sold for $7,183.58. The auctioneer and supervisors billed $199.69 for their services. When all other expenses were deducted the bank received $6,715.59. Among the assets sold were warehouses full of Meeker's crop of 1895, all in bales, stored neatly, awaiting a buyer.

As to his 1896 hop crop Meeker wrote, "The last crop I raised costing me eleven cents per pound, and selling for three under the hammer at sheriff's sale. At that time I had more than $100,000 advanced to my neighbors and others upon their hop crops, which was lost. These people simply could not pay, and I forgave the debt, taking no judgments against them, and have never regretted the action."[7]

Meeker was not present at either auction. He was in Grand Forks, British Columbia, embarking upon his new career as the President of the International Mine Development Company.

The bank retained ownership of Meeker's hop farms and leased the land. Hops were grown on them for a number of years. Prices, however, remained at depressed levels until 1900 when they rose to fourteen cents. In 1902 hops sold for twenty-three cents per pound and the following year twenty-five cents per pound. In 1902, six years after Meeker lost his hop farms, the bank sold 110 acres of Meeker's old property for $30,000 to Herman Klaber, who had been managing the property since the 1896 foreclosure. Klaber, who owned a large hop ranch near Chehalis, had control through purchase and lease of 306 acres of hop land in western Washington, making him the new Northwest "hop king."[8]

Herman Klaber died in 1912, one of 1,517 casualties of the sinking of the *Titanic*.[9] He was probably on his way home from the London Hop Borough. The valley hop business also died, as farmers made the transition to growing berries of various varieties along with daffodils and other such products.[10] Today all that can be seen of the golden times of the valley hop years are a few remnants: a restored hop kiln near the city of Snoqualmie; a 1907 hop barn on Valley Avenue in Alderton; a few wild hops vines growing on power poles here and there in the valley; and a hop display near the entrance to the Meeker Mansion in Puyallup.

Afterword

Over the years many have speculated on the reasons for the collapse of Meeker's financial empire. The common view usually blames the hop lice invasion. Indeed, *Phorodon humuli* reduced the quality of Northwest hops and increased the costs of growing a marketable product. It is the answer Meeker himself supplied in his various books, claiming, "that, in killing the louse, we virtually destroyed the hops, and instead of being able to sell our hops at the top price of the market, our product fell to the foot of the list."[1] But Europe and New York had been successfully selling lice-ravaged hops for decades, and Meeker's own sales figures refute the notion that Northwest hops suddenly became so inferior as to be unmarketable.

Yes, Northwest farmers lost the competitive edge they had enjoyed for years, but the lice first appeared in 1890 and by 1893 Meeker and others had mastered European spraying techniques and even improved upon them. Part of the problem was that many growers could not afford to spray as Meeker did and the total harvest was much reduced as a result. But this damaged brokerage business much more than it did his own hop growing operation. Indeed, Meeker said he made money on his own hops every year from 1890 through 1894. And in the contemporary press he always claimed that his sprayed hops were of fine quality. Fred Meeker said of the 1893 crop, "The lice have been dealt with much more effectively this year than last. At the first indication the farmers went to work, and if any yards have lice in them it is the fault of the farmers themselves." He blamed any reduction in yield to a damp summer season rather than lice.[2] While a factor, the lice invasion was not the fatal blow.

Others have suggested the bailout of the Puyallup Bank at Meeker's own expense was a primary reason for his demise. In his books Meeker in a roundabout way hinted at this possibility. He told the story without mentioning a dollar amount. His readers were left to believe that the amount was quite large. After all, not many individuals have the resources to bail out a bank and repay all its depositors. This author accepted the explanation at face value until discovering how small the sum involved actually was.

So, while both of the above concerns played a role in Meeker's fall, other factors were at work as well. The chief complicating factor was Meeker himself. Even as he developed into an extremely skilled businessman, he had long forgotten his 1882 advice that hops should be handled like dynamite—"with care."[3] His entire farming enterprise was invested in growing hops; his brokerage business was entirely invested in selling hops.

Meeker was also afflicted by his self-identified tendency to always think big, not just building castles in the air but investing in actual foundations on the ground. By the beginning of the 1890s Meeker was at the height of his prosperity. If not the wealthiest man in the state, he was surely among the elite. He had finally been elected to a political office (mayor), and his self-confidence was at its apex. This success encouraged Meeker to embark on four substantial projects that literally sucked up money—the Puyallup-Tacoma Railway, the Park Hotel, the Puyallup Light Company, and the Meeker mansion. The railroad in particular was a huge financial gamble, and his nephew Frank's dishonest dealings added to the toll. These projects were primarily funded by Meeker's hop business. Although Meeker claimed the mansion was built with his wife's money, it seems likely that some of his own was involved in that project as well. The mansion was completed and became the new family home. However, the depression of 1893 dealt the death blow to the other three projects. They all went bankrupt, and with their demise went much of Meeker's liquidity.

Starting in 1890 Meeker began the practice of advancing money to local hop-growers to cover their planting and harvesting costs, with the loans to be paid back when the fall harvest was sold. For a time he convinced eastern hop-buyers to advance the money, but eventually most of it came out of his own pocket. Meeker noted unpaid loans due him in the sum of $100,000 (the equivalent of $2.5 million in today's dollars). Whether that was for the final year of his hop business or cumulative since the appearance of the lice in 1890, he does not make clear. Either way, it was a huge sum of money, all predicated on successful hop harvests.

By 1894 Meeker was drastically overextended. When the price of hops plunged to seven cents a pound that fall, a price below the cost of production, Meeker simply put his hops in a warehouse and waited. Many growers couldn't afford to wait. The crop eventually sold and Meeker claimed he made a profit on this harvest, but he never said how much of a profit. One speculates it was meager at best. Certainly his brokerage business could not have prospered at that price. And when prices stayed at seven cents for the 1895 harvest Meeker again put his hops in warehouses and waited. But this time he found no buyers. And then he made a fatal error.

Meeker mortgaged his hop yards and business to fund the planting and harvesting of the 1896 crop. No doubt he reasoned prices had to come up, as they had never before stayed below the cost of production for more than two consecutive years. Instead they plunged even lower—to an unprecedented three cents per pound. Meeker now had no way to repay the mortgage.

There is no mention in any of his correspondence, nor is there any evidence in any other document in the historical record, that Meeker ever tried to recover any of the $100,000 he had loaned his fellow growers. As he wrote, "I forgave the debt, taking no judgments against them, and have never regretted the action."[4] It would be 1900 before the price of hops finally returned to pre-1894 levels. By then only a handful of hop growers were left on the west side of the Cascade Mountains, and Meeker was not among them.

There is little doubt that he saw it coming. The wheels had been coming off for a long time. He probably knew when he returned from England after his fourth and final trip across the Atlantic in the spring of 1896 that his days as "hop king" were over. He was now sixty-five years old but without the luxury (fortune) or temperament to retire. Meeker made the transition from hop grower to mine investor almost seamlessly. By the end of 1896 he was in British Columbia working under the banner of the International Mine Development Company and in the Yukon from 1898 to 1901, a story that is told in the author's volume *Slick as a Mitten*.

Meeker lived thirty-two years beyond the loss of his hop empire. Never once in any of his correspondence did he look back with regret or mourn that loss. Instead he kept moving forward, always operating at energy levels that would challenge younger men. He served a term as president of the Washington State Historical Society, wrote a history of early Washington Territory, and traveled multiple times over the remnants of the old Oregon Trail (by covered wagon, automobile, train, and airplane) in a years-long campaign to memorialize and mark it for future generations. He founded the Oregon Trail Memorial Association to that end, wrote several more books, championed the vision of a national highway, testified multiple times before Congressional hearings, and met five presidents. He built big again for the Alaska-Yukon-Pacific Exposition of 1909, experimented with motion pictures, hobnobbed with the rich and famous, and became somewhat of a national celebrity himself. In a very short time his hop king/businessman identity faded entirely away to be replaced in the national consciousness by his Oregon Trail persona of the "old pioneer." Meeker continued to build "castles in the air" until the end of his life. Some of them are still standing.[5]

A Short History of Beer

Humans have been fermenting grains, rice, juices, and honey to make alcoholic beverages for thousands of years. There is evidence of an alcoholic drink in China as early as 7,000 BCE and in India as early as 3,000 BCE Wine and mead appeared in Babylon and Greece as early as 2,700 BCE. The making of ale is nearly as old and has been recorded in the writings of ancient Egypt and Mesopotamia.

Historically "ale" was a drink made from fermented malt (a dried grain) without using hops. The downside of this brew was that it had a very short shelf life before spoiling and going sour. When hops came into the picture beer was born. "Beer," like ale, was a drink made from fermented malt, but with one important difference: the use of hops. Hops acted as a preservative, giving the beverage a shelf life of years rather than weeks. It also imparted a unique bitter taste to the drink. But this did not happen for a good long time.

The first documented link between hops and brewing appeared in the year 822 in the writings of Abbot Adalhard of the Benedict Monastery of Corbie in northern France. All previous mentions of hops referred to its use in making dyes or in the making of rope and paper from the stalks, but this was the first writing to link hops with the brewing process. A book called *Physica*, published in 1150 by Abbess Hildegard of Beingen, Germany, clearly demonstrated that the use of hops as a preservative was well known by that date. By 1400 hop culture as an industry had appeared in Belgium and Holland and by 1500 had made its way to England, primarily in the Kent district southeast of London. In 1574 Reginald Scot published *A Perfite Platform of a Hoppe Garden*, the first English treatise on the subject. Taxes on the English growers and regulations on the brewers began to appear by 1700. By 1878 there were 71,789 acres of hops under cultivation in England

Of course it didn't remain quite so simple. At some point in the Middle Ages the Germans discovered that if you brewed your beer in the fall and stored it until spring, covered with ice harvested from nearby lakes, it came out mellow and smoother tasting than traditional beer. The colder temperatures resulted in a slower fermentation process. This new entry was called "lager" beer, referring to the long storage period. Refinements with yeast soon made lager the primary beer on the block. But ale did not go away. It metamorphosed. And while the rest of the world drank beer, this "new" ale (the older version of hop-brewed beer that fermented more quickly at warmer temperatures) became the national drink of Britain and Belgian. Today ales are enjoying a renaissance, especially with the emergence of microbrewing. Aficionados might regard ale and beer as two different commodities as they are brewed differently, but both are made from malt and both have hops in their mix.

Hop culture came to the United States with the English in 1628 in Massachusetts and with the Dutch who erected a brewery in New Amsterdam (New York) in 1633.[1] For much of the 1700s New England was the epicenter of the new nation's hop industry, but by the mid-1800s New York had surpassed its eastern neighbors and became the leader in U.S. hop production. It was the new giant in the industry.

Next into the field was the state of Wisconsin. Early settlers found hops growing wild in the southern part of the state and immigrants from New York brought their knowledge of hops and hop growing with them. By 1850 a large and growing number of acres were under hop cultivation. Despite a few dips, within two decades production reached over four million pounds. It was a short-lived boom, however, for by 1880, as diseases and pests took their toll, output had been cut in half. New York's sigh of relief did not last long as hops grown in California, Oregon, and Washington soon offered the Empire State serious competition.

The New England hop industry succumbed to competition from New York and is non-existent today. Wisconsin suffered from the ravages of mold, lice, and competition. By 1920 the industry there was dead. In 1880 New York produced twenty-one million pounds of dried hops, but by 1920 commercial hop growing came to an end there as well. Disease from mildew in the early 1900s and Prohibition (1920–1933) both had a hand in killing the industry. Hop yards disappeared, replaced by other crops. Barns and kilns were converted to other uses or left to rot. The great hop industry of New York became just a memory. California was the next to fold. Hops are no longer grown there to any extent, with only around fifty acres of commercial hops under cultivation today, primarily in the area north of San Francisco.[2] While growing grapes and other crops proved more profitable for California, efforts today are being made in New York and Wisconsin to encourage new farmers back into the field to revive the hop industry.

Oregon's Willamette Valley hop industry survived Prohibition by taking advantage of a burgeoning international market after WWI destroyed much of European agriculture. In the early 1900s the region proclaimed itself the "hop capital of the world." Today Oregon and Idaho account for around 25 percent of U.S. production.[3]

In Washington the great hop yards of the Puyallup and White River Valleys and the huge Snoqualmie yards of Puget Sound are gone. Currently, there are small-scale efforts being made in Thurston County and elsewhere in western Washington to revive the industry, but it is the Yakima Valley, east of the Cascade Mountains, that has prospered. It was here that Ezra Meeker purchased property in the 1890s. If he was contemplating an eventual expansion or move of his hop-growing operations, it never happened. He was overtaken by his collapsing empire and lost fortune.

Today the United States is the world's second largest producer of hops, trailing only Germany, and 70 percent of the nation's hop production comes from the Yakima Valley. Sitting in the heart of that valley is the city of Toppenish, home of the American Hop Museum. According to their records, Charles Carpenter planted the first rootstock in the valley in 1868 but the industry was slow to take off. In 1876 valley growers shipped a mere eighty bales of hops to Puget Sound. However, twenty years later hop growing was well established with Moxee City and Toppenish becoming the major market centers. By the mid-1890s when the Puget Sound industry faltered, the Yakima Valley became the major hop growing area in Washington. Today hop yards blanket the valley. Meeker would have been wise to make the move.

In 2015, Washington State was the leader in U.S. commercial hop production, with 32,205 acres devoted to the crop. Oregon was second with 6,807 acres, Idaho third with 4,975 acres. All other states combined have just 1,244 acres in hops.

Hop plants grow naturally in many places around the world and local conditions have led to the natural evolution of many varieties. By 1900 in Europe alone there were some eighty different types of hops, often named after the geographic location of their origin. Scientific breeding of hops began at Wye College in Kent, England, around 1900, eventually resulting in a plethora of varieties that has in turn helped create the growth of the microbrewery industry. Small brewers can now choose from a wide variety of hops and experiment with the brewing process to produce varieties and flavors of beer. Growing hops and brewing beer has become to a large extent a scientific endeavor as well as a craft. As modern consumer tastes have moved to lighter and less hopped beer, the demand for massive quantities of hops as required in Meeker's time has lessened. Instead, brewers today are asking for quality and variety.

Notes

Notes to Chapter 1: Two Brothers

1. Ezra Meeker, *Ventures and Adventures of Ezra Meeker* (Seattle: Rainier Printing Co., 1908), 151.

2. "An Exciting Time," *Puget Sound Herald*, November 25, 1859, 2.

3. "Arrival of the *Columbia*. Wreck of the *Northerner*," *Pioneer and Democrat*, January 20, 1860, 2.

4. Most interestingly, Ezra was not listed as the administrator of Oliver's estate. Antonio Rabbeson and Robert S. More [Moore] were given that title. "Administrators Notice." *Puget Sound Herald* (Steilacoom), January 20, 1860, 2.

5. "Religious Service," *Puget Sound Herald*, February 24, 1860, 2.

6. The 1860 census recorded incorrect ages for a number of the Meeker household members. As of February 1860, Ezra (born December 29, 1830) was 29; Eliza Jane (born October 13, 1834) was 25; Amanda (born January 26, 1839) was 21; Marion (born March 9, 1852) was 7; Ella (born February 26, 1854) was 6; Frank (born May 3, 1855) was 4; and Caroline (born January 16, 1859) was 1. Caroline was interchangeably called Carrie or Caddie throughout her life in all correspondence and in various published writings. Her formal name was never used. For consistency Carrie is used in this work. The census listed Thomas Mallit's age as 32.

7. Ezra's adopted Indian child grew up on the Meeker Puyallup farm and in due course married a woman named Sally. "For a time the couple lived in a small cabin nearby, but they eventually moved to the Puyallup Indian Reservation where 160 acres were allotted to them and where they lived until their deaths…Their child, Jerry Meeker, was sent to school…and developed into a shrewd business man and has fallen heir to an estate valued at $50,000 or more of which he had taken good care and is now a rich man, and maintains an office in Tacoma." Jerry Meeker went on to become an activist for the northwest Indian tribes and a Tacoma attorney of some note. "The Case of Jerry Meeker," Meeker Papers, Box 10, Envelope 1.

8. "Depreciated," *Puget Sound Herald*, June 29, 1860, 2.

9. "Apples," *Puget Sound Herald*, August 31, 1860, 3.

Notes to Chapter 2: Politics and the Law

1. Ezra Meeker to Clarence Bagley, August 18, 1912, Meeker Papers, Box 4, Folder 12C; Ezra Meeker to Eben Osborne, August 17, 1912, Meeker Papers, Box 6, Vol. 18.

2. Wallace died February 7, 1879, and is interred in the Fort Steilacoom cemetery, now located on the grounds of Western State Hospital in Lakewood, Washington. His tombstone, long in disrepair, has recently been restored.

3. "The Election," *Puget Sound Herald,* July 11, 1861, 2.

4. In the early days of the territory a hot political issue was the location of the territorial capital. There was a strong rivalry between Olympia, which was in Thurston County, and Steilacoom, in Pierce County, for the prize, and both cities had newspapers. The *Washington Standard* was an Olympia newspaper. The *Puget Sound Herald* was in Steilacoom. The accusation that Meeker, who was running for office in Pierce County, was supporting Olympia's bid to remain the capital city would be deadly for his campaign.

5. "Communicated. To the Editor," *Puget Sound Herald,* July 4, 1861, 2. In 1854 the Washington Territorial Legislature created Sawamish County, whose name was chosen to honor the Indian tribes of southern Puget Sound. The name was changed to Mason County ten years later. Pierce and Sawamish Counties made up Meeker's election district.

6. "Organization of the Legislature," *Vancouver (WA) Register,* December 16, 1865, 2.

7. Meeker lost to James Gallagher 116-138. "Official Vote of Pierce County," *Vancouver Register,* July 3, 1869, 1.

8. W. Victor Wortley, trans., *Louis Rossi: Six Years on the West Coast of America* (Fairfield, WA: Ye Galleon Press, 1983), 142.

9. Richard Klugar, *The Bitter Waters of Medicine Creek: A Tragic Clash Between White and Native America* (New York: Vintage Books, 2012), 260, 284.

10. *Washington Territory vs. Ezra Meeker,* Case PRC-944, Washington State Archives.

11. "Administrators Notice," *Puget Sound Herald,* January 20, 1860, 4.

12. The paperwork was a deed, which Meeker failed to fully explain. Oliver had a Donation Land Claim at Fern Hill, part interest in the Steilacoom store, and was an owner along with his brother of a blockhouse constructed in Steilacoom during the Indian war. Any one of these could have been the document referred to. But why Eliza Jane Meeker's signature would be needed for these properties is unclear. There is another possibility. Meeker stated that as surviving partner in the store he had the right to settle up the debts of the business by posting a bond. The most probable source of income for that bond would have been to satisfy it with a lien against their Fern Hill property. The Title Abstract of Ezra and Eliza Jane's Fern Hill DLC specifies that half of the property belonged to him and half belonged to his wife. The abstract goes further, actually delineating the specific land parcels that belonged to each. This perhaps is what required both Ezra's and Eliza Jane's signatures. This abstract is in the collection of the Puyallup Historical Society at the Meeker Mansion in Puyallup, Washington.

13. "Tribute to My Wife," Meeker Papers, Box 10, Envelope 1. Rabbeson and Meeker would cross paths again, in a literary fashion, in 1886. Rabbeson wrote a story of his activities during the Indian war that was published in the *Seattle Daily Press.* Meeker responded by writing a lengthy account of his version of those years that later formed part of the structure for his book *Pioneer Reminiscences and the Tragedy of Leschi* (Seattle: Lowman & Hanford Printing Company, 1905). "In Stirring Times," *Seattle Daily Press,* September 14, 1886, 3.

14. *Ezra Meeker vs. B. M. and C. H. Spinning*, Case PRC-372, Washington State Archives.

Notes to Chapter 3: A New Start

1. "Sale Continued," *Puget Sound Herald*, October 24, 1861, 2.

2. "Soap, etc.," *Puget Sound Herald*, February 20, 1862, 2.

3. "Union Soap Works," *Puget Sound Herald*, March 27, 1862, 2.

4. "Our Soap Factory," *Puget Sound Herald*, April 17, 1862, 2.

5. Smith complained that Ezra endorsed "foul articles in the *Northwest*." The *Northwest* was one of Port Townsend's short-lived weekly newspapers. It is likely that Meeker sent a letter to the editor castigating Smith. Thomas Camfield, *An Illustrated History of Port Townsend: Shanghaiing, Shipwrecks, Soiled Doves and Sundry Souls* (Port Townsend: Ah Tom Publishing, Inc., 2000), 157 and 190.

6. "Collector Victor Smith." *Puget Sound Herald*, January 30, 1862, 2. The editor of the *Herald* added this comment at the beginning of the letter. "The last two lines [of text] of Victor's letter, in reference to Mr. E. Meeker, so amused us that we could not refrain from printing them in italic; the reader will therefore not charge him with underlining them, as is usual in such cases."

7. "Appointed," *Puget Sound Herald*, March 27, 1862, 2, and "J. R. Meeker's Appointment," *Puget Sound Herald*, April 10, 1862, 2.

8. "Narrow Escape," *Puget Sound Herald*, August 14, 1862, 2.

9. Meeker spelled the name Stilly. Jeremiah's tombstone in the Sumner, Washington, cemetery spells it Stilley. The latter spelling will be used in this work.

10. Ezra Meeker, *The Busy Life of Eighty-Five Years of Ezra Meeker* (Indianapolis: Wm. B. Burford Press, 1916), 352-353, provides an interesting depiction of Stilley. Meeker describes him as a lover of Shakespeare and Gibbon and a student of the Bible. He wrote that Stilley moved too often to "gather much of the world's riches around him." But he did "raise a crop of ten children, made no pretension in dress, seldom went to church, but was exemplary in his habits, though inclined toward pessimism in his later life." Ezra kept in contact with him over the years even with the frequent moves. Two of those moves have been documented—a 160-acre homestead claim near today's Buckley, Washington, and a move to the Okanogan Valley in eastern Washington just prior to 1900.

11. Ezra Meeker and Howard R. Driggs, *Covered Wagon Centennial and Ox Team Days* (New York: Yonkers-on-Hudson, 1932), 196.

12. The Donation Land Claim Act went into effect on September 27, 1850, and expired in late 1855. It originally granted a claim of 320 acres to the male filer with an additional 320 acres available to his wife. When amended on February 14, 1853, the amount of land a settler might have was reduced in half. Four steps were needed in order to receive a DLC: (1) File a claim notification with the Registrar and Receiver of Lands within three months of settlement; (2) Nine months later file sworn proof of culti-

vation and one year's residence with affidavits from two disinterested witnesses; (3) Resubmit proof four years later; (4) Surveyor General awards land certificate, which is forwarded to the General Land Office, which issues a patent or deed to the claimant, finalizing the land claim.

The Homestead Act signed by President Abraham Lincoln on May 20, 1862 granted a claim of 160 acres to anyone 21 years of age or older who was head of a household (including free slaves and women), and who had never taken up arms against the U.S. government. No extra provision was made for wives. It required simply filing an application, after which you had five years to improve the land, at which point you were granted a deed. Settlers could obtain title outright after six months by paying $1.25 an acre. As Meeker made clear, a person could file for both a DLC and a Homestead claim. Homesteading was allowed in Alaska until 1986.

13. Meeker, *Busy Life*, 370.

14. Williamson was Anthony R. Williamson, with whom Meeker had several dealings over the years. He was part of Meeker's surveying crew in 1867 and partner with Meeker in growing hops the next year. In 1869 Williamson moved to the Skagit Valley and became a hop grower in that vicinity, suggesting that was the year Ezra bought him out and made a square out of his Puyallup Homestead claim.

15. The claim consisted of Sections 2 and 3 in Township 19 North, Range 3 East; the west half to Ezra and the east half to Eliza Jane.

16. One account has him moving from his South Tacoma Donation Land Claim in 1860. If this is accurate then Jacob moved to the valley two years ahead of his son Ezra. "The Settlement and Growth of the Puyallup Valley," *Snohomish (WA) Northern Star*, September 29, 1877, 3.

17. Nancy's children were Lynus Burr, age 14; Samuel Burr, 12; and Sarah Burr, age 9.

18. It is not known for certain if John Meeker arrived in Steilacoom before Oliver left for San Francisco. If Oliver had gone south on the *Northerner* from Steilacoom in mid- to late December, or if he had gone south on the *Columbia* that arrived in Steilacoom on December 22, 1859, the two brothers would have had an opportunity for a brief reunion.

19. Lori Price stated that John Meeker lived in James Stewart's cabin for a year before filing his Homestead claim. Lori Price and Ruth Anderson, *Puyallup: A Pioneer Paradise* (Charleston: Arcadia Publishing, 2001), 24.

20. John and Mary Jane Meeker's children were: Mary Frances, born February 27, 1858 in Eddyville, Iowa; Joseph Pence, born May 15, 1860, and Lucy Jane, born October 7, 1861, both in Steilacoom, Washington Territory; Harriet Elizabeth, born December 1, 1863, and Maggie A., born June 8, 1865, both in Puyallup, Washington Territory.

21. His son Marion was fourteen, his nephew Frank was eleven, and his stepbrother Lynus was sixteen.

22. "Danger of an Indian Difficulty," *Washington Standard* (Olympia), August 17, 1867, 2.

23. Julha, Pat Thompson, and Loretta Finnerty Bilow, *Index to Marriage Records, Pierce County, Washington, Territorial Marriages 1853-1889* (Tacoma: Tacoma-Pierce County Genealogical Society, 1988), 61. Amanda's obituary states that this marriage took place in 1870. Pierce County records say otherwise.

Notes to Chapter 4: Birth of the Puyallup Valley Hop Industry

1. Ezra Meeker, *Hop Culture in the United States* (Puyallup: E. Meeker & Co., 1883), 8.

2. Until 1891 Washington had two Woodlands. That year a federal commission said that it was too confusing to the U.S. Postal Service, and thus Isaac Wood's Woodland became Lacey.

3. George Himes to Ezra Meeker, January 11, 1915, Meeker Papers, Box 4, Folder 12B.

4. "Brewery," *Pioneer and Democrat*, July 22, 1859, 2.

5. Ibid., May 24, 1861, 2.

6. www.thurstontalk.com/2015/02/22/olympia-brewery-history.

7. George Himes to Ezra Meeker, August 18, 1919, Meeker Papers, Box 4, Folder 12B.

8. "Acres of Hops," *Tacoma Daily Ledger*, July 7, 1887, 2. This article was repeated in "First Washington Hops," *Washington Standard*, September 23, 1887, 1.

9. "The Hop Fields of the Puyallup," *Northern Star*, September 29, 1877, 4.

10. Ibid.

11. "A Puyallup Hop Farm," *Seattle Daily Pacific Tribune*, August 30, 1877, 2.

12. John Meeker confirms this in a story titled "Hops and Their Cultivation," *Tacoma Daily Ledger*, July 25, 1894, 2. "The roots were furnished him by a Mr. Wood, a brewer in Olympia, who had induced the old gentleman to make the trial, sending him the roots free of charge."

13. Ibid.

14. "Hop Growing in the Pacific Northwest," *Pacific Rural Press*. Volume 24, Number 9, August 26, 1882, 134. (This California newspaper article supplies a wealth of material about the early history of the Puyallup Valley hop industry.) Contradicting the *Pacific Rural Press*, John Meeker said, "Meantime the old gentleman obtained some roots from John Loch, a brewer in Steilacoom, paying the rate of $100 per thousand for the cuttings. These were a variety called the Canada red and were also found to be undesirable. These have been eradicated from the fields after a long and earnest warfare." "Hops and Their Cultivation," *Tacoma Daily Ledger*, July 25, 1894, 2.

15. "Hop Growing in the Pacific Northwest," 134.

16. Ezra confirmed the seventy-five cents per pound price and stated that the yield was four bales or around eight hundred pounds. "Acres of Hops," *Tacoma Daily Ledger*, June 7, 1887, 2.

17. THR-673 and 680, 1867, United States vs. Isaac Wood, Criminal, Liquor sales to Indians.

18. Meeker, *Hop Culture*, 8.

19. "Puyallup Hop Growing," *Willamette Farmer*, August 11, 1882, 1. This long article gives a rather thorough and accurate history of the beginning of the Puyallup Valley hop industry.

20. Meeker, *Busy Life*, 225.

21. "Hops and Their Cultivation," *Tacoma Daily Ledger*, July 25, 1894, 2.

22. Anthony Williamson is the person from whom Ezra had purchased enough land to make his Puyallup homestead claim contiguous.

23. Michael Tomlan gives credit for introducing hops to California to Wilson G. Flint, who imported roots from Vermont in the winter of 1855-56. *Tinged With Gold* (Athens and London: University of Georgia Press, 1992), 26. His brother, Daniel Flint, planted a trial yard near Sacramento, California, in the spring of 1857 and is usually credited with starting the hop industry in that state. Tom Gregory, *History of Yolo County, California* (Los Angeles: Historic Record Company: 1913), 659–661.

24. "Hop Growing in the Pacific Northwest," 134.

25. Exactly what the E. Meeker & Company looked like in 1867 is unclear. It was probably an umbrella organization that included the farms and businesses of both Jacob and Ezra, and probably John. This would be similar to what was done in the 1850s and 1860s with the Steilacoom store. It was a few years before the company became solely identified with hops. Even during its peak hop years the company was involved in other enterprises—businesses such as operating a sawmill and road construction.

26. "The Chase," *Walla Walla Statesman*, August 9, 1867, 2.

27. "Hop Growing in the Pacific Northwest," 134.

28. Meeker, *Ventures and Adventures*, 254.

Notes to Chapter 5: Suddenly Wealthy

1. "Acres of Hops," *Tacoma Daily Ledger*, July 7, 1887, 2.

2. "Hops," *Tacoma Herald*, October 16, 1879, 3.

3. David Buerge, "Ezra Meeker Goes to Wall Street," *Columbia: The Magazine of Northwest History* 2, no. 1 (1988), 14.

4. The *Willamette Farmer* (Salem, Oregon) of August 11, 1882, 1, in an article titled "Puyallup Hop Growing," stated that prior to 1871 there were only three hop yards in the Puyallup Valley: Jacob Meeker's, Ezra Meeker's, and Meade and Thompson's. The article goes on to say that in 1871 John Meeker and James Stewart joined the mix. "The History of Puyallup," *Puyallup Valley Tribune*, July 30, 1904, 6, gives a few details about Stewart's entry into the hop business. "In the spring of 1871 he [James Stewart] planted one acre of hops, securing the roots from L. F. Thompson, who was plowing his up because the price was only .06 cents per pound. He raised 763 pounds the first year and gave Ezra Meeker one-half for picking, bailing, and drying them. These hops sold for 45 cents per pound in the fall. Thompson, Meeker and Judge Stewart were the only persons raising hops in the territory at that time, but the business rapidly spread."

Larry Kolano, *Puyallup Perspectives* (Tacoma: Graphic Press, 1976), 60, said Romulus Nix planted an acre of hops as early as 1870 but cites no source for this claim. The above sources make no mention of Nix.

5. "Puyallup Valley; Its Excellent Development," *Puget Sound Express*, December 5, 1872, 2.

6. This total likely included the hop yards of Ezra, John V., and Jacob Meeker. Nancy Burr Meeker continued to manage the farm founded by her husband until her death in 1906, probably with Ezra's help for the first few years after Jacob's death. Nancy's two sons from her first marriage helped run the farm.

7. "Hops," *Olympia Daily Pacific Tribune*, July 11, 1872, 2.

8. Blinn was a lumberman who operated a sawmill at Seabeck on Hood Canal.

9. Buerge, 14.

10. Ibid., 13.

11. Ken Keigley, "Summary of Meeker Land Transactions," (Unpublished: Puyallup Historical Society, 2005), 1.

12. On January 11, 1919, Meeker wrote to Clarence Bagley of Seattle complimenting him on finding a copy after a fifteen-year search. In 2011 while looking through the Edward Jay Allen materials at the Hillman Library, University of Pittsburgh, the author found a pristine copy of the booklet. It was undoubtedly a gift from Meeker to Allen, as the two pioneers were friends. Meeker appended a poor quality copy of the booklet to his 1921 work *Seventy Years of Progress in Washington* (Tacoma: Allstrum Printing Company).

13. Meeker and Woodard were both members of the Puget Sound Farmers' Club which met monthly in the Olympia library. Meeker served for a time as chairman of the club. Woodard, like Meeker, was a pioneer of 1852. "Puget Sound Farmers' Club," *Olympia Weekly Pacific Tribune*, January 13, 1872, 4.

14. Beriah Brown (1815-1900) was the editor of the *Portland Herald* from 1866-1868. He moved to Seattle in 1870 and became the mayor of that city in 1878. His primary career was that of newspaper editor, taking on that role in many cities in the west. At that time he had a reputation as one of the best editors in the country. How he and Meeker met is not known.

15. Meeker, *Seventy Years of Progress*, 50.

16. Ibid., 52.

17. Buerge, 17.

18. Keigley, "Meeker Land Transactions," 1. The complete story of this fascinating journey may be found in Meeker's book *Seventy Years of Progress*, 48-54, and in Buerge, 12-21.

19. Keigley, "Meeker Land Transactions," 1.

20. Klootchman is Chinook jargon meaning "woman."

21. "Puget Sound Farmers' Club," *Olympia Weekly Pacific Tribune*, May 11, 1872, 4.

22. The steamship *California* took ten tons of hops that fall from Puget Sound to Portland. "Exports," *Olympia Weekly Pacific Tribune*, October 10, 1872, 3.

23. "Hops and Their Cultivation," *Tacoma Daily Ledger*, July 25, 1894, 2.

24. "Mr. E. Meeker," *Washington Standard*, November 22, 1873, 2. These hops would have been first shipped to San Francisco, and from there sent to New York via the new transcontinental railroad.

25. "New Store," *Tacoma Daily Pacific Tribune*, November 10, 1873, 3.

26. "E. Meeker received 90 packages Oregon produce per steamer *Gussie Telfair*," "Local News," *Tacoma Daily Pacific Tribune*, December 3, 1873, 3.

27. In 1874 Marion married Mary L. Weller, a native of Oregon who was living near Enumclaw with her uncle Alan L. Porter, a longtime Washington Territory resident. Financial success and independence seemed to elude Marion. Throughout much of his adult life he worked for his father. In 1877 he built a water system for his father's Puyallup properties. In 1881 he replaced his father as the Puyallup postmaster. When Meeker purchased a sawmill in 1883, Marion managed it. In 1884 he took on the management of the Meeker Puyallup store, along with a three-year lease of some of his father's hop yards—a lease on which he lost money. In the 1890s he worked as an agent for his father's hop brokerage business, and in 1901 he left his family in Puyallup to spend two years in the Klondike operating and closing down his father's Dawson City store. Marion seemed to handle these assignments competently but could never quite get out from under his father's shadow. He finally struck out on his own in 1907 when he moved his family to southern California.

28. Keigley, "Meeker Land Transactions," 1.

29. Ezra Meeker, *Uncle Ezra's Short Stories for Children* (Tacoma: 1912), 33.

30. "A Voice from the Hop Fields, *Tacoma Herald,* December 10, 1877: 3.

31. Meeker said that he was the exclusive supplier of hops to Weinhard for thirteen out of fourteen years. Meeker, *Busy Life*, 225-226.

32. "Hops," *Tacoma Herald*, July 28, 1877, 2.

33. Michael Tomlan said it cost five dollars a ton to haul hops to Tacoma by wagon in the early 1870s and twenty to twenty-five dollars to ship them to San Francisco. He probably meant Steilacoom as Tacoma barely existed in the early 1870s. Tomlan, *Tinged With Gold*, 104.

34. The initial news reports stated that the *Pacific* struck a rock.

35. The story of the sinking of the *Pacific* is chronicled in the *Seattle Daily Pacific Tribune* of November 8, 10, and 11, 1875.

36. "San Francisco Hop Market," *Tacoma Herald*, October 20, 1877, 3.

37. "The Report," *Puget Sound Weekly Argus*, May 4, 1877, 5.

38. Some growers paid railroad fares for the pickers who came from the southern and eastern parts of the territory. Of course, they preferred to hire those who provided their own transportation.

39. "Local News," *Tacoma Daily Ledger*, August 22, 1883, 4.

40. "Indians as Hop Pickers," *Tacoma Daily Ledger*, October 28, 1894, 1.

41. Paige Sylvia Raibmon, *Authentic Indians: Episodes of Encounter from the Late Nineteenth Century Northwest Coast* (Ann Arbor: Bell & Howell Information and Learning Company, 2001), 153.

42. "Farm and Home," *Seattle Post-Intelligencer*, August 7, 1887, 3.

43. Ezra Meeker, *Uncle Ezra's Short Stories for Children* (Tacoma: 1912), "Hops," 33-34.

44. In maritime terms the head or high point of Puget Sound is its southernmost tip. Everything south of the Puyallup River would be considered up sound and everything north of the river would be considered down sound. The meaning in this passage is that the Indians were coming from the north (down sound), i.e. British Columbia and Alaska.

45. "From the Hop Fields," *Tacoma Herald*, September 29, 1877, 2.

46. Coll Thrush, *Native Seattle: Histories from the Crossing Over Place*, (Seattle: University of Washington Press, 2007), 106-107.

47. "Out in the Hop Fields," *Tacoma Daily Ledger*, September 6, 1889, 5.

48. "Tacoma and Puyallup Valley," *Seattle Daily Pacific Tribune*, September 8, 1875, 3.

49. "Off for the Hop Fields," *Tacoma Herald*, September 6, 1878, 3.

50. "Late News from the Hop Fields," *Tacoma Herald*, September 15, 1877, 2.

51. "Hops," *Tacoma Weekly Pacific Tribune*, October 9, 1874, 2.

52. As mentioned earlier, with the sinking of the *Pacific*, ten percent of this crop went to the bottom of the Pacific Ocean. "Puyallup Hops and Pickers," *Seattle Daily Pacific Tribune*, August 20, 1877, 3.

53. "The Hop Crop," *Washington Standard* (Olympia), September 9, 1876, 2.

54. "Local and News Items," *Washington Standard*, July 22, 1876, 2.

55. "Local and News Brevities," *Washington Standard*, July 25, 1879, 1; Ezra Meeker to Eliza Jane Meeker, 20 April 1882, Meeker Papers, Box 4, Folder 1A; Meeker, *Ventures and Adventures*, 24-25.

56. "Attempt to Burn E. Meeker's Hop Houses," *Tacoma Herald*, September 6, 1878, 3. Burning hop houses seemed to be a valley hazard. Three years after the above incident, this article appeared: "On Wednesday evening a hop-house belonging to Marion Meeker was burned, loss about $1,100, insured for $500. The fire is supposed to be the work of an incendiary." "Puyallup Items," *Pierce County News*, October 5, 1881, 2.

57. "Incendiarism," *Washington Standard*, September 21, 1878, 5.

58. "Hop Growing in Washington Territory," *Pacific Rural Press*, August 26, 1882, 2.

59. General John Sprague was a Northern Pacific Railroad executive and the first mayor of Tacoma. John Hosmer was the manager of the Tacoma Land Company. Harry and Pitt Cooke were brothers and partners of Jay Cooke. Olive Meeker was four years old, not five. She was born October 24, 1869.

60. "Pioneer Reminiscences about the First Railroad," Address prepared for the Commercial Club of Tacoma, December 1913, Meeker Papers, Box 8, Envelope 3.

Notes to Chapter 6: Building a Town

1. In 1862 Meeker's brother-in-law, Jesse Dunlap, carried the mail from Fort Steilacoom to Franklin once a week for twenty dollars a month. Price and Anderson, *Puyallup*, 26.

2. Meeker, *Busy Life*, 205.

3. W. P. Bonney, *History of Pierce County Washington*, Volume I (Chicago: Pioneer Historical Publishing Company, 1927), 395; and "Guy Reed Ramsey," edited by Jeanne Engerman, *Postmarked Washington, Pierce Count.* (Tacoma: Washington State Historical Society, 1981), 8.

4. Ramsey, 8.

5. Bonney, 392.

6. "The Pierce County Fair," *Tacoma Herald*, May 20, 1877, 3.

7. Bonney, 405.

8. Amanda received her teaching certificate in 1864. Bowden, Angie Burt, *Early Schools of Washington Territory* (Seattle: Lowman and Hanford Company, 1935), 250–51 and 262.

9. By 1874 John Meeker had become the county school superintendent.

10. Charles Henry Carey, "Hon. Thomas Ray Coon." *The History of Oregon, Volume II*, (Chicago-Portland: The Pioneer Historical Publishing Co., 1922), 653–55.

11. See the previous chapter for more information about Porter.

12. Thomas Ray Coon, "A School of Fifty Years Ago." Lori Price Collection, Puyallup Historical Society.

13. It is not known whether the school in Franklin was in session at this time. If so, it seems likely that Mrs. Meeker would have feted them instead, since this was the school her children attended. Perhaps the Franklin schoolchildren traveled to Elhi with Mrs. Meeker to join the party there. "School at Elhi, Pierce County, Washington Territory 1873-74. Taught by Miss Delia McNeil," Lori Price Collection, Puyallup Historical Society.

14. Charles Henry Cary, "Hon. Thomas Ray Coon." *The History of Oregon*. Chicago-Portland: The Pioneer Historical Publishing Co., Volume II, 1922: 653-5.

15. It is unknown if the Elhi school was discontinued with the departure of Mrs. Coon.

16. "Franklin School—1874 Mrs. Delia M. Coon, Teacher," Lori Price Collection, Puyallup Historical Society.

17. Bonney, 403.

18. "Tribute to My Wife," Meeker Papers, Box 10, Envelope 1.

19. Bonney, 421-23.

20. Ezra Meeker to Gordon Powers, January 27, 1912, Meeker Papers, Box 6, Volume 16.

21. "Here and Hereabouts," *Pierce County News*, November 9, 1881, 3.

22. "Here and Hereabouts," *Pierce County News*, November 23, 1881, 3.

23. "State of Washington," *Pierce County News*, November 23, 1881, 3.

24. "Council Proceedings," *Pierce County News*, November 23, 1881, 3.

25. "Mr. Meeker's Letter," *Tacoma Daily Ledger*, October 17, 1885, 2.

26. Larry Kolano, *Puyallup Perspectives* (Tacoma: Graphic Press, 1976), 69.

27. "Mr. Meeker's Letter," *Tacoma Daily Ledger*, October 17, 1885, 2.

28. "Puyallup Items," *Pierce County News*, November 30, 1881, 3.

29. Ibid.

30. Hunt, *History of Tacoma*, 279.

31. "Small Pox Expense," *Pierce County News*, January 18, 1882, 2.

Notes to Chapter 7: The Feud

1. "Farquharson, A. S., reminiscence." MsSC 137A, Washington State Historical Society, 1913.

2. Staves were the strips of wood used to make wooden barrels. The mill would make two of the parts needed to create a wooden barrel—the side slats or staves and the hoops that bound them together. It is not clear if the mill was also making the end of the barrels, although an article in the *Tacoma Herald* suggests this was the case. "All About Puyallup," *Tacoma Herald*, June 16, 1877, 2.

3. "Pacific Slope News," *Puget Sound Weekly Argus* (Port Townsend, WA), November 24, 1876, 1.

4. "All About Puyallup," *Tacoma Herald*, June 16, 1877, 2.

5. "Puyallup Water Works," *Tacoma Herald*, July 28, 1877, 2.

6. "The water used for mechanical and other purposes is brought one and one half miles in a flume. The works are owned and controlled by Ezra Meeker." "Puyallup Items," *Northern Star*, October 5, 1878, 4.

7. "Puyallup," *Tacoma Herald*, September 8, 1877, 3. This article describes the Puyallup railroad station and Meeker's store. The closing date of Meeker's store in Tacoma is unknown but the two events likely coincided with each other.

8. "Puget Sound Manufacturing Co.," *Tacoma Herald*, September 15, 1877, 3. Farquharson's stave factory was referred to as the Puget Sound Manufacturing Company. Meeker formally deeded the company the land from Main to Pioneer and from Meridian to West 3rd on July 19, 1877. Keigley, "Meeker Land Transactions," 1.

9. "Notes from Puyallup," *Tacoma Herald*, March 15, 1878, 3.

10. This occurred in October 1877 according to Farquharson's manuscript. This was just one month after the stave factory opened. Farquharson, Folder 5.

11. *Ezra Meeker vs. Puget Sound Manufacturing Company*, Case PRC-824, Washington State Archives.

12. Bonney, 407.

13. *Washington Territory vs. E. Meeker, F. M. Slythe, F. O. Meeker and Robert Wilson*, PCR-430, Washington State Archives.

14. Alexander Farquharson married Roxanne Wagner, daughter of William Wagner of Yelm, on October 7, 1877. Herbert Hunt, *Washington West of the Cascades, Vol. III* (Chicago: S.J. Clarke Company, 1917), 298-302.

15. "Puyallup Valley," *Tacoma News* (Weekly), March 22, 1883, 2.

16. "From Puyallup," *Tacoma Daily Ledger*, March 27, 1886, 7.

17. "Puyallup Pickings," *Tacoma Daily Ledger*, June 22, 1886, 6.

18. "Ezra Meeker Days Are Here Again," *Tacoma Times*, July 18, 1941, 12.

19. Meeker, *Busy Life*, 203-204.

20. "After Many Years," *Tacoma Times*, May 9, 1935, 18. "Farquharson Breaks up Ezra Meeker's Hanging Party," *Tacoma Times*, August 6, 1941, 16.

21. Farquharson, Folder 6. Farquharson apparently wanted his version of this incident to become historical fact. The year before Herbert Hunt, in his *History of Tacoma*, published Farquharson's version of Meeker's 1886 run for Congress, thus putting that fallacy into the historical record. On November 22, 1917, Farquharson wrote a long letter to Hunt, who was then preparing his *History of Washington*, repeating the Sproul story contained in his manuscript and suggested that Sproul was persecuted by several prominent Tacoma businessmen as a way to obtain his Tacoma homestead claim and his Carbonado mine property. Farquharson, Folder 7. Farquharson also failed to note that Mrs. Taylor, in whose hotel he supposedly held Sproul, was a Meeker in-law, whose daughter was married to Meeker's son, Marion. This would seem an odd place to protect Sproul from Meeker's wrath.

22. *Washington Territory vs. Robert Sproul*, PCR 317, Washington State Archives.

23. "Burned Barns," *Seattle Daily Pacific Tribune*, September 13, 1878, 3.

24. Washington State Archives, Case #317, *Territory of Washington vs. Robert Sproul*.

25. Dr. Gandy was elected to the territorial legislature in 1879.

26. "The Sproule Murder Case," *Spokane Falls Weekly Review*, March 6, 1886, 3.

27. Sproul, however, did not ultimately escape the noose. In 1886 he was hanged for murder in Victoria, British Columbia, likely on trumped-up charges according to both Farquharson and Gandy. "Sproule's Execution," *Tacoma Daily Ledger* of November 3 1886, 5.

28. Farquharson, Folder 3.

29. Larsen, *Slick as a Mitten: Ezra Meeker's Klondike Enterprise*, 36-37.

30. Meeker, *Pioneer Reminiscences*, 12.

31. Ezra Meeker to Eliza Egbert, May 7, 1903, Meeker Papers, Box 6, Vol. 2.

Notes to Chapter 8: The Hop King

1. The Boatmans came to Puyallup over the Oregon Trail in the early 1850s and were one of the first families to settle in the valley.

2. "Puyallup, W. T.," *Tacoma News* (Weekly), November 9, 1882, 3.

3. "Puyallup Valley," *Tacoma News* (Weekly), April 5, 1883, 2.

4. "Personal and Social," *Tacoma News* (Weekly), October 12, 1882, 3.

5. While written in New York, *Hop Culture* was published in Washington.

6. "Washington Territory Hops," *Willamette Farmer* (Salem, OR), August 31, 1883, 1.

7. Ibid.

8. Eben married Carrie Meeker in 1879. He attended the Territorial University and was admitted to the bar in 1878. In addition to working for his father-in-law, Eben served as the Clerk of the City of Seattle for seven years, from 1878 to the summer of 1885, and at various times as vice-presidents of the Washington Title Insurance Company and the Seattle Trust Company, and as manager and vice-president of Osborne, Tremper & Co., Inc.

9. Ezra Meeker to Eliza Jane Meeker, February 25, 1883, Meeker Papers, Box 4, Folder 1C.

10. "Hop Wrinkles," *Tacoma Daily Ledger*, May 17, 1883, 2.

11. "Puyallup Valley Letter," *Tacoma News* (Weekly), January 11, 1883, 2.

12. "Puyallup Valley," *Tacoma News* (Weekly), June 14, 1883, 2.

13. "Hop Acreage—1883," *Tacoma News* (Weekly), May 24, 1883, 2.

14. "The Acreage of Hops," *Tacoma Daily Ledger*, May 18, 1883, 4 and "Local Matters." *Tacoma Daily Ledger*, June 14, 1883, 4.

15. "The Hop Outlook," Irvin Terry of Syracuse, N.Y. to A. C. Campbell of W.T., April 17, 1883, in the *Tacoma Daily Ledger*, May 8, 1883, 3.

16. "The Acreage of Hops," *Tacoma Daily Ledger*, May 18, 1883, 4.

17. "Instead of Hops," *Tacoma Daily Ledger*, August 1, 1883, 2.

18. "Hops," *Tacoma Daily Ledger*, August 15, 1883, 4.

19. "Fascination of Hop Culture," *Tacoma Daily Ledger*, August 28, 1883, 3.

20. "Telegraphic Hop Report," *Tacoma Daily Ledger*, August 25, 1883, 3.

21. The taxes are documented in Hunt, *History of Tacoma*, 306. The two hundred acres are documented in the November 1884 issue of *The West Shore* magazine. The cost and average sale price come from the same issue of *The West Shore* and also from a long article written by Meeker published as "The State Hop Crop," *Seattle Post-Intelligencer*, August 26, 1891, 5. The remainder is basic mathematics.

Notes to Chapter 9: The London Hop Trade

1. "CIF," Meeker Papers, Box 10, Envelope 1.

2. The hop broker who sent Meeker the CIF cable was identified in the *Yakima Herald*, November 17, 1892, 3. "J. R. Short, of the firm of Thomas & Short, hop factors of London, was in the city Tuesday endeavoring to effect arrangements by which his house could handle Yakima hops. Messrs. Thomas & Short lay claim to being the first importers of Pacific coast hops, having commenced to handle these 'goods' thirty years ago. Mr. Short is of the opinion that he also handled the first hops sent to London from this state, being the crop of Ezra Meeker, of Puyallup." "CIF." Meeker Papers, Box 10, Envelope 1.

3. "Puyallup Items," *Tacoma Daily Ledger*, December 10, 1884, 3.

4. "Letter From Ezra Meeker," *Tacoma Daily Ledger*, January 29, 1885, 4.

5. "CIF," Meeker Papers, Box 10, Envelope 1.

6. Ibid.

7. "Letter From Ezra Meeker," *Tacoma Daily Ledger*, February 3, 1885, 4.

8. Ibid.

9. "CIF," Meeker Papers, Box 10, Envelope 1.

10. "Hops," *Tacoma Daily Ledger*, August 5, 1885, 6.

11. "A London Letter," *Tacoma Daily Ledger*, February 10, 1885, 4.

12. "Letter From Germany," *Tacoma Daily Ledger*, March 11, 1885, 4.

13. Ibid.

14. Ibid.

15. Ibid.

16. Ibid.

17. "Letter From Paris," *Tacoma Daily Ledger*, March 25, 1885, 6.

18. "Local News," *Tacoma Daily Ledger*, March 19, 1885, 5.

Notes to Chapter 10: Diversification

1. "Puyallup Pickings," *Tacoma Daily Ledger*, July 31, 1885, 6.

2. "Local. The First Boring." *Tacoma Daily Ledger*, August 23, 1885, 4.

3. "Discovering Gas." *Tacoma Daily Ledger*, September 30, 1885, 1.

4. Hunt, *History of Tacoma*, 315.

5. Meeker, *Busy Life*, 230-231.

6. Meeker, *Busy Life*, 230. The *Tacoma Daily News* offered the following confirmation of Meeker's *Busy Life* story. "Mr. E. Meeker has shipped ten tons of beets raised in the Sound country to California where they will be manufactured into sugar for exhibition at the New Orleans Exposition. They were shipped from Seattle and are on their way to San Francisco." "Brieflets," *Tacoma Daily News*, October 10, 1885, 3.

7. "Mr. Fred S. Meeker has returned to Puyallup from California where he has been studying the scientific parts of beet sugar manufacturing. He will look after his father's large interests here while the latter is at New Orleans." "Puyallup Pickings." *Tacoma Daily Ledger*, November 3, 1885, 3.

8. Meeker, *Busy Life,* 231.

9. "The Iowa Editors," *Tacoma Daily News,* June 16, 1885, 4.

10. "Puyallup Pickings," *Tacoma Daily Ledger,* September 2, 1885, 3.

11. "Puyallup Pickings," *Tacoma Daily Ledger.* November 3, 1885, 3.

12. "Puyallup Hops," *Tacoma Daily News,* October 19, 1885, 1.

Notes to Chapter 11: The Chinese Expulsion

1. Three secondary sources offer an in-depth look at these events. *Puget's Sound* by Murray Morgan, 212-252, gives a comprehensive account of Tacoma's Chinese expulsion and discusses Meeker's opposition. *Washington Territory*, by Robert Ficken, 190-195, offers an insight into how indispensible the 3,000-plus Chinese workers were to the territory's economy, highlights the racial bigotry that poured forth from many of the territory's white citizens, and gives a graphic account of the murders of Chinese hop pickers in the territory. *Northwest Gateway* by Archie Binns tells the story with an emphasis on events in Seattle.

2. Murray Morgan, *Puget's Sound: A Narrative of Early Tacoma and the Southern Sound.* (Seattle: University of Washington Press, 1979), 221-223.

3. "The Chinese Question," *Tacoma Daily Ledger*, October 6, 1885, 4.

4. Morgan, 232-233.

5. Morgan, 233.

6. Various accounts supply different numbers for the casualties. Despite the confession of one of the white murderers, the jury took just thirty minutes to acquit the accused. "Trouble in the Hop Fields." *Tacoma Daily News,* September 9, 1885, 3. Morgan, 227. Raibmon, 154.

7. Morgan, 233.

8. Comerford was fired by the publisher of the *Ledger* when he refused to stop his anti-Chinese tirades in the newspaper. "Mr. Comerford's Address, True Inwardness of the Mongolian Question, Ezra Meeker and the Parsons." *Tacoma Daily News*, October 19, 1885, 3.

9. "Puyallup Deputies, Men Sworn to Preserve the Peace During the Chinese Agitation." *Tacoma Daily News,* October 21, 1885, 3.

10. "Brieflets," *Tacoma Daily News,* October 19, 1885, 3.

11. "At Puyallup, An Enthusiastic Demonstration among a Law Abiding People." *Tacoma Daily News,* October 22, 1885, 4.

12. "The Chinese Go, From the Village of Sumner—Thirteen Mongolians Obey the Order of a Committee—Arriving at Tacoma Under Escort." *Tacoma Daily Ledger*, November 6, 1885, 5.

13. "Arrested for Assault," *Tacoma Daily Ledger*, November 12, 1885, 5.

14. Morgan, 243.

15. "Coming Home," *Tacoma Daily Ledger*, November 12, 1885, 1 and Morgan, 246.

16. "Mr. Fred S. Meeker has returned to Puyallup from California where he has been studying the scientific parts of beet sugar manufacturing. He will look after his father's large interests here while the latter is at New Orleans." "Puyallup Pickings," *Tacoma Daily Ledger*, November 3, 1885, 3.

Notes to Chapter 12: The American Exhibition at New Orleans

1. The official title was the North Central and South American Exposition at New Orleans, November 10, 1885, to March 31, 1886. It was more generally referred to as the American Exposition at New Orleans.

2. "American Exhibition at New Orleans," *Tacoma Daily Ledger*, August 13, 1885, 6.

3. Ibid.

4. Pamela Hale to Eliza Jane Meeker, January 31, 1886, Meeker Papers, Box 5, Folder 1.

5. "Report of E. Meeker," *Tacoma Daily Ledger*, July 20, 1886, 6.

6. Ibid.

7. Ibid.

8. "Washington Territory. Enjoyable Entertainment at Commissioner Meeker's Head-quarters," *Tacoma Daily Ledger*, April 6, 1886, 6.

9. "The Exposition Closes," *Tacoma Daily Ledger*, April 11, 1886, 4.

10. "Report on the London American Exposition," Meeker Papers, Box 13, Folder 4.

11. "Mr. Ezra Meeker," *Tacoma Daily Ledger*, June 27, 1886, 2.

12. "Report of E. Meeker," *Tacoma Daily Ledger*, July 20, 1886, 6.

13. Catalogue of exhibits of Washington Territory at the American Exposition, New Orleans, November 10, 1885, to April 1, 1886. Published by Press of W. B. Stansbury & Co. 1886. Pacific Northwest History Collection. WSU MASC. F891 .C38 1886. WSU 000680540.

14. "Puyallup Notes," *Tacoma Daily Ledger*, May 12, 1886, 6.

Notes to Chapter 13: Hop Tramping

1. "The Outlook For Hops," *Tacoma Daily Ledger*, June 29, 1886, 6.

2. "Personal and Social," *Tacoma Daily Ledger*, June 20, 1886, 5.

3. "The Outlook For Hops," *Tacoma Daily Ledger*, June 29, 1886, 6.

4. "Personal," *Tacoma Daily Ledger*, June 26, 1886, 5.

5. "The Outlook For Hops," *Tacoma Daily Ledger*, June 29, 1886, 6.

6. "A Hop Light Lew," *Tacoma Daily Ledger*, July 16, 1886, 4.

7. "A Horoscope 'O Hops," *Tacoma Daily Ledger*, July 20, 1886, 4.

8. "The Freight On Hops," *Tacoma Daily Ledger*, July 22, 1886, 4.

9. "Puyallup Pickings," *Tacoma Daily Ledger*, June 1, 1886, 6.

10. "True Blue Republican," *Tacoma Daily Ledger*, September 12, 1886, 5.

11. "A Few Remarks," *Tacoma Daily Ledger*, October 12, 1886, 5.

12. "Tribute to my Wife," Meeker Papers, Box 10, Envelope 1. A persistent story in Meeker circles and on the internet is that after touring Europe Eliza Jane came home and demanded a home similar to those she saw in Europe. As Eliza Jane had not yet been to Europe and would not visit the continent until 1893, and since the mansion is not of a European design, the story is obviously false. But it is a story that refuses to die.

Notes to Chapter 14: Meeker for Congress

1. Voorhees' name was often spelled Vorhees in contemporary accounts. The Congressional Biographical Directory spells it Voorhees.

2. Farquharson, Folder 3.

3. http://www.feefhs.org/links/other/1886nenc/86gar1.html.

4. Reprinted in "Notes and Comments," *Tacoma Daily Ledger*, September 8, 1886, 2.

5. "Republican Convention," *Seattle Post-Intelligencer* September 9, 1886, 1.

6. "Republican Convention," *Seattle Post-Intelligencer*, September 14, 1886, 1.

7. "Claiming the Honor," *Seattle Daily Press*, September 10, 1886, 2.

8. The last line in Hunt's history stated: "At the November election, Bradshaw defeated Vorhees." Hunt, *History of Tacoma*, 390. This is one more item that Hunt got wrong in his telling of Meeker's run for Congress. Charles Stewart Voorhees (1853-1909) was, in fact, reelected. "Biographical Directory of the United States Congress, 1774-Present," http://bioguide.congress.gov; http://www.historylink.org/index.cfm?DisplayPage=output.cfm&file_id=5463.

9. "Puyallup Pickings," *Tacoma Daily Ledger*, June 21, 1886, 6.

Notes to Chapter 15: Farm and Home

1. "The town council met last night. The main subject was the question of sewage…J. V. Meeker expressed his opinion that the city would have to content itself with a system of drainage and adopt the dry earth closet system." From "Puyallup Pickings," (Tacoma) *Daily Ledger*, December 6, 1888, 3.

2. "Farm and Home," *Seattle Post-Intelligencer*, October 16, 1887, 3.

3. Over the years Meeker acquired much more land than his original 160-acre homestead. Various parcels like Junction Farm seemed to acquire nicknames. Many of the land holdings are documented in Keigley, "Meeker Land Transactions."

4. "Farm and Home," *Seattle Post-Intelligencer*, July 24, 1887, 3.

5. "Farm and Home," *Seattle Post-Intelligencer*, August 7, 1887, 3.

6. "Acres of Hops," *Tacoma Daily Ledger*, July 7, 1887, 3.

7. Ibid.

8. "Washington Territory," *Pacific Rural Press*, November 5, 1887, Volume 34, No. 19, 363.

Notes to Chapter 16: A Woman's Right to Vote

1. Meeker, *Seventy Years of Progress*, 150.

2. The Olympia newspaper gave lengthy coverage to the convention, its officers and speakers, but did not list those who attended. "Woman Suffrage Convention," *Olympia Weekly Standard*, November 11, 1871, 1+.

3. The document is kept at the University of Washington. When unrolled it is nearly five feet long. Much of the handwriting is exceptionally difficult to make out. "Petition Supporting Woman Suffrage Presented to the Washington Territory Constitutional Convention June 17, 1878, Petition of 581 citizens." Pacific Northwest Historical Documents Collection, Accession No. 4284-1, Box 3, Digital ID No. PNW00539, University of Washington Libraries, Special Collections Division.

4. The 1893 Puyallup city directory listed her as the widow of James Ross and the proprietor of a millinery store.

5. Besides being fellow postmasters (Ezra at Puyallup and Elizabeth at Sumner) Mrs. Spinning seemed to be a family friend to the point of exchanging Christmas presents.

6. William and Maynard Crounse are listed in the 1893 city directory as a drayman and a carpenter.

7. The 1893 city directory listed Thomas S. Hubbard as a harness and saddle maker.

8. "Women at Work," *Tacoma Daily Ledger*, April 18, 1889, 3.

9. Clara Bewick Colby, "Far-Off Sounds, Number IV." *Woman's Tribune*, May 11, 1889, 164.

10. "Farm Field and Fireside." *Tacoma Daily Ledger*, August 9, 1896, 12.

11. Ida Husted Harper, *The Life and Work of Susan B. Anthony: Including Public Addresses, Her Own Letters and Many From Her Contemporaries Over Fifty Years*, Volume II, (Indianapolis: The Hallenbeck Press, 1898), 676.

12. There is correspondence in the Meeker Papers between Abigail Scott Duniway and Ezra Meeker praising each other's work. And there are several letters from Ezra to his daughter Carrie and his granddaughter Olive Osborne about voting, all seemingly approving. Meeker's good friends, George Himes and Elizabeth Laughlin Lord, were deeply involved in the suffrage movement in Oregon. Thus far, little beyond this has surfaced.

13. "Puyallup," *Tacoma Daily Ledger*, May 7, 1890, 5.

14. "Echoes of the Visit," *Tacoma News*, May 7, 1891, 1.

15. "The News of Puyallup." *Tacoma Daily News*, July 22, 1891, 8.

16. "Farm, Field and Fireside," *Tacoma Daily Ledger*, August 23, 1896, 12.

17. "Four Score, but She is Still Fighting," *Seattle Times*, September 29, 1907, 3.

Notes to Chapter 17: Society News and Real Estate

1. "Puyallup," *Tacoma Daily Ledger*, May 29, 1890, 6.

2. "Puyallup," *Tacoma Daily Ledger*, June 11, 1890, 6. Martin Davidson Ballard (1832-1907) and his brother Dr. David Wesley Ballard (1824-1883) crossed the Nebraska plains with Meeker in 1852. When Oliver Meeker fell ill early in the trip, Ezra pulled out of the wagon train and waited for his brother to recover. The Ballards went on to Oregon. David Ballard was appointed the third governor of Idaho Territory by President Andrew Johnson in 1866. After many adventures in the west, in 1883 Martin founded the Seattle Hardware Store. Dayton Ballard was a third brother, visiting from Nebraska. The complete story of the Ballards and Meeker may be found in the spring 2012 issue of *Northwest Trails Journal* at www.octa-trails.org/chapters/northwest/newsletter.php.

3. "Puyallup Personals," *Tacoma Daily Ledger*, August 5, 1890, 4.

4. "Puyallup Personals," *Tacoma Daily Ledger*, July 16, 1890, 3.

5. "For Sale at Puyallup," *Tacoma Daily Ledger*, January 25, 1888, 3.

6. "Now on the Market," *Tacoma Daily Ledger*, March 23, 1888, 4.

7. "Puyallup Pickings," *Tacoma Daily Ledger*, December 4, 1888, 6.

8. "Puyallup Pickings," *Tacoma Daily Ledger*, December 7, 1888, 3.

9. Fred Meeker sent a report on the mansion progress to his father in December 1889. "Mason began to put on the 2nd coat of paint today. I have not seen it yet but will report how it looks later." Fred Meeker to Ezra Meeker, December 23, 1889, Meeker Papers, Box 4 Folder 1A.

10. "Puget Sound Locals," *Tacoma Daily Ledger*, April 1, 1888, 5.

11. William Templeton of Brownsville, Oregon, married Ella Meeker in 1872. Besides running the family farm, Billy as he was called, served for years as Meeker's Willamette Valley agent, buying and selling hops for E. Meeker & Company. In 1895 Templeton was elected a representative to the Oregon legislature. According to documents in the Templeton collection held in the Brownsville Museum, Billy and his brothers obtained a number of hop roots from Meeker, and from these roots sprang the Willamette Valley hop industry. In fact, the beginnings of the Willamette Valley hop industry predated the Templetons. George Leasure raised the first commercial crop in the valley in 1869 and others followed. Kopp, Peter, "Hop Fever in the Willamette Valley," *Oregon Historical Quarterly* 112, no. 4 (Winter 2011): 411.

12. Meeker's brokerage business will be discussed more fully in Chapter 20.

13. For a number of years E. Meeker & Company published a monthly one-page hop circular giving the current news about the business and the company. The company also published a *Hop Annual and Hand Book* on January 1 of each year. This pocket-sized paperback was a primer on how to successfully grow hops. Inside were pages of information on such mundane topics as proper methods of cultivation, how to train hop vines, and how to dry and bale hops properly. At the end of the handbook was an assessment of the previous year and an outlook for the future.

14. The *Ledger* was likely referring to Fort Rupert, British Columbia, home to the Kwakiutl Indians.

15. Meeker and Campbell were joint owners of a 183 acre farm, of which fifty were in hops. They divided the farm in 1890. "The News of Puyallup: A Farm Divided," *Tacoma Daily News*, October 20, 1890, 1.

16. "Out in the Hop Fields," *Tacoma Daily Ledger*, September 6, 1889, 5.

17. "Puyallup," *Tacoma Daily Ledger*, May 20, 1890, 3.

18. Mrs. Francis Victor Fuller, *Atlantis Arisen or, Talks of a Tourist about Oregon and Washington* (Philadelphia: J. B. Lippincott Company, 1891), 300.

19. "Farm and Home," *Seattle Post Intelligencer*, October 16, 1887, 3.

20. "Farm and Home," *Seattle Post-Intelligencer*, August 7, 1887, 3.

21. "Hops for Japan," *Daily Alta California*, October 6, 1887, 5.

22. "Hops for Japan," *Tacoma News*, September 29, 1888, 4.

23. "The first shipment of 1000 pounds went to Yokohama, and are to fill orders that Americans are taking from the natives, who are, according to the American account, gradually acquiring a taste for beer." "From the Hop Fields," *Tacoma Daily Ledger*, September 30, 1889, 3.

24. "Hops for Japan," *Tacoma News*, September 29, 1888, 4.

25. "Journal of my trip from Puyallup to London Written Expressly for <u>My Dear Wife</u> E. J. Meeker," November 11, 1895, Meeker Papers, Box 4, Folder 6B, 52.

26. Fred and Clara met in California as Fred attended the University of California at Berkeley. They were married on March 15, 1886, in Portland, Oregon, while Ezra and Eliza Jane worked the New Orleans Exposition. Their story is told more fully in Dennis Larsen, *Slick as a Mitten: Ezra Meeker's Klondike Enterprise* (Pullman: Washington State University Press, 2009).

27. Clara Meeker to Ezra Meeker, March 14, 1890, Meeker Papers, Box 4, Folder 16.

28. "Puyallup Personals," *Tacoma Daily Ledger*, June 26, 1890, 5.

29. "Puyallup Brevities," *Tacoma Daily Ledger*, July 31, 1890, 4.

30. "Puyallup Brevities," *Tacoma Daily Ledger*, August 5, 1890, 4. Amanda Clement (Meeker) Spinning's brother, Henry Newell Clement, lived in San Francisco, California. His two children, Jabish, age 20 and Ada age 13, Frank Meeker's cousins, were the visitors being feted.

31. See Chapter 18 for the story of Mayor Meeker.

32. Roderick McDonald emigrated from Scotland in 1888, made his way to Puget Sound and in 1889 became Ezra Meeker's bookkeeper. After his marriage to Olive Meeker Roderick moved out of his bookkeeping job and into more of a partnership in several of his father-in-law's business ventures. Roderick's story is fully told in Larsen, *Slick as a Mitten*.

33. "Double Celebration." *Tacoma Daily Ledger*, October 16, 1890, 5.

34. "News From Puyallup," *Tacoma Daily Ledger*, December 10, 1890, 3.

35. "News From Puyallup," *Tacoma Daily Ledger*, February 4, 1891, 6.

36. "The News of Puyallup," *Tacoma Daily News*, February 10, 1891, 6.

Notes to Chapter 18: "Inclined to be Pugnacious"

1. "Puyallup Happening," *Tacoma Daily Ledger*, February 19, 1890, 5.

2. Price and Anderson, *Puyallup*, 47-49.

3. "Puyallup Election," *Tacoma Daily Ledger*, August 19, 1890, 4.

4. "Puyallup Fire," *Tacoma Daily News*, September 17, 1890, 1.

5. Price and Anderson, *Puyallup*, 48-49.

6. "The News of Puyallup," *Tacoma Daily News*, December 2, 1891, 5.

7. "Alleged Fraud in Election," *Tacoma News*, December 17, 1891, 1.

8. "News About the City," *Puyallup Citizen*, December 9, 1892, 4; and "Populists Carry Puyallup," *Tacoma Daily Ledger*, December 7, 1892, 1.

9. *Meeker et ux. v. City of Puyallup* (Supreme Court of Washington, Feb. 17, 1893). Dedication of Park—Change of Grantee. The court ruled the gift was made to the public, and that the city indeed represented that public and that the city had sufficiently complied with the conditions of the gift.

10. "The News of Puyallup," *Tacoma Daily News*, February 22, 1893, 5.

11. Some of these exhibits were truly unique. "Any of the pioneers who came to the Territory before 1870 who will send a lock of their hair to Mrs. N. J. Ross will greatly assist her in completing her picture of Mount Tacoma, to be made from the hair of pioneers, which she is making for the exposition. By a key attached to the picture any pioneer can find his lock of hair, name and date of arrival." "The News of Puyallup," *Tacoma Daily News*, August 26, 1891, 5.

12. "All Are Enthusiastic," *Tacoma Daily Ledger*, March 27, 1891, 4.

13. "The News of Puyallup," *Tacoma Daily News*, June 16, 1891, 8.

14. "The Washington Building." *Yakima Herald*, July 9, 1891, 3.

15. "Ezra Meeker has returned from his trip to Chicago." "The News of Puyallup," *Tacoma Daily News*, July 29, 1891, 8.

16. "Ezra Meeker," *Yakima Herald*, September 10, 1891, 2.

17. "The Press is After the Scalp of E. S. Meany," *Yakima Herald*, December 22, 1892, 2.

18. "Charges By Meeker," *Tacoma Daily Ledger*, February 5, 1893, 5; "World's Fair Inquiry." *Tacoma Daily Ledger*, February 10, 1893, 1; "Where the Fund Went," *Tacoma Daily Ledger*, February 15, 1893, 1.

Notes to Chapter 19: Railroads, Swindles, and the Troubled Life of Frank Meeker

1. Spinning apparently went by the name Frank, rather than Ben, as that is how he is listed in later census records.

2. "Off to College," *Daily Pacific Tribune* (Olympia, WA), November 23, 1872, 3.

3. This August 18, 1866, Deed of Trust from Amanda C. Meeker to E. Meeker for Frank O. Meeker may be found in the Puyallup Historical Society's collection.

4. The exam included questions that required knowledge of algebra, geometry, trigonometry, English grammar, French, German, Greek, Latin, and physiology.

5. A broader glimpse of Frank's college years can be found in Thomas Hewett Waterman, *Cornell University Register for 1877-78* and *Cornell University: A History*. Ithaca, 1905.

6. It is quite likely that Frank Meeker, for the most part home-schooled by his mother and Uncle John, was the first Washington Territorial resident to graduate from an Ivy League college.

7. Oliver died November 22, 1978, in Los Angeles. Felix died in nearby Reseda in May 1972.

8. Ken Keigley, "Meeker Land Transactions," 3. (The late Ken Keigley, a descendent of Ezra's brother John Meeker, spent years transcribing and cataloging the various legal documents located at the Meeker Mansion in Puyallup. It was his work that enabled the two of us to piece together Frank Meeker's complex story.)

9. After her husband's death Louise Ackerson remained close to the Meekers, and in 1893 she accompanied them to the Chicago World's Fair. In 1905 she financed the publication of Meeker's book *Pioneer Reminiscences*.

10. Levant F. Thompson was one of the oldest hop growers in the Puyallup Valley. George McAllister worked for the *Ledger* as a printer and reporter.

11. "Twenty-Five Years Ago, Tacoma, March 22, 1889. Election Among Indians on Question of Opening the Puyallup Reservation to the Puyallup Valley Railroad," *Daily Oregonian*, March 23, 1914, 6.

12. "Bribery is Charged," *Tacoma Daily News*, March 22, 1889, 4. The bribery story was covered in full by the *Tacoma Daily News* in stories printed on March 22 and March 23, 1889. The *Ledger* offered a brief story on March 22.

13. "That Alleged Bribery," *Tacoma Daily Ledger*, March 23, 1889, 4.

14. The various legal documents cited in this chapter were catalogued by Ken Keigley and arranged in an unpublished document titled "Timeline of the Tacoma Puyallup Railroad Company."

15. Apparently Meeker's efforts reached as far as the presidency. Although President Harrison discussed opening the Indian Reservation in his May 6, 1891, address to the citizens of Puyallup, it was rather too little, too late for the railroad. See Chapter 16.

16. George McAllister to Ezra Meeker, February 14, 1890, Meeker Papers, Box 5, Folder 1.

17. "Tacoma & Puyallup," *Tacoma Daily Ledger*, May 5, 1890, 3.

18. "Puyallup," *Tacoma Daily Ledger*, June 14, 1890, 6.

19. "Rumble of the Railroads," *Tacoma Daily News*, June 27, 1890: 8.

20. "Tacoma & Puyallup. The Line to Be Completed by Middle of June," *Tacoma Daily Ledger*, May 5, 1890, 3.

21. "Tacoma to Puyallup," *Tacoma Daily Ledger*, June 30, 1890, 8.

22. "Puyallup Is Hustling," *Tacoma Daily Ledger*, July 16, 1890, 3.

23. Private communication from Ken Keigley to Dennis Larsen, December 13, 2012.

24. Fred Meeker to Ezra Meeker, April 5, 1890, Meeker Papers, Box 4, Folder 16.

25. Full Page Advertisement, *Tacoma Daily Ledger*, June 21, 1890, 6. The advertising that started in May began, "The Garden of Earth. If you buy a lot out there you won't go hungry next winter no matter what happens." *Tacoma Daily Ledger*, May 15, 1890, 3.

26. "Meeker Meets Defeat," *Tacoma Daily News*, September 3, 1895, 3.

27. "Summons," *Tacoma Daily News*, July 16, 1894, 2.

28. "South Enders Kick," *Tacoma Daily News*, November 21, 1892, 1.

29. "To Sell the Road," *Tacoma Daily News*, February 2, 1893, 7.

30. "Puyallup News," *Tacoma Daily Ledger*, October 25, 1894, 1.

31. A. L. Polk & Co., Publisher, *Tacoma City Directory 1893, Including Puyallup, Sumner and Steilacoom* (Tacoma: Puget Sound Printing Co., 1893), 86.

32. *Les Pedens, London & San Francisco Bank vs. Frank O. Meeker, Ettella W. Meeker, his wife; Tacoma & Puyallup Railroad Company, a corporation; Otis Sprague, as assignee of the Tacoma & Puyallup Railroad Company; Ezra M. Meeker and Eliza J. Meeker, his wife; and Roderick McDonald and Olive McDonald, his wife.* Keigley, "Timeline of Tacoma Puyallup Railroad Co.," 2-3.

33. Radebaugh in his retirement wrote a serialized history of early Tacoma that appeared every Saturday in the *Tacoma News Tribune* from April 22 to September 28, 1922. "Veteran Tacoma Newspaper Founder Writes Reminiscences of Early Days." *Tacoma News Tribune*, April 22, 1922, 1.

34. Louisa's parents were members of Dr. Wilhelm Keil's communal living colony, established in Bethel, Missouri, in 1844. The colony immigrated to Willapa Bay on the west coast of Washington in 1855, traveling over the Oregon Trail in the famous wagon train led by Dr. Keil's oldest son, Willie, who died shortly before the trip started. His lead-lined coffin, filled with colony-made Golden Rule whisky, headed the procession. Later Dr. Keil declared the Willapa country an unfit site for permanent settlement and moved the fledgling colony to Aurora, Oregon, where Herman and Margaret

were married on August 8, 1860. Shortly thereafter they left the colony and moved to Bucoda, WA, the future home of the territorial prison, and incidentally, the future home of Eliza Jane Meeker's parents and siblings.

35. Aurora colony records and U.S. Census records differ on Louisa's birth year.

36. The story of the killing of Frank Dewitt is told in "Spencer's Acquittal." *Tacoma News* (Weekly), November 30, 1882, 2.

37. Frances Louisa DeWitt, Case PRC-268, Probate Court, Washington State Archives.

38. Ibid.

39. "Frank Meeker Shot." *Seattle Post-Intelligencer*, December 14, 1894, 2.

40. Most of the information about the Knox family comes from a history of George Washington Knox that may be found in the "Charles Ross Papers" at the Washington State Historical Society Research Center in Tacoma, Washington.

41. According to family history she was also the art supervisor for the Portland Public Schools and introduced a system of watercolors into the school's curriculum. Apparently several of her paintings remained in family hands up to the 1930s.

42. "Miss Anna Knox of Portland is visiting at her sisters, Mrs. Wm. Seaman and Mrs. Chas. Ross," "Puyallup Pickings," *Tacoma Daily Ledger*, September 2, 1885, 3.

43. "Miss Anna Knox, teacher in the high school in Portland, has been spending the holidays with her sister, Mrs. E. R. Ross. Miss Knox purchased a lot when here." "Puyallup Matters," *Tacoma Daily Ledger*, January 2, 1889, 4.

44. "Puyallup Personal," *Tacoma Daily Ledger*, August 19, 1890, 4, and "Puyallup Matters," *Tacoma Daily Ledger*, January 2, 1889, 4. Anna's father died in 1875.

45. "Shot For Revenge," *Tacoma Daily News*, December 14, 1894, 1.

46. Ibid.

47. Ibid.

48. Frank Meeker to Ezra Meeker, January 1, 1895, Meeker Papers, Box 4, Folder 6A. This must have been a very disheartening time for the Meekers. Adding to their woes, we find in Meeker's correspondence with his wife mention of their youngest son Fred's drinking problem.

49. "The Meeker Case," *Tacoma Daily News*, December 15, 1894, 1.

50. "Obituary," *Ft. Morgan Times*, March 31, 1905, 1. The Riverside & Memorial Garden's cemetery book lists Ettella's birth year as 1861. The obituary reads 1862. Her Riverside Cemetery tombstone is inscribed 1863.

51. Ezra Meeker to Carrie Osborne, January 14, 1908, Meeker Papers, Box 4, Folder 2D.

52. Carrie Osborne to Ezra Meeker, July 11, 1914, Meeker Papers, Box 4, Folder 3A.

53. Carrie Osborne to Ezra Meeker, February 25, 1917, Meeker Papers, Box 4, Folder 4C.

Notes to Chapter 20: Hop Lice

1. "Ezra Meeker's Office Hop Capital's Bank," *Tacoma News Tribune*, April 7, 1952, E-4.

2. *E. Meeker & Co's Hop Circular*, June 24, 1890, Meeker Papers, Box 17, Folder 2A.

3. Meeker, *Busy Life,* 227.

4. Meeker, *Busy Life,* 228.

5. Ibid.

6. "Fred S. Meeker, who has been representing the great hop fields of Washington in the London market, will return to his Puyallup home in a few weeks." "Puyallup Pointers," *Tacoma Daily Ledger*, January 15, 1889, 6.

7. Fred Meeker to Ezra Meeker, November 27, 1890. Meeker Papers, Box 4, Folder 16.

8. The formula was sixty-five pounds of quassia chips, sixty pounds of whale oil soap, and one thousand pounds of water to spray an acre four times.

9. *E. Meeker & Co's Hop Circular*, November 14, 1890. Meeker Papers, Box 17 Folder 2A.

10. *E. Meeker & Company's Hop Circular*, February 19, 1891. Meeker Papers, Box 17, Folder 2A.

11. "Washington State News," *Tacoma Daily News*, June 4, 1891, 6.

12. "The News of Puyallup," *Tacoma Daily News*, June 16, 1891, 8.

13. Some interesting ideas on how to combat the hop louse appeared in the local press. "James Wilson foreman of the Shaw & Alger hop ranch near Seattle found an insect that devours the hop lice at work on the leaves. The insect not only eats the louse but it also destroys the eggs. It is a sort of an ant lion and of the family known to etymologists as neuroptera. It has six legs on each side and claws or nippers leading from the mouth, which are not unlike the claws or feelers of a crab or lobster. To what extent the insect destroyer exists here is not known, but if the species can be extensively propagated it is said that it will be a boon to our hop and vine growers." "Enemy of the Hop Louse," *Tacoma Daily News*, September 4, 1891, 2.

14. Riley served as the entomologist for the U.S. Department of Agriculture 1878–1879 and 1881–1894.

15. When soaked in cold water, wood and bark from the quassia tree produces a chemical whose value as an insecticide had been known since 1730. Quassia trees, indigenous to the West Indies and tropical South America, grow fifty to one hundred feet in height and reach a diameter of three feet. Meeker imported quassia logs from Brazil and ground them up into chips and shavings, which he sold for ten cents per pound.

16. In March 1891 Ezra Meeker, Albert Provine, Roderick McDonald, Frank Spinning, and Charles Hood established the Puyallup Hardware Company. Meeker was the president and Albert Provine served as vice president. Charles Hood later bought out the partners and took over sole ownership of the Puyallup firm.

17. "The State Hop Crop," *Seattle Post-Intelligencer*, August 26, 1891, 5.

18. "The Hop Crop," *Tacoma Daily Ledger*, September 5, 1891, 1.

19. *E. Meeker & Co's Hop Circular*, February 19, 1891, Meeker Papers, Box 17, Folder 2A.

20. *E. Meeker & Co's Hop Annual and Handbook*, (Puyallup:1893), 41, Meeker Papers, Box 17, Folder 2B.

21. "The State of Hop Crop," *Seattle Post-Intelligencer*, August 26, 1891, 5.

22. "Mr. Meeker Interviewed," *Puyallup Citizen*, August 18, 1893, 2.

23. Several of these ledgers may be found in Box 2 of the Meeker Papers.

24. "News of Puyallup," *Tacoma Daily News*, December 10, 1891, 2.

25. "State News," *Washington Standard*, December 18, 1891, 1.

26. See Chapter 5.

27. "Mr. Meeker Interviewed," *Puyallup Citizen*, August 18, 1893, 1.

Notes to Chapter 21: Travels with Ezra

1. Jabez Thomas Sunderland, ed. "Northwest Conference," *The Unitarian, Vol. VIII*, January 25-27, 1893, 58.

2. Ibid.

3. "Unitarians Adjourn: Alameda Is Selected as the Place for the Next Annual Convention," *San Francisco Call*, May 4, 1895, 1.

4. "Tribute to My Wife," Meeker Papers. Box 10, Envelope 1.

5. "Do you know, I have long felt lonesome because my belief would not square with that of should I say favorite children, the two daughters—you know who I mean." Ezra Meeker to Reverend Harry Templeton, June 18, 1911, Meeker Papers, Box 6, Letterbook, Volume 14.

6. *Journal of Ezra Meeker's 1910 Old Oregon Trail Monument Expedition*, Meeker Papers, Box 8, Folder 5E, May 15, 1910.

7. "News About the City," *Puyallup Citizen*, March 7, 1893, 4.

8. A yellow-flowering plant of the parsley family, whose swollen leaf bases are eaten as a vegetable.

9. Ezra Meeker to Eliza Jane Meeker, July 10, 1893, Meeker Papers, Box 4, Folder 6B.

10. Ezra Meeker to Eliza Jane Meeker, July 15, 1893, Meeker Papers, Box 4, Folder 6B. July 13, 1893, Meeker Papers, Box 4, Folder 6B.

11. "Hop Notes," *Puyallup Citizen*, August 18, 1893, 1.

12. "Mr. Meeker Interviewed," *Puyallup Citizen*, August 18, 1893, 1, quoting a story about Meeker in the *New York Mail and Express*. As the Puyallup newspaper also said Meeker started home August 17, it may be assumed that he left New York City on that date and stopped at Waterville on his way home.

13. A partial journal of this trip is in the Meeker Papers, Box 11, Folder 4.

14. Michael Tomlan in *Tinged With Gold*, 36, states that Meeker served as the judge of hops at the exposition. Someone may have appointed him as such, but Meeker attended the fair only on November 6, the day he met his wife in Chicago. Ezra and Eliza Jane continued on the next day to New York and then to Europe and returned directly to Puyallup five months later.

15. Robert Alexander to Ezra Meeker, January 6, 1894, Meeker Papers, Box 5, Folder 3.

16. "Letter from Paris," *Tacoma Daily Ledger*, March 25, 1885, 6.

17. "Journal of my trip from Puyallup to London Written Expressly for <u>My</u> <u>Dear</u> <u>Wife</u> E. J. Meeker," Meeker Papers, Box 4, Folder 6B.

18. The mention of the audience with Queen Victoria appears in the obituaries in the Puyallup and Tacoma newspapers, but not in the Seattle newspapers where two of Meeker's daughters lived and where Eliza Jane died. It is possible that Charles Ross wrote the Puyallup and Tacoma obituaries, fully believing the story.

19. Meeker Papers, Box 11, Envelope 1-2, Folder 5.

20. Notes in the Box 11 diary suggest a possible origin for the gown. "Paris Bon Marche, ask for Mr. Go. Farmer, give name of Mrs. Ackerson. Paris Cloak Maker Loir 4 Rue San Joseph."

Notes to Chapter 22: The Siege of Puyallup

1. "Hops Low In Price," *Tacoma Daily Ledger*, March 27, 1894, 6.

2. Governor McGraw to Ezra Meeker, April 25, 1894, Meeker Papers, Box 5, Folder 3.

3. "Ezra Meeker was in the City Yesterday," *Washington Standard*, April 27, 1894, 3.

4. Six miles south of downtown Seattle would have placed the Industrials near today's Tukwila, Washington. "In Camp at Kent," *Tacoma Daily Ledger*, April 28, 1894, 1.

5. Ibid.

6. Ibid.

7. "No Deputy Sheriff," *Tacoma Daily News*, April 29, 1894, 1.

8. "The Army Has Gone," *Tacoma Daily Ledger*, April 29, 1894, 5.

9. "On the March," *Tacoma Daily News*, April 28, 1894, 1.

10. "The Army Has Gone," *Tacoma Daily Ledger*, April 29, 1894, 5.

11. Ibid.

12. Ibid.

13. Ibid.

14. "Strike Possible," *Tacoma Daily News*, May 1, 1894, 1.

15. "Toil Not, Nor Do They Spin," *Tacoma Daily Ledger*, May 2, 1894, 5.

16. Ibid.

17. John P. Hartman Jr. was an attorney for the Northern Pacific Railroad in addition to being Meeker's attorney and business partner. He was instrumental in the creation

of Mount Rainier National Park. In 1899 Hartman, along with five others, founded the Northwest Steamship Company. From 1905 to 1911 he was a regent for the University of Washington and he was on the Board of Directors during the Alaska Yukon Pacific Exposition in 1909. Hartman was personally acquainted with every U.S. president from McKinley to Harding.

18. "Gov. McGraw Visits Puyallup," *Tacoma Daily Ledger*, May 3, 1894, 5.

19. "Jumbo Moves," *Tacoma Daily News*, May 4, 1894, 4.

20. Morgan, 287-292.

Notes to Chapter 23: Troubled Times

1. "The Latest Hop News," *Yakima Herald*, September 8, 1892, 2.

2. "Heraldings," *Yakima Herald*, August 25, 1892, 3.

3. "Trying to Corner Hops," *Capital Journal* (Salem, OR), August 30, 1893, 2.

4. Running these numbers through the inflation calculator yields, in today's dollars, thirty million pledged by Lindsay, Bird & Co. with about six million of that brought to the Northwest by Meeker.

5. "The Hop Men In Form," *Capital Journal* (Salem, OR), August 28, 1893, 1.

6. "Hop Items," *Capital Journal* (Salem, OR), September 21, 1893, 2.

7. "Hops and Hop Pickers," *Tacoma Daily Ledger*, September 16, 1894, 2.

8. "Home From The Hop Fields," *Tacoma Daily Ledger*, September 22, 1894, 3.

9. "Indians as Hop Pickers," *Tacoma Daily Ledger*, October 28, 1894, 1.

10. Ezra Meeker to John P. Hartman Jr., December 19, 1894, Meeker Papers, Box 5, Folder 7.

11. Frank H. Adams to Ezra Meeker, August 1, 1895, Meeker Papers, Box 5, Folder 13.

12. L. H. Hale to Ezra Meeker, August 1, 1895, Meeker Papers, Box 5, Folder 13.

13. Balfour, Guthrie & Co. to Ezra Meeker, October 22, 1895.Meeker Papers, Box 5, Folder 14.

14. Meeker, *Busy Life*, 228-229.

15. J. W. Raymond to Ezra Meeker, September 7, 1895, Meeker Papers, Box 5, Folder 14.

16. The prospectus for the "Puyallup Hop Company" may be found in the Meeker Papers, Box 17, Folder 2B. It was incorporated on May 16, 1891.

17. "Outlook For Hops Is Gloomy," *Tacoma Daily Ledger*, August 29, 1895, 3.

18. Albert Heilig, a Pennsylvania native and Kansas judge, came to Tacoma in 1889 and opened a law office. In the 1890s he worked in partnership with John Hartman Jr. Heilig served in the Washington State House of Representatives from 1898 to 1900. In 1900 he became the Clerk of the Court for U.S. district judge James Wickersham in Fairbanks, Alaska. Heilig served on the Fairbanks city council and became a founding member and president of the Board of Trustees of the Alaska College and School of Mines.

19. Meeker, *Busy Life*, 236-237.

20. "Tried to Stop Mr. Meeker," *Tacoma Daily Ledger*, October 19, 1895, 5.

21. According to Meeker, George Macklin, the bank cashier, Charles Hood, and John P. Hartman Jr. made up the remainder of party. Meeker, *Busy Life*, 237.

22. Meeker's office and bank were torn down in February 1934 to make room for a new building. The massive iron doors, bearing Meeker's name in gold leaf, were removed to the office of a local attorney.

23. "A Run on Bank Depositors," *Tacoma Daily Ledger*, October 20, 1895, 1.

24. John P. Hartman Jr. to all, October 25, 1895, Meeker Papers, Box 5, Folder 14.

25. A George Hedges was married to Ezra's niece, Chloe Dunlap Hedges. It is not known if George was related to Treasurer John. B. Hedges.

26. "County Money All in Sight," *Tacoma Daily Ledger*, November 19, 1895, 8.

Notes to Chapter 24: The End of the Hop Empire

1. Meeker Papers, Box 4, Folder 6B.

2. Sickels was the General Western Agent of the Atlantic Transport Line, the company that shipped Meeker's hops to London.

3. Dennis Larsen, *Slick as a Mitten: Ezra Meeker's Klondike Enterprise*, 17-18.

4. The thick tuberous root of skunk cabbage has been used historically as a medicine that opens air passages in cases of whooping cough, asthma, and bronchitis.

5. Meeker used code in many of his hop communications, especially if they involved overseas cables. His codebook may be found in Box 3, Folder 23 of the Meeker papers.

6. Ezra Meeker to Eliza Jane Meeker, February 26, 1896, Meeker Papers, Box 4, Folder 1C.

7. Meeker, *Busy Life*, 228.

8. "Meeker Farm Sold," *Tacoma Daily Ledger*, November 4, 1902, 3.

9. Bart Ripp, "King of Hops: The Legacy of Herman Klaber." *Tacoma News Tribune*, April 12, 2001, A1.

10. Hops continued to be grown in the valley on a few farms in small amounts until the 1960s.

Notes to the Afterword

1. Meeker, *Busy Life*, 228.

2. "How the Crop Looks," *Tacoma Daily Ledger*, August 19, 1893, 5.

3. "Hop Wrinkles," *Tacoma Daily Ledger*, May 17, 1883, 2.

4. Meeker, *Busy Life*, 228.

5. Michael Tomlan noted in *Tinged with Gold*, 37-38, that in 1899 hop "growers in Washington were the first in the country to become subject to state legislation that

appointed a state hop inspector. Henceforth, if there was a disagreement, the inspector determined the grade and quality of the crop. Joseph N. Fernandez of Puyallup was appointed by the governor as the first inspector." What Tomlan failed to mention was that Fernandez was John Meeker's son-in-law. The Meeker reach continued long after Ezra and John had quit the business.

Notes to Appendix: A Short History of Beer

1. The best current history of hop culture in the United States is Michael Tomlan's *Tinged With Gold* (Athens and London: University of Georgia Press, 1992). Also of interest is the American Hop Museum's database of U.S. microbreweries at www.americanhopmuseum.org/microbrew.htm.

2. sfbrewersguild.org/blog/northern-california-fresh-hop-season-is-here.

3. See Peter Kopp, "Hop Fever in the Willamette Valley," *Oregon Historical Quarterly* 112, no. 4 (Winter 2011), for an excellent history of the Willamette Valley hop industry.

Bibliography

ARCHIVAL SOURCES:

The Meeker Papers

The Meeker papers are stored at the Washington State Historical Society Research Center in Tacoma, Washington. They may be viewed by appointment Tuesday through Thursday. Seventeen archival boxes in the collection contain over 50,000 documents and letters, along with a large number of photographs. A large binder contains photocopies of the photographs allowing the researcher to peruse the photographic collection quickly, and a number of photographs may also be viewed online.

A general index of the documents and letters, created by Frank Green in 1969, is available at the research center and is quite helpful in locating written materials. Unfortunately for the researcher, no item index exists. You must go through the boxes folder by folder if you are looking for a specific item. The earliest letter in the collection is from Carrie Meeker Osborne to her brother Fred Meeker dated February 23, 1882. Most of the correspondence in the collection covers the time period after 1890. If the researcher is interested in events prior to 1882 he must generally look elsewhere.

After a decade of transcribing much of the correspondence in these boxes I have become quite familiar with their contents. Accordingly I supply the reader with the following brief guide to the parts of the collection that pertain to this work.

Box 2 contains a few business ledgers of interest but little more. Box 3 holds hop correspondence from 1890 through 1895 consisting mostly of business minutia. Of much more use to the researcher are Meeker's monthly hop circulars, yearly hop handbooks, and the Prospectus of the Puyallup Hop Company that may be found in Box 17, Folders 2A and 2B. Meeker's hop contracts for 1888-1890 are in Box 17, Folder 2. The family correspondence is found primarily in Box 4. Folders 1-4 cover the time period of this work. Separate folders in Box 4 contain Meeker's correspondence with George Himes and Clarence Bagley. Business correspondence is found primarily in Box 5 and begins in 1886. Box 6 contains 27 letterbooks, bound carbons of correspondence, both personal and business. Only volume 1 covers the time period before 1896. Box 8 holds a number of Meeker's speeches and some day calendars. Box 10 contains a number of essays and speeches written over the years on various topics, several of which are incorporated into this work. Box 11 holds Meeker's diaries and day calendars. It also contains Eliza Jane's 1889-1890 Journal, the only writing of hers that has been located. Here also is Meeker's journal of their 1893 trip to Europe. Box 15, Folder 7 is the repository of two interesting scrapbooks. The first is a collection of Meeker's "Farm and Home" columns published in the *Seattle Post-Intelligencer*. The second is a scrapbook of articles clipped from the suffrage newspaper *Woman's Tribune*.

Letters from the Meeker Papers

Ezra Meeker to Eliza Jane Meeker, April 20, 1882, Box 4, Folder 1A.

Ezra Meeker to Eliza Jane Meeker, February 25, 1883, Box 4, Folder 1C.

Pamela Hale to Eliza Jane Meeker, January 31, 1886, Box 5, Folder 1.

Fred Meeker to Ezra Meeker, December 23, 1889, Box 4, Folder 1A.

B. N. Baker to E. Meeker, December 26, 1889, Box 5, Folder 1.

B. N. Baker to Messrs. Williams, Torrey & Field, December 26, 1889, Box 5, Folder 1.

George McAllister to Ezra Meeker, February 14, 1890, Box 5, Folder 1.

Clara Meeker to Ezra Meeker, March 14, 1890, Box 4, Folder 16.

Fred Meeker to Ezra Meeker, April 5, 1890, Box 4, Folder 16.

Fred Meeker to Ezra Meeker, November 27, 1890, Box 4, Folder 16.

Clara Meeker to Eliza Jane Meeker, November 27, 1890, Box 4, Folder 16.

Ezra Meeker to Eliza Jane Meeker, July 11, 1891, Box 4, Folder 18B.

Ezra Meeker to Eliza Jane Meeker, July 13, 1893, Box 4, Folder 6B.

Robert Alexander to Ezra Meeker, January 6, 1894, Box 5, Folder 3.

Governor McGraw to Ezra Meeker, April 25, 1894, Box 5, Folder 3.

Ezra Meeker to John P. Hartman Jr., December 19, 1894, Box 5, Folder 7.

Frank Meeker to Ezra Meeker, January 1, 1895, Box 4, Folder 6A.

E. O. Graves to Ezra Meeker, July 2, 189, Box 5, Folder 13.

Frank H. Adams to Ezra Meeker, August 1, 1895, Box 5, Folder 13.

L. H. Hale to Ezra Meeker, August 1, 1895, Box 5, Folder 13.

C. W. Vance to Ezra Meeker, September 2, 1895, Box 5, Folder 14.

J. W. Raymond to Ezra Meeker, September 7, 1895, Box 5, Folder 14.

J. A. Acton to Ezra Meeker, September 30, 1895, Box 5, Folder 14.

Balfour, Guthrie & Co. to Ezra Meeker, October 4, 1895, Box 3, Folder 21A.

Balfour, Guthrie & Co. to Ezra Meeker, October 22, 1895, Box 5, Folder 14.

John P. Hartman Jr. to all, October 25, 1895, Box 5, Folder 14.

Ezra Meeker to Eliza Jane Meeker, February 26, 1896, Box 4, Folder 1C.

Carrie Meeker to Ezra Meeker, January 5, 1908, Meeker Papers, Box 4, Folder 2C.

Ezra Meeker to Carrie Osborne, January 14, 1908, Meeker Papers, Box 4, Folder 2D.

Ezra Meeker to Clarence Bagley, August 18, 1912, Meeker Papers, Box 4, Folder 12C.

Ezra Meeker to Gus Johnson, March 24, 1913, Meeker Papers, Ms. 2 #20.

Carrie Osborne to Ezra Meeker, July 11, 1914, Meeker Papers, Box 4, Folder 3A.

George Himes to Ezra Meeker, January 11, 1915, Meeker Papers, Box 4, Folder 12B.

Carrie Osborne to Ezra Meeker, February 25, 1917, Meeker Papers, Box 4, Folder4C.

George Himes to Ezra Meeker, August 18, 1919, Meeker Papers, Box 4, Folder 12B.

Others Items from the Meeker Papers

Several business ledgers may be found in Box 2.

The hop business code book may be found in Box 3, Folder 23.

"Journal of my [1895] trip from Puyallup to London Written Expressly for <u>My Dear Wife</u> E. J. Meeker," Box 4, Folder 6B.

"Pioneer Reminiscences About the First Railroad." Address prepared for the Commercial Club of Tacoma, December 1913, Box 8, Envelope 3.

"The Case of Jerry Meeker," Box 10, Envelope 1.

"Tribute to My Wife," Box 10, Envelope 1.

"CIF," Box 10, Envelope 1.

"Report on the London American Exposition," Box 13, Folder 4.

E. Meeker and Company Hop Annual and Hand Book. Puyallup: January 1, 1892, Box 17, Folder 2B.

E. Meeker and Company Hop Annual and Hand Book. Puyallup: January 1, 1893, Box 17, Folder 2B.

"Prospectus of The Puyallup Hop Company," Box 17, Folder 2B.

"E. Meeker & Company Monthly Hop Circulars," Box 17, Folder 2A.

The E. Meeker Company Balance Sheet, November 1, 1895, Box 3, Folder 22.

A partial journal of the 1893 trip to England is in Box 11, Folder 4.

Box 11, Envelope 1-2, Folder 5 contains Olive Osborne's notes on her grandmother and the Paris gown.

Other Collections held at the Washington State Historical Society

Farquharson, A. S., reminiscence (MsSC 137A), Washington State Historical Society, 1913.

Charles H. Ross Papers (MsSc 116), Washington State Historical Society.

Puyallup Historical Society at the Meeker Mansion

(In 2013 the Ezra Meeker Historical Society officially changed its name to the above. References in previous works obviously refer to the society's original name.)

"School at Elhi, Pierce County, Washington Territory 1873-74. Taught by Miss Delia McNeil." Lori Price Collection.

"Franklin School—1874 Mrs. Delia M. Coon, Teacher." Lori Price Collection.

August 18, 1866 Deed of Trust from Amanda C. Meeker to E. Meeker for Frank O. Meeker.

Keigley, Ken. "Summary of Meeker Land Transactions." Puyallup: Unpublished, Ezra Meeker Historical Society, 2005.

Keigley, Ken. "Timeline of the Tacoma Puyallup Railroad Company." Puyallup: Unpublished, Ezra Meeker Historical Society, 2010.

LEGAL ACTIONS

The Meeker family was involved in an incredible number of court cases during the second half of the nineteenth century. Ezra, his wife, children, nephews, and in-laws all found their way to the front of the docket at one time or another. Ezra himself had fifty-three appearances in court during the territorial days alone. The Washington State Archives has created a finding aid titled "Frontier Justice" for the court records that took place from the beginning of the territory in 1853 to statehood in 1889. To actually look at the court records, one must venture to the Archives office at Olympia for court cases that took place in Thurston or Pierce County. King County cases require a trip to Bellevue. A researcher will find two separate case numbers listed—a modern number and the original case number. To view the documents, which are on microfilm, you will need to use the original case numbers. Accordingly, these are cited below. All but a few of the court actions were either civil or probate cases. Criminal cases are identified as such.

Washington Territorial Court Records

PCR-40, 1860, Oliver P. Meeker Probate.

PCR-944, 1860, Washington Territory vs. E. Meeker, Criminal, Public Nuisance.

TCR-372, 1861, E. Meeker vs. C. H. and B. M. Spinning, Account Collection.

THR-673 and 680, 1867, United States vs. Isaac Wood, Criminal, Liquor sales to Indians.

PCR-105, 1872, Probate Court, Guardianship of Malinda and Aaron Meeker.

PCR-159, 1876, E. Meeker vs. A. Gardella, Account Collection.

PCR-452, 1879, M. T. Ward vs. C. Spinning and E. Meeker, Defamation.

PCR-317, 1879, Washington Territory vs. Robert Sproul[e], Criminal, Arson.

PCR-707, 1879, E. Meeker and Margaret Walker vs. A. Gardella, Mortgage Foreclosure, Restraining Order.

PCR-334, 1879, A. Gardella vs. Byron Young (Sheriff), C. O. Bean, and E. Meeker, Farm Lease Dispute, Change of Venue.

PCR-824, 1879, E. Meeker vs. Puget Sound Mfg. Co., Water Rights Dispute.

PCR-347, 1882, A. Gardella vs. Mary J. Walker, Conveyance of Deed.

PCR-268, 1882, Frances Louise DeWitt, Pierce County, W. T. Probate Court, Adoption of Frances Louise DeWitt, aka Grace Meeker.

PCR-1365, 1883, A. Gardella, A. Farquharson, and William Wagner vs. E. Meeker, Recovery of Property.

PCR-1370, 1883, A. Gardella, A. Farquharson, William Wagner, and John Morgan vs. E. Meeker, Restraining Order.

PCR-430, 1883, Washington Territory vs. E. Meeker, F. M. Slythe, Frank O. Meeker, and Robert Wilson, Criminal, Petit Larceny.

PCR-1209, 1884, E. Meeker vs. R. J. Weisbach, Account Collection.

State Supreme Court Decisions

Kreider, Eugene Genroy, *Reports of Cases Determined in the Supreme Court of the State of Washington*, Olympia: Washington State Supreme Court, 1893, 242.
  Ezra Meeker vs. Otis Sprague and R. F. Radebaugh; No. 707, Decided November 23, 1892.

Kreider, Eugene Genroy, *Reports of Cases Determined in the Supreme Court of the State of Washington*, Olympia: Washington State Supreme Court, 1890, 139.
  Ezra Meeker vs. Augustus Gardella, Alexander S. Farquharson, Christina Wagner and Allen J. Miller, administrator of the estate of William Wagner, deceased; No. 602, Decided February 24, 1890.

Kreider, Eugene Genroy, *Reports of Cases Determined in the Supreme Court of the State of Washington*, Olympia: Washington State Supreme Court, 1893, 718.
  Ezra Meeker and Fred Meeker vs. Ira Johnson; No. 550, Decided February 14, 1893.

Kreider, Eugene Genroy, *Reports of Cases Determined in the Supreme Court of the State of Washington*, Olympia: Washington State Supreme Court, 1893, 759.
  Ezra Meeker and Eliza Jane Meeker vs. City of Puyallup; No. 161, Decided February 17, 1893.

Kreider, Eugene Genroy, *Reports of Cases Determined in the Supreme Court of the State of Washington*, Olympia: Washington State Supreme Court, 1897, 185.
  A. C. Utterback, et al. vs. E. Meeker, et. Ux.; No. 2305, Decided December 14, 1896.

District Court Decision

*Les Pedens, London & San Francisco Bank vs. Frank O. Meeker, Ettella W. Meeker, his wife; Tacoma & Puyallup Railroad Company, a corporation; Otis Sprague, as assignee of the Tacoma & Puyallup Railroad Company; Ezra M. Meeker and Eliza J. Meeker, his wife; and Roderick McDonald and Olive McDonald, his wif*e. March 1, 1898.

Other

DeWitt, Grace, King County Birth Certificate #12050-P, March 15, 1943.

DeWitt, Grace, and Merton J. Corwin Marriage License #369869, Cook County, Illinois, July 10, 1903.

CENSUS AND GENEALOGICAL RECORDS

Donation Land Claim Notes. Washington, U.S. Bureau of Land Management, http://www.blm.gov/or/landrecords/survey. Also available on microfilm at the Washington State Library, Micro. 333.16.

United States Census various years, available at http://www.digitalarchives.wa.gov.

Washington Territorial Census, available at http://www.digitalarchives.wa.gov.

Washington Territory Donation Land Claims. Seattle: Seattle Genealogical Society, 1980.

INFLATION CALCULATOR

http://www.in2013dollars.com/1890-dollars-in-2015?amount=30268.

PERSONAL CORRESPONDENCE

Harris, Patrick, director of the Aurora Colony Museum. Personal correspondence via email regarding Louisa DeWitt's connections with the Aurora Colony. July 12, 2012.

Keigley, Ken, a direct descendant of John Valentine Meeker. Many, many emails and discussions over the years in regard to Meeker items. The email cited was from December 13, 2012.

MANUSCRIPTS, BOOKS, ARTICLES

Alexander, Benjamin F. *Coxey's Army: Popular Protest in the Gilded Age.* Baltimore: Johns Hopkins University Press, 2015.

Bagley, Clarence. *History of Seattle, Vol. III.* Chicago: S. J. Clarke Publishing Co., 1916.

Beers, J. H. *Representative Men and Old Families of Southeastern Massachusetts, Vol. II.* Chicago: J.H. Beers & Co., 1912.

Binns, Archie. *Northwest Gateway: The Story of the Port of Seattle.* Portland: Binfords and Mort, 1941.

"Biographical Directory of the United States Congress, 1774-Present," bioguide. congress.gov.

Bonney, William P. *History of Pierce County Washington. Volume 1.* Chicago: Pioneer Historical Publishing Company, 1927.

Bowden, Angie Burt. *Early Schools of Washington Territory.* Seattle: Lowman and Hanford Company, 1935.

Buerge, David. "Ezra Meeker Goes to Wall Street." *Columbia: The Magazine of Northwest History.* Tacoma: Washington State Historical Society. Vol. Two, No. One, Spring 1988.

Camfield, Thomas. *An Illustrated History of Port Townsend: Shanghaiing, Shipwrecks, Soiled Doves and Sundry Souls.* Port Townsend: Ah Tom Publishing, Inc., 2000.

Carey, Charles Henry. "Hon. Thomas Ray Coon." *The History of Oregon, Volume II.* Chicago-Portland: The Pioneer Historical Publishing Co., 1922.

Catalogue of Exhibits of Washington Territory at the American Exposition, New Orleans, November 10, 1885 to April 1, 1886. Published by Press of W. B. Stansbury & Co. 1886, Pacific Northwest History Collection. WSU MASC F891.C38 1886. WSU 000680540, 32 pages: ill.

Ficken, Robert E. *Washington Territory.* Pullman: Washington State University Press, 2002.

Fuller, Mrs. Francis Victor. *Atlantis Arisen or, Talks of a Tourist About Oregon and Washington.* Philadelphia: J. B. Lippincott Company, 1891.

Green, Frank. *Ezra Meeker-Pioneer A Bibliographical Guide.* Tacoma: Washington State Historical Society, 1969.

Gregory, Tom. *History of Yolo County, California.* Los Angeles: Historic Record Company, 1913.

Harper, Ida Husted. *The Life and Work of Susan B. Anthony: Including Public Addresses, Her Own Letters and many From Her Contemporaries Over Fifty Years, Volume II.* Indianapolis: The Hallenbeck Press, 1898.

Harper's Weekly. New York, October 20, 1888.

History Link. "Congressional Delegations from Washington." www.historylink.org/index.cfm?DisplayPage=output.cfm&file_id=5463

Hunt, Herbert. *History of Tacoma, Volume 1.* Chicago: S. J. Clarke Pub. Co., 1916.

_____. *Washington West of the Cascades, Volume III.* Chicago: S. J. Clarke Company, 1917.

Julha, Pat Thompson, and Loretta Finnerty Bilow. *Index to Marriage Records, Pierce County, Washington, Territorial Marriages 1853-1889.* Tacoma: Tacoma-Pierce County Genealogical Society, 1988.

Kluger, Richard. *The Bitter Waters of Medicine Creek: A Tragic Clash Between White and Native America.* New York: Vintage Books, 2011.

Kolano, Larry. *Puyallup Perspectives.* Tacoma: Graphic Press, 1976.

Kopp, Peter. "Hop Fever in the Willamette Valley," *Oregon Historical Quarterly*, Winter 2011/Volume 112, Number 4.

Larsen, Dennis. *Slick As a Mitten: Ezra Meeker's Klondike Enterprise.* Pullman: Washington State University Press, 2009.

_____. "The Ballard Family on the Oregon Trail in 1852." *Northwest Trails* Volume 28, No. 1 Spring 2013. www.octatrails.org/chapters/northwest/newsletter.php.

Meany, Edmund, "Living Pioneers of Washington," Seattle Genealogical Society, 1995.

Meeker, Ezra. *Washington Territory West of the Cascade Mountain.* Olympia: Transcript Office, 1870.

_____. *Hop Culture in the United States.* Puyallup: E. Meeker & Co., 1883.

_____. *Pioneer Reminiscences of Puget Sound and the Tragedy of Leschi.* Seattle: Lowman & Hanford Printing Company, 1905.

_____ *Ventures and Adventures of Ezra Meeker.* Seattle: Rainier Printing Company, 1909.

_____. *Uncle Ezra's Short Stories for Children.* Tacoma: 1912.

_____. *The Busy Life of Eighty-Five Years of Ezra Meeker.* Indianapolis: Wm. B. Burford Press, 1916.

_____ *Seventy Years of Progress in Washington.* Tacoma: Allstrum Printing Company, 1921.

Morgan, Murray. *Puget's Sound: A Narrative of Early Tacoma and the Southern Sound.* Seattle: University of Washington Press, 1979.

"Petition Supporting Woman Suffrage Presented to the Washington Territory Constitutional Convention June 17, 1878, Petition of 581 citizens." Pacific Northwest Historical Documents Collection, Accession No. 4284-1, Box 3, Digital ID No. PNW00539, University of Washington Libraries, Special Collections Division.

Polk, A. L. & Co., Publisher, *Tacoma City Directory 1889, Including Puyallup, Sumner and Steilacoom.* Tacoma: Puget Sound Printing Co., 1889.

_____. *Tacoma City Directory 1893, Including Puyallup, Sumner and Steilacoom.* Tacoma: Puget Sound Printing Co., 1893.

_____. *Tacoma City Directory 1894, Including Puyallup, Sumner and Steilacoom.* Tacoma: Puget Sound Printing Co., 1894.

Price, Lori and Ruth Anderson. *Puyallup: A Pioneer Paradise.* Charleston, SC: Arcadia Publishing, 2002.

Raibmon, Paige Sylvia. *Authentic Indians: Episodes of Encounter from the Late Nineteenth Century Northwest Coast.* Ann Arbor: Bell & Howell Information and Learning Company, 2001.

Ramsey, Guy Reed, edited by Jeanne Engerman. *Postmarked Washington, Pierce County.* Tacoma: Washington State Historical Society, 1981.

Sunderland, Jabez Thomas, ed. "Northwest Conference." Boston: *The Unitarian, Vol. VIII,* January 25-27, 1893.

Thrush, Coll. *Native Seattle: Histories from the Crossing Over Place.* Seattle: University of Washington Press, 2007.

Tomlan, Michael. *Tinged With Gold.* Athens and London: University of Georgia Press, 1992.

Waterman, Thomas Hewett. *Cornell University Register for 1877-78* and *Cornell University: A History.* Ithaca: 1905.

The West Shore Magazine. Portland: November 1884.

Wortley, W. Victor, translated, annotated and introduced. *Louis Rossi: Six Years On the West Coast of America.* Fairfield, WA: Ye Galleon Press, 1983.

Wright, E. W., Editor. *Lewis & Dryden's Marine History of the Pacific Northwest.* First published in 1895 by Lewis and Dryden Printing Company. Reprinted with corrections, New York: Antiquarian Press, 1961.

NEWSPAPERS

A large part of Meeker's story must be gleaned from contemporary newspaper accounts of his activities and those of his associates and family members. The Washington State Library located in Tumwater has most of the state newspapers on microfilm. The Washington Secretary of State's office maintains a searchable website containing many of the early territorial newspapers. Plans are to expand the listing as finances become available. The Northwest Room at the Tacoma Public Library and the University of Washington Library also maintain fairly extensive collections of state and territorial newspapers on microfilm. Many other repositories of newspapers are online, some for a fee, some free. Below are the newspapers I found useful.

Capital Journal (Salem, OR)
Centralia Chronicle
Centralia News Examiner
Chicago Tribune
Daily Alta California (San Francisco)
Daily Oregonian (Portland, OR)
Fort Morgan (CO) Times
Olympia Daily Pacific Tribune
Olympia Weekly Pacific Tribune
Olympia Weekly Standard
Pacific Rural Press
Pierce County News
Pioneer and Democrat
Puget Sound Express
Puget Sound Herald (Steilacoom, WA)
Puget Sound Weekly Argus (Port Townsend, WA)
Puyallup Citizen
Puyallup Republican
Puyallup Valley Tribune
Rogue River Courier (Grants Pass, OR)
San Francisco Call
Seattle Daily Pacific Tribune
Seattle Daily Press
Seattle Post-Intelligencer
Seattle Times
Spokane Falls Weekly Review
Spokane Times
Tacoma Daily Ledger
Tacoma Daily News
Tacoma Daily Pacific Tribune
Tacoma Herald
Tacoma News
Tacoma News (Weekly)
Tacoma News Tribune
Tacoma Times
Tacoma Weekly Pacific Tribune
Vancouver (WA) Register
Walla Walla Statesman

Washington Standard (Olympia)
Willamette Farmer (Salem, OR)
Woman's Tribune (Beatrice, NE)
Yakima Herald
Yakima Republic

Index

About the Author

Dennis M. Larsen is a retired history teacher residing in Olympia, Washington. For the past fifteen years he has been researching and writing about Northwest pioneers. He is author of *Slick as a Mitten: Ezra Meeker's Klondike Enterprise* (WSU Press, 2009), and co-author with Karen L. Johnson of *A Yankee on Puget Sound: Pioneer Dispatches of Edward Jay Allen, 1852–1855* (WSU Press, 2013). His articles have appeared in *Overland Journal*, the *Lewis County Historian*, *Northwest Trails* (the newsletter of the Northwest Chapter of the Oregon-California Trails Association), and other publications. He is a frequent presenter on topics including Ezra Meeker, the Oregon Trail, and Northwest pioneers.